Dwelling in the Household of God

Dwelling in the Household of God

Johannine Ecclesiology and Spirituality

Mary L. Coloe, P.B.V.M.

A Michael Glazier Book

LITURGICAL PRESS

Collegeville, Minnesota

www.litpress.org

A Michael Glazier Book published by Liturgical Press

Cover design by Ann Blattner. *Trinity* by Andrei Rublev, 1425.

Old Testament Scripture quotations are from the New Revised Standard Version Bible, © 1989 by the Division of Christian Education of the National Council of Churches of Christ in the U.S.A. Used with permission. All rights reserved.

New Testament Scripture quotations are the author's own translation.

| 1 | 2 | 3 | 4 | 5 | 6 | 7 | 8 |

Library of Congress Cataloging-in-Publication Data

Coloe, Mary L. 1949–
    Dwelling in the household of God : Johannine ecclesiology and spirituality / Mary L. Coloe.
      p. cm.
    "A Michael Glazier Book."
    Includes bibliographical references and indexes.
    ISBN-13: 978-0-8146-5988-5
    ISBN-10: 0-8146-5988-8
      1. Bible. N.T. John—Criticism, interpretation, etc.   I. Title.

BS2615.52.C65   2006
226.506—dc22

                                               2006034178

Contents

Foreword

It is a pleasure to introduce this fine study in the Fourth Gospel, to those who know Mary Coloe's first major study of John's Gospel, *God Dwells with Us*, and especially to those who do not. This new book, *Dwelling in the Household of God*, grows organically out of its predecessor in which Coloe explored the development of the community of the Fourth Gospel—from its roots in the Jewish perception of the Temple in Jerusalem as God's dwelling in Israel, to its experience of God's dwelling in the Christian community in Jesus. This new study looks at the Gospel of John, as it were, from "the other end," that is, from the post-Resurrection perspective from which the Johannine community experiences itself as God's household or dwelling place, as a new Israel in which the risen Jesus is the New Temple.

While just as rigorous, exegetically and critically, as the first volume this new study is theologically and spiritually richer and deeper. It is quite explicitly a work of biblical theology and biblical spirituality solidly grounded in excellent scholarship. Coloe attempts, very successfully, to discern and explicate the religious, indeed mystical, experience of mutual indwelling of believers and Jesus, which grounds their experience of community life as life in the household of God. This community experience is the matrix out of which the text arises and to which it bears witness. By her careful scholarship enriched by an unobtrusive but unmistakable personal engagement with the subject matter Coloe invites the reader not only to appropriate intellectually the information that the text conveys but to enter personally into its revelatory, that is, its transformational dynamics. Coloe's text makes the implicit claim that the Fourth Gospel cannot be read neutrally.

Dwelling in the Household of God is a highly original contribution to the understanding of the Fourth Gospel, making excellent use of previous and contemporary scholarship but rife with new insights. At the same time it demonstrates the fruitfulness of a methodological choice to read the entire gospel through a particular theological-spiritual lens, a choice that could have resulted in a forced or selective or even tendentious reading but in this case has simultaneously deepened and broadened the interpretive perspective while offering a coherent and unified reading of the gospel. Finally, it provides a fine example of biblical spirituality both as hermeneutical practice and as existential product. The book will be a valuable resource for scholars but also a fine textbook for upper level university students, seminarians, and thoughtful pastors. Educated laity will find in this volume both an incentive to serious study of John's Gospel and robust nourishment for their life of faith and commitment. I hope it will have the breadth of readership it so richly deserves.

Sandra M. Schneiders

Preface

The Rublev icon of the Trinity draws the viewer into the scene, to take her place at the table, to fill the empty space and complete the circle. The three figures are depicted in a moment of deep communion. The central figure, Jesus, holds his hand in blessing over the cup containing the head of the sacrificial calf. His eyes are turned to the Father, whose face bears infinite sadness as he returns the gaze of the Son. The third figure, robed in green, is the vivifier, the eternally young Spirit, whose face also depicts a depth of sadness in contemplating the costliness of love.

Andrei Rublev, the great Russian master of the early fifteenth century, has captured the essence of the Johannine vision of God. Here is a communion of love and a communion of invitation. In the final discourse we read: "Make your home in me, as I make mine in you" (John 15:4). The invitation is offered—to dwell in God as God dwells in us, to participate in this divine communion of life and love.

My first book, *God Dwells With Us: Temple Symbolism in the Fourth Gospel*, explored one pole of this invitation: the dwelling of God with and in us. In that book the Temple, "my Father's House," was the symbol in the gospel text that expressed God's dwelling in history. As the narrative unfolded, the Temple shifted in its symbolism: from a building, to the person of Jesus, to the believers.

The current book explores the second pole of the invitation: Make your home in me. Again I have focused on a symbol within the text, "my Father's household" (14:2), which evokes both the Temple tradition and the people who are part of the household. The phrase "my Father's household" expresses the reciprocity inherent in the invitation: "make your home in me, as I make mine in you." It is my belief that underlying the Gospel of John is a profound experience, a mysticism of divine mutual indwelling. This book is my attempt to test this belief, to see if within the narrative we can read the traces of a profound mystical experience of God at the origins of the Christian story.

As I write about a communion of life I am conscious that this book emerged from within such a communion. While the final product bears the imprint and limitations of my own skills, I have received support and insight from a range of people. My religious congregation, the Presentation Sisters, has continued to encourage and enable my research. My experience of living within a Presentation community and the ongoing love of women whose spirits run deep and true enables me to glimpse at times the subject of this book, the love and life of the divine communion. My colleagues at the Australian Catholic University and St. Paul's College of Theology have listened to and critiqued papers given in seminars. The biblical academies in Australia, Europe, and North America have provided further opportunities to test the development of my ideas and to receive helpful advice and directions from other academics. I am most grateful to the Australian Research Council, which provided me with a large research grant, releasing me from my teaching responsibilities and enabling me to attend a number of international conferences and to spend a year in Berkeley, California. This book could not have been written without that financial support by the Australian government. During the year at Berkeley I experienced the hospitality of the Jesuit School of Theology and the caring support of a community of men and women living in the Salesian residence, Don Bosco Hall. My time in Berkeley also gave me the opportunity to renew my collaboration and friendship with Professor Sandra Schneiders. Sandra's interest in symbolism dates back to the 70s, and her work has continued to awaken and deepen my own insights. A course on hermeneutics offered by Sandra and Professor Barbara Green was of particular help to me in articulating the theoretical perspective that underlies this work. I have been truly blessed through my ongoing friendship with both Sandra Schneiders and Frank Moloney. These two outstanding Johannine scholars have read parts of this text, offered suggestions, and guided me to some of the important studies by European scholars. I am grateful again to all at Liturgical Press, especially Linda Maloney and Peter Dwyer who provided skilled editing and recommendations. Their publishing expertise and support make it possible for my writing to reach a wider reading community.

I extend my heartfelt thanks to all these people. Academic writing must be a time of intense solitude. The encouragement, friendship, and support of my sisters, friends, and colleagues enable solitude to be a creative rather than a lonely experience.

Mary L. Coloe, P.B.V.M.

Abbreviations

AB	Anchor Bible
ABD	*Anchor Bible Dictionary*
ABR	*Australian Biblical Review*
ABRL	Anchor Bible Reference Library
AnBib	Analecta Biblica
ATANT	Abhandlungen zur Theologie des Alten und Neuen Testaments
BETL	Bibliotheca Ephemeridum Theologicae Lovaniensis
Bib	*Biblica*
BT	*Bible Translator*
BZNW	*Beihefte zur Zeitschrift für die neutestamentliche Wissenschaft*
CahRB	Cahiers de la Revue Biblique
CBET	Contributions to Biblical Exegesis and Theology
CBQ	Catholic Biblical Quarterly
ConBNT	Coniectanea Biblica, New Testament Series
CRINT	Compendia rerum Iudaicarum ad Novum Testamentum Section 1
EstB	*Estudios Bíblicos*
ExpT	*Expository Times*
HTCNT	Herder's Theological Commentary on the New Testament
HUT	Hermeneutische Untersuchungen zur Theologie
IDB	*The Interpreter's Dictionary of the Bible*
Int	*Interpretation*
JBL	*Journal of Biblical Literature*
JSNT	*Journal for the Study of the New Testament*

JSOT	*Journal for the Study of the Old Testament*
JSNTSup	Journal for the Study of the New Testament Supplement Series
JSOTSup	Journal for the Study of the Old Testament Supplement Series
LD	Lectio Divina
LXX	The Septuagint (Greek Old Testament)
MT	The Masoretic Text (Hebrew Old Testament)
NCB	New Century Bible
NovT	*Novum Testamentum*
NovTSup	Supplements to Novum Testamentum
NRTh	*Nouvelle revue théologique*
NTL	New Testament Library
NTS	*New Testament Studies*
OTL	Old Testament Library
QD	Quaestiones Disputatae
RSR	*Recherches de science religieuse*
SANT	Studien zum Alten und Neuen Testament
SBFA	Studium Biblicum Franciscanum Analecta
SBLDS	Society of Biblical Literature Dissertation Series
SBLSCS	Society of Biblical Literature Septuagint and Cognate Studies
SBT	Studies in Biblical Theology
SNTSMS	Society for New Testament Studies Monograph Series
SNTSU	*Studien zum Neuen Testament und seiner Umwelt*
SP	Sacra Pagina
TDNT	*Theological Dictionary of the New Testament*
TDOT	*Theological Dictionary of the Old Testament*
TLNT	*Theological Lexicon of the New Testament*
TS	*Theological Studies*
WUNT	Wissenschaftliche Untersuchungen zum Neuen Testament
ZNW	*Zeitschrift für die neutestamentliche Wissenschaft und die Kunde der älteren Kirche*

Introduction

"In my Father's house are many dwellings," what else can we suppose the house of God to mean but the temple of God? And what that is, ask the apostle, and he will reply, "For the temple of God is holy, which [temple] ye are."[1]

These words of Augustine concluded my study of the Temple in the Fourth Gospel.[2] In that book I traced the way the Temple functioned across the text of the gospel and came to the conclusion that the Temple was not only the major image of the person and mission of Jesus, but also an image of the identity and mission of the Johannine community. Just as Jesus could be described as the tabernacling presence of God (1:14), and as a temple (2:21), so too the Johannine community was a living "temple" in which God continued to dwell (14:10, 17, 23, 25).[3] But there was a problem. While the gospel narrative could express its theology through the symbol of the Temple, in the post-70 experience of the Johannine community the Temple was no longer appropriate as a means of expressing its own identity. The Temple building, along with its elaborate cult, no longer existed, nor is there

[1] Augustine, *The Gospel of John.* Tractate 68. John 14:1-3.

[2] Mary L. Coloe, *God Dwells with Us: Temple Symbolism in the Fourth Gospel* (Collegeville: Liturgical Press, 2001).

[3] For a discussion of the significance of these verses see Coloe, *God Dwells with Us,* ch. 8. The gradual theological development of Israel's relationship with God and sense of God's presence is discussed in ibid., ch. 3. Under the influence of Canaanite mythology, a royal ideology developed during the early period of the Solomonic Temple, which in turn led to a simplistic, almost literalizing view of YHWH's presence in the Jerusalem Temple, so that God can be called "YHWH of Zion" (Ps 110:2) and "Resident of Jerusalem" (Ps 135:21). In response to this the Deuteronomists, the prophets, and the Priestly tradition set about a spiritualization of the cult (see ibid., especially 36–51).

anything in the Johannine gospel to suggest a community that had a cultic sense of its identity. Nothing in the text shows interest in Christian priesthood, sacrifice, hierarchies, formal rituals to be re-enacted, or prayers to be said.[4] On the contrary, Jesus' actions in the Jerusalem Temple (2:13-25) disrupt and overturn its cultic significance,[5] and his words to the Samaritan woman speak of worship in Spirit rather than in sacred places (4:19-26).[6] This gospel makes no distinction between "apostle" and "disciple"; instead, all are disciples. There is no eucharistic institution narrative, nor is there a baptismal formula such as that found at the end of Matthew's gospel (Matt 28:16-20). There is no teaching about offering sacrifice, or about prayer. Nothing therefore in the text gives any indication that the Johannine community took to itself the meaning of "Temple" as a cultic institution.

While I was experiencing some disquiet about the Temple as an appropriate symbol for the community, even as that first book came to its end a second was beginning to emerge, for there was another symbol in the text, a symbol capable of meaning Temple and of being transferred to the community in a post-70 context. This symbol was the household. When Jesus enters the Temple for the first Passover he names the building "my Father's house" (2:16); later, within the final discourse, he speaks again of "my Father's house" (14:2). Although the expression obviously refers to the building in chapter 2, in the Old Testament "my father's house" is never used in this architectural sense; instead, it always has the personal sense of "my father's household."[7] The double meaning of this expression, in its reference to the Temple and to a group of people, suggested a way of understanding the transferral of Temple imagery to the community—not in a cultic sense, as the house of God, but in a more interrelational sense, that is, as the household of God. The focus shifts from the Temple as a place of human activity, of doing cultic things, to the Temple as a place of divine activity, of God's dwelling within creation.[8] In the life of Jesus, God's dwell-

---

[4] This is not an exhaustive list of expressions of Israel's cult but a description of aspects of the cult linked to the Temple.

[5] *God Dwells with Us*, ch. 4.

[6] *God Dwells with Us*, ch. 5.

[7] For example, "So Joseph said to his brothers and to his father's house, 'I will go up and tell Pharaoh, and will say to him, "My brothers and my father's house have come to me"'" (Gen 46:31); similarly Gen 24:38; 28:21; Josh 2:13; Judg 6:15; 9:18; 16:31; 1 Sam 22:15; 2 Sam 14:9; 1 Chr 28:4). Often the expression "father's house" is translated as "family" in the Revised Standard Version and "household" in the New Revised Standard Version.

[8] The understanding of the Temple as God's dwelling place is already present in the Old Testament, for in the Hebrew text the most frequent name for the Jerusalem Temple was "the House of God."

ing in creation became God's incarnation in a human person. The incarnation makes personal the mode of God's being in the world, first in Jesus; then, in and through his departure and gift of the Spirit, God's dwelling has its locus in the community of believers, born into the Father's household.[9] Understanding the Temple raised up by Jesus as "my father's household" provided me with an initial entry point into a second reading of the gospel. The task in my first book was christological: to explore the identity and mission of Jesus through the narrative symbol of the Temple. The aim of this study is ecclesial: to explore the identity and mission of the community through the narrative symbol of the household.

In his work on interpreting texts, Paul Ricoeur speaks of a "second naïveté" to describe the process of returning to a literary work a second time, bringing to this second reading the insights gained from the first reading.[10] The second reading therefore has a certain level of perception that makes possible the disclosure of deeper levels of meaning. Thus the reader is involved in an ongoing hermeneutical circle of reading, understanding, raising questions, new readings, new perceptions, and new questions. Perhaps it is more accurate to speak of a hermeneutical spiral as the new readings open the reader to ever deepening layers of interpretive possibilities that were not evident at first. Such is the ongoing nature of interpretation.

Once again I will pay attention to the symbolic potential of the narrative, to its characters, its indicators of time, its religious and social customs. The symbolic dimension will be even more important in this second reading, as in my earlier work the focus on the Temple meant overlooking other significant aspects of the narrative. My hermeneutics of suspicion will therefore be more obvious in this book, as experience has taught me to look beyond the surface meaning of the text, for this writer is a skilled artist whose apparently straightforward narrative discloses depths of theological insight to the perceptive reader. These initial comments lead me to a more nuanced and explicit statement of my hermeneutical approach and method.

Interpretive Approach and Method

The work of Paul Ricoeur has been foundational for my understanding of text and its interpretation. According to Ricoeur the written form of communication gives a particular autonomy to the text in that the author is

---

[9] See my examination on the meaning of the crucifixion in John as the destruction and raising of the Temple in *God Dwells with Us,* ch. 9.

[10] Paul Ricoeur, *Interpretation Theory: Discourse and the Surplus of Meaning* (Fort Worth: Texas Christian University Press, 1976) 4.

no longer available to question directly, nor is the author in a position to control directly how a text is read.[11] In a conversation, if there is any ambiguity there is opportunity to make sure that what the speaker means and what the words mean coincide. In a written text the immediacy of clarification is no longer possible, "the author's intention and the meaning of the text no longer coincide."[12] This creates a distance between the author and the reader, and this distance offers interpretive possibilities not available to its original recipients. The text is the only medium possible for the reader today to appropriate the meaning of its author, and even then what can be grasped by the reader is not so much the mind of the author as the author's, or more accurately the implied author's, point of view, his/her particular way of making sense of the world.[13] This point of view can be discovered only within the rhetorical features of the text. The reader is involved in trying to understand not only what the author writes, the grammar of the sentences, the meaning of the words, but what the author is writing about.[14] This is the task of interpretation, for words can have a multiplicity of meanings and a singular meaning can be determined only by the context. In scientific writing an attempt is made to provide an explanation of the context so that only one meaning is possible. By contrast, in poetic writing and literature the author deliberately exploits the possibility of multiple meanings to engage the reader more directly, so that *understanding* involves a creative task on the part of the reader similar to what *expression* involves on the part of the author.[15]

In the case of the gospel, the private experience of the first community is made public and available to me, the reader, through the author's intention to disclose meaning in his written text. Ricoeur speaks of the "intentional exteriorization" of the author. Here he makes the distinction between

---

[11] See Ricouer's analysis of writing as discourse in ibid., 25–29, 43–44.

[12] Ibid. 29.

[13] In making the distinction between the real author and the implied author revealed within the text, Francis Moloney notes that, unlike contemporary narratives, "it can be assumed (but never proved) that the real author *of* and the implied author *in* New Testament narratives speak with the same voice." See Francis J. Moloney, *John.* SP 4 (Collegeville: Liturgical Press, 1998) 16.

[14] Ricoeur speaks of a "verbal meaning" of the text and a "secondary metaphoric and symbolic meaning"; see *Interpretation Theory*, 75–78.

[15] Paul Ricoeur, *Hermeneutics and the Human Sciences: Essays on Language, Action and Interpretation*, trans. J. B. Thompson (Cambridge: Cambridge University Press, 1981) 151: "Understanding seeks to coincide with the inner life of the author, to liken itself to him (*sich gleichsetzen*), to reproduce (*nachbilden*) the creative processes which engendered the work."

the actual historical event, the impact of Jesus on the first disciples, which today I can no longer enter into, and the meaning of the event as it has been set down in writing. "What we write, what we inscribe is the *noema* [the thought content] of the act of speaking, the meaning of the speech event, not the event as event."[16] This meaning will have both a sense, insofar as the narrative makes sense, and a reference beyond the narrative to the symbolic world by which the first community articulates for itself the meaning of the Christ event. Within the community this symbolic world would be expressed in various forms: in liturgy, in ways of speaking, in ritual, in community organization, in the times and places it considers sacred, in the living commitment of its members, in its evangelistic outreach to others, in all the many tangible and intangible ways this community gives expression to its faith in Jesus. This world is called "symbolic," for it attempts to bring to human sensory perception what is essentially spiritual: the community's ongoing experience of Jesus' presence now mediated through the Spirit. The gospel narrative is one of these sensory experiences that tries to communicate what transcends the human senses but is no less real. For this reason the gospel needs to be read as a symbolic narrative. Not only will the gospel at times use symbols, but the entire narrative is itself a symbol of the faith expression of the community. The task of interpretation, then, is to grasp not just the meaning at the level of the narrative, but also the deeper meaning that the narrative simultaneously enfolds and discloses.[17]

Because the gospel narrative is set in first-century Judaism, and was produced by a community writing toward the end of that century, possibly in Ephesus,[18] a first level of understanding the narrative will be to grasp this historical context, for the author will use the words, faith expressions, geography, religious and cultural customs of his time. Even the symbolic world he creates in and through the narrative will be bounded necessarily by the limitations of a particular time and place. My reading of the text must therefore take note of, but not be confined by its particularity and specificity in order to bring a first-century world into dialogue with a third-millennium

[16] Ricoeur, *Interpretation Theory*, 27.

[17] "The sense of a text is not behind the text, but in front of it. It is not something hidden, but something disclosed. . . . Understanding has less than ever to do with the author and his situation. It seeks to grasp the world-propositions opened up by the reference of the text." See Ricoeur, *Interpretation Theory*, 87.

[18] For recent discussions of the possible location of the Johannine Community and the conclusion that Ephesus seems the most likely proposal see Moloney, *John*, 5, and Raymond E. Brown, *An Introduction to the Gospel of John: Edited, Updated, Introduced and Concluded by Francis J. Moloney*. ABRL (New York: Doubleday, 2003) 202–206.

world. Even in this task I must acknowledge my own specificity and limitations in that I am not just any reader anywhere; I am an educated white Australian woman, a believing Christian for whom this gospel is part of my scriptural tradition. I read, then, with a hermeneutic of faith, as well as a hermeneutic of suspicion, as I critically engage with the text and wrestle with its multiple layers of meaning to retrieve a meaning that offers faith and life for me and for others today.

The dialogue between my twenty-first-century world and the world of the gospel presumes that there is historical continuity between these two worlds, making possible what Hans-Georg Gadamer refers to as a "fusion of horizons."

> [T]he horizon of the present cannot be formed without the past. There is no more an isolated horizon of the present than there are historical horizons. Understanding, rather, is always the fusion of these horizons which we imagine to exist by themselves. . . . In a tradition this process of fusion is continually going on, for there old and new continually grow together to make something of living value.[19]

This understanding of interpretation, particularly of historical works, as a fusion of horizons is important for naming what understanding means. Real understanding occurs when we have made a text our own, when we have appropriated its meaning for ourselves.[20] However, what we make our own is not an alien experience or another's mental insights, for that is impossible. What I make my own is the referential meaning of the text, the "what it is about," which is what the text is directed toward. This is the horizon of meaning that an author attempts to inscribe in a text. Insofar as I am able to place myself in the ongoing traditioning process that has its origins in the first century but continues to be effective today, the gospel has possibilities for enlarging my own current horizon. So understanding is not my empathetic entering into the past world inscribed in the text, but my allowing the text to impact on me and to work a transformation of my current vision of reality. Understanding a text will necessarily involve a change. This insight into the effectiveness of understanding was discussed by Gadamer particularly in relation to the law and the gospel. "[T]he text, whether law or Gospel, if it is to be understood properly, i.e., according to

---

[19] Hans-Georg Gadamer, *Truth and Method*, trans. John Cumming (2nd ed. New York: Seabury Press, 1975) 273.

[20] Ricoeur, *Hermeneutics and the Human Sciences*, 82–93.

the claim it makes, must be understood at every moment, in every situation, in a new and different way. Understanding here is always application."[21]

This study will use various methods. Historical and social criticism will provide some insights into the first-century world of the author and his community. It will provide the essential background for the author's narrative and for a reader's first understanding of what the text means. In conjunction with these historical considerations, my major methodology is best described as narrative criticism. I will attempt to discover the narrative world the author has created by use of characterization, dialogues, chains of events, irony, Old Testament quotations and allusions, figurative language, and particularly by the structure through which the narrative unfolds, both in small discrete units and in larger sections.[22] As my focus in this study is on the possible symbolic meaning of the household, I have selected scenes that relate to households, namely, Jesus' initial invitation to disciples to come and stay with him (John 1), the wedding at Cana (John 2), birth (John 3), the household of Lazarus, Martha, and Mary (John 11 and 12), the last discourse, when Jesus gathers with his own (John 13–17), and the Jerusalem household where disciples first experience the Risen Lord (John 20). The questions I bring to these pericopes are:

- Does the narrative offer any indication that the household scene within the text has as its reference the post-Easter household of the Johannine community?
- Does the household narrative suggest a deeper level of meaning that gives expression to the symbolic world of the community, to its faith, its spirituality, and its sense of identity?
- Is it possible to detect in these household scenes any hints that we are not only dealing with "time past," i.e., the time of Jesus, but also "time present," i.e., the time of the Johannine community?
- Is the living "household of God" casting its own shadow on those scenes when Jesus gathers his own?

As the study develops, I will, where necessary, review aspects of my study of the Temple, which, as I explained above, provided my first level of understanding the symbolic world of this gospel.

---

[21] Gadamer, *Truth and Method*, 275.

[22] This list of narrative techniques is descriptive rather than exhaustive. One of the early pioneers in narrative criticism of the Gospel of John is Alan Culpepper; his study provides a more thorough listing of narrative devices. See R. Alan Culpepper, *Anatomy of the Fourth Gospel: A Study in Literary Design* (Philadelphia: Fortress Press, 1983).

Presuppositions and Cautions

The gospel we now have is the narrative formulation of one community's insight into the person and ministry of Jesus. This theology developed over some decades of oral teaching, Spirit-guided recollection, and ongoing community praxis in different historical circumstances. Underlying the theology, which determined the particular narrative shape of this gospel, was a community's experience of the living presence of Jesus, mediated now through "another Paraclete" (John 14:16). As Sandra Schneiders writes,

> it was a particular *lived experience* of union with God in the risen Jesus through his gift of the Spirit/Paraclete within the believing community (spirituality) that gave rise gradually to a particular *articulated understanding* of Christian faith (theology). This theology was encoded in the Gospel text, and through it we gain access to the experience, the spirituality, that gives this Gospel its unique character.[23]

In Ricoeur's terms, the theology and christology are the primary reference of the narrative; the story of Jesus is *about* the incarnation of the divine Word. My other book, *God Dwells with Us,* explored this primary reference by examining the christological significance of the Temple as symbol. The present study aims to reach behind the theology, behind the primary reference, to the lived experience, and to ask what would be the living "spirituality" or sense of religious identity of a community that would articulate its theology in this manner? This is a more difficult task, since the primary reference of the gospel is the meaning of the life, death, and resurrection of *Jesus.* The narrative is *for* the community, but is not *about* the community. But, taking the theology of the gospel as a clue into the community's spirituality, I presume there may be some traces of this community life, however subtle, within the narrative. David Aune's words express my fundamental hermeneutic and its inherent difficulties.

> It would therefore be incorrect to claim, with Ernst Käsemann, that basic elements of congregational life, worship, sacraments and the ministry play only insignificant roles in the Fourth Gospel.[24] *Such elements do not receive explicit treatment precisely because they are the presuppositions of the ecclesial context out of which the Gospel arose.* Since the Fourth Gospel was not

---

[23] Sandra M. Schneiders, *Written That You May Believe: Encountering Jesus in the Fourth Gospel* (New York: Crossroad, 1999) 48.

[24] Ernst Käsemann, *The Testament of Jesus according to John 17* (Philadelphia: Fortress Press, 1968) 27.

written for the consumption of modern scholars, it is necessary for us to break the code in which the Gospel is written, and which it presupposes.[25]

This study begins with an intuition, or guess,[26] that the household scenes in the gospel may provide access to "the code" in which the community's experience has been inscribed. It will be the task of this book to test if this intuition is accurate, and to validate it through careful exegesis of the text, alert always to the danger of reading more into the text than it can rightfully sustain. The dialogue between the first-century world and my world will therefore need to be both rigorous and receptive. According to Ricoeur, "Hermeneutics seems to me to be animated by this double motivation: willingness to suspect, willingness to listen."[27] My faith-filled lived experience may alert me to nuances or clues in the text suggesting the faith-filled experience of the Johannine community, but the final arbiter of the accuracy of my reading must be the text itself in its holistic integrity.[28]

Recent Studies on the Household

There is a growing number of books exploring the phenomenon of the early Christian *ekklesia* and its relationship to first-century Jewish/Greco-Roman households.[29] Some writers take the gospel as the starting point and

---

[25] David E. Aune, *The Cultic Setting of Realized Eschatology in Early Christianity.* NovTSup 28 (Leiden: Brill, 1972) 73 (italics supplied).

[26] "In the beginning, understanding is a guess." See Ricoeur, *Interpretation Theory,* 74. In the following pages Ricoeur goes on to speak of the necessity and process of validating the initial guess.

[27] Paul Ricoeur, *Freud and Philosophy,* trans. Denis Savage (New Haven: Yale University Press, 1970) 27.

[28] In describing the interpretive value of clues Ricoeur writes: "A clue serves as a guide for a specific construction, in that it contains at once a permission and a prohibition; it excludes unsuitable constructions and allows those which give more meaning to the same words. Second . . . one construction can be said to be more probable than another, not more truthful. The more probable is that which, on the one hand, takes account of the greatest number of facts furnished by the text, including its potential connotation, and on the other hand, offers a qualitatively better convergence between the features which it takes into account. A mediocre explanation can be called narrow or forced" (Ricoeur, *Hermeneutics and the Human Sciences,* 175–76).

[29] See, for example and for further bibliographical works, Roger W. Gehring, *House Church and Mission: The Importance of Household Structures in Early Christianity* (Peabody, MA: Hendrickson, 2004); Joseph H. Hellerman, *The Ancient Church as Family* (Minneapolis: Fortress, 2001); David L. Balch and Carolyn Osiek, eds., *Early Christian Families in Context: An Interdisciplinary Dialogue* (Grand Rapids: Eerdmans, 2003). One issue of the *Journal for the Study of the New Testament* was devoted entirely to this

read this text with the aid of sociological studies on ancient Mediterranean families.[30] Other writers take for their text the archaeological and epigraphical remains and interpret these in order to construct a picture of a first-century household and its many complex activities and associations.[31] These studies provide helpful background in a general way to Mediterranean family life, but historical reconstructions have necessary limitations. Documentary evidence may only be available for certain types of households and in certain locations, either because the type of household did not keep documents, as in the case of nomadic Bedouins, or because these documents have not been preserved. A similar difficulty applies to archaeological and epigraphical remains. It is possible that the picture constructed through such evidence is quite skewed and not applicable to a specific location. There is also the problem of locating the Johannine community with utter certainty. While these limitations suggest that it is not possible to propose a precise picture of a household that would apply to the Johannine setting, nonetheless there is sufficient evidence to recreate a general idea of some customs.[32]

One such general feature is the patriarchal organization of family and social life in the first century. This immediately raises serious hermeneutical difficulties for modern interpreters. In suggesting "household" as a possible symbol for the self-identity of the Johannine community, am I implying that this gospel community organized itself along patriarchal lines? Studies of the New Testament that restrict themselves to sociological analysis can suggest this. A proper understanding of symbol will liberate the term "household" from its sociological meaning and allow it to take on a theo-

---

theme, and a bibliography of recent studies can be found in the editors' introduction; see Margaret MacDonald and Halvor Moxnes, "Domestic Space and Families in Early Christianity: Editors' Introduction," *JSNT* 27 (2004) 5–6.

[30] For example, Michael H. Crosby, *House of Disciples: Church, Economics and Justice in Matthew* (Maryknoll, NY: Orbis, 1988); Michael F. Trainor, *The Quest for Home: The Household in Mark's Community* (Collegeville: Liturgical Press, 2001).

[31] For example, Carolyn Osiek and David L. Balch, *Families in the New Testament World: Households and House Churches* (Louisville: Westminster John Knox, 1997).

[32] An important study from this perspective on the Fourth Gospel is Jan Gabriël van der Watt, *Family of the King: Dynamics of Metaphor in the Gospel According to John*. Biblical Interpretation Series 47 (Leiden: Brill, 2000). The author provides an excursus on the use and limitations of socioeconomic models for investigating family life in John (pp. 163–65). In some respects my study is similar to *Family of the King* in its exploration of symbol and a focus on "family" terminology in the gospel. However, my starting point has been the symbol of the Temple, which has opened up for me the possibilities of the expression found in the phrase "my Father's house," with its reference to the household of God.

logical meaning that is more appropriate, given the theological nature of the gospel text. In other words, the household model for the Johannine community is not to be found in the social sphere of the first century, but must be located in the world of divine relationships.

The Symbol of the Father's Household in this Study

Ricoeur begins his work on symbol by examining the dynamics of a metaphor, which has a more restricted semantic context. A metaphor is a linguistic double meaning. Two realities from different contexts or domains are brought together in such a way that, simply at a verbal level, the statement does not make sense.[33] The reader is then forced to grapple with the assimilation of these two realities into some meaningful relationship beyond the verbal sense, creating something new out of what would otherwise be absurd. In speaking of God dwelling in a temple, or of God's household, we are speaking metaphorically. Whatever we mean by the word "God," it has the sense of a transcendent, spiritual, divine reality beyond containment "in" either the spatial or temporal dimensions of human experience. We may speak of sacred times or places, but these are terms we use to describe our embodied experience of the numinous. In this metaphorical sense we may say God is present or dwells in a temple, but the theory of metaphor also notes that there is both an "is" and an "is not" operating in this type of speech. Literally God, the full reality of divinity, is not present or dwelling "in" a temple/house. The linguistic tension between the "is" and the "is not" is the dynamic that enables a metaphor to create a new perception of reality. The meaning of a metaphor transcends the literalness of the words in the sentence, and the image evoked by the metaphor creates a new reality in the mind of the reader that cannot be exactly translated.

In a similar manner a symbol looks beyond its factual reality for its meaning; it refers to another level of reality and truth that is only accessible through the symbol. This last point is critical for understanding the theological necessity of symbols. Our primary way of knowing is mediated through sensory experiences: what we see, hear, taste, touch, and smell. However, in itself the divine or spiritual world is beyond such sensory experience. For that reason the process of revelation occurs through symbolic experience. God's presence is known through what God does: in creation, in the history of Israel, through prophetic teaching and writing, and for

---

[33] The following brief description of metaphor and symbol draws on Ricoeur's *Interpretation Theory*, 45–69.

Christians in the incarnation of the divine Word. The reality of Jesus' humanity provides access to the reality of the divine Word. The transcendent is present in the symbol.[34]

In the Fourth Gospel, particularly in the last discourse, Jesus refers to aspects of his relationship with God as a model for human relationships: "Holy Father, protect them in your name that you have given me so that they may be one as we are one" (17:11); "that they may all be one. As you, Father, are in me and I am in you, may they also be in us" (17:21, also 22).[35] This explicit comparison with the divine world provides a hermeneutic for examining household not in reference to Jewish/Greco-Roman patriarchal models, but using the relationships between the Father, Jesus, and Spirit as the primary reference.[36] While the term "Father's house/hold" comes from the social context of the gospel, it must be understood in a symbolic sense as referring to people in relationship with God and each other. Its reference is to a household "not of this world."[37]

Similarly, the word "Father" as a reference to God must be understood in a metaphorical sense and may not be reduced to equating God with a

---

[34] Sandra Schneiders' early work on symbolism in the Fourth Gospel remains foundational for appreciating the symbolic nature of biblical texts from a theological perspective, especially the Fourth Gospel. See Sandra M. Schneiders, "History and Symbolism in the Fourth Gospel," in Marinus de Jonge, ed., *L'Évangile de Jean: Sources, Rédaction, Théologie.* BETL 44 (Louvain: Louvain University Press, 1977) 371–76, and eadem, "Symbolism and the Sacramental Principle in the Fourth Gospel," in Pius-Ramon Tragan, ed., *Segni E Sacramenti Nel Vangelo Di Giovanni.* Studia Anselmiana 67 (Rome: Editrice Anselmiana, 1977) 221–35. Craig Koester, *Symbolism in the Fourth Gospel: Meaning, Mystery, Community* (Minneapolis: Fortress Press, 1995) has contributed a study of many symbols found across the gospel, and most recently Ruben Zimmermann published a major study of the phenomenon of symbolism in John, using John 10 to demonstrate his theory; see Ruben Zimmermann, *Christologie der Bilder im Johannesevangelium: Die Christopoetik des vierten Evangeliums unter besonderer Berücksichtigung von John 10.* WUNT 171 (Tübingen: Mohr Siebeck, 2004).

[35] Other examples of this correlation between the divine and human worlds can be seen in John 6:57; 10:14-15; 13:15, 34; 15:9, 10, 12; 17:18; 20:21.

[36] The use of "household" as a way of speaking of the divine relationships will be explored in more detail in this study. I am not suggesting here that the Fourth Gospel is already using a full Trinitarian concept of God that will develop in later centuries. To read the formulations of Nicea and Chalcedon back into the Fourth Gospel is anachronistic.

[37] In speaking of his kingship, Jesus says to Pilate: "My kingship is not of this world" (19:36). I am applying this same principle to the notion of household. While the metaphor of household or kingship uses the language of first-century culture, the reference is to the divine world.

male patriarch. The frequency of the word "Father" in the Fourth Gospel has attracted a number of studies and a variety of responses.[38] The gospel itself provides a clue to why the image of "father" is so significant. In the discussion following the Sabbath healing in chapter 5, Jesus claims he has the authority to give life and to judge on the Sabbath because these are two works God is permitted to do on the Sabbath (5:17).[39] In his argument with "the Jews"[40] he provides a brief parable of a son learning a trade by copying his father.[41] "Very truly I tell you, the son can do nothing by himself, but only what he sees the father doing; for whatever he does, the son does likewise. The father loves the son and shows him everything that he does" (5:19-20). The son apprenticed to his father and therefore able to do what his father does provides "the underlying imagery of Father and Son in the Fourth Gospel."[42] Dorothy Lee draws on C. H. Dodd's work to examine the meaning of "Father" within the gospel text; in other words, she allows the evangelist to create his own world of meaning. In this way fatherhood is properly interpreted from within the narrative by asking what kind of father-figure is described in the gospel. She points to the number of times "the Father-symbol occurs in narrative contexts that are concerned with the surrender of power."[43] The Father's love for the world renders him vulnerable through the gift of his son, given over to death. Power and authority are not held

---

[38] In 1999 an entire edition of *Semeia* was devoted to the use of "Father" in this gospel without resolving the problems created by the use of paternal God-language; see Adele Reinhartz, ed., *God the Father in the Gospel of John. Semeia* 85 (Atlanta: Society of Biblical Literature, 1999).

[39] On the prerogatives of God's Sabbath work see M. Asiedu-Peprah, *Johannine Sabbath Conflicts as Juridical Controversy.* WUNT 2nd ser. 132 (Tübingen: Mohr Siebeck, 2001) 76–77.

[40] See Moloney, *John,* 9–11 for the meaning of "the Jews" as a characterization of disbelief rather than of actual historical persons. He writes: "The expression 'the Jews' in this gospel must always be placed within quotation marks because it does not represent the Jewish people. A critical reading of the Johannine Gospel makes it clear that 'the Jews' are those characters in the story who have made up their minds about Jesus. . . . *They do not accurately represent the experience of the historical Jesus*" (italics in the original, p. 10). On the purpose of this narrative strategy see the recent study by Raimo Hakola, *Identity Matters: John, the Jews and Jewishness*, NovTSup 118 (Boston and Leiden: Brill, 2005) esp. 232–38.

[41] See the study by C. H. Dodd, "A Hidden Parable in the Fourth Gospel," in his *More New Testament Studies* (Manchester: Manchester University Press, 1968) 30–40.

[42] Dorothy A. Lee, "The Symbol of Divine Fatherhood," *Semeia* 85 (1999) 179.

[43] Lee, "Divine Fatherhood," 180. Lee develops her critical understanding of the symbol of God as Father in her recent title, *Flesh and Glory: Symbolism, Gender and Theology in the Gospel of John* (New York: Crossroad, 2002) 110–34.

onto by the Father, but are relinquished freely to the Son. This is in sharp contrast with the figure of the *paterfamilias* in the Greco-Roman world. Lee contrasts the gospel language of intimacy and mutuality with that of duty and fear associated with Roman family life and points out that the mutual love between Father and Son is opened out to include others. "Unlike patriarchal kinship, those outside the immediate family are drawn into the paternal embrace (*kolpon*, 1:18)."[44] Even the master-slave model is rejected and deconstructed by the model of friendship (15:11-17).

I find Lee's methodology and arguments convincing. With her, I want to insist that the symbolism of the gospel be taken seriously. God in God's-self is beyond gender categories, beyond names and representations, and would be utterly unknowable without God's condescending self-revelation in ways accessible to human apprehension. Even then the language used to speak of this revelation is necessarily metaphorical because of the limitation of language in adequately expressing the divine reality. The God we speak of always "is" and "is not" communicable. In becoming flesh, the divine has allowed a specific particularity, Jesus, to be the means of God's presence in history. The male Jesus is symbol of the divine Word, and the Father in this gospel is a symbol of the life-giving, self-surrendering God who invites all to be embraced as children (1:13). The fatherhood of God functions in the text as a way the evangelist tries to articulate the experience of being drawn into participation in God's own life mediated through Jesus and the Spirit. A father-son relationship becomes a symbol for the believer's post-Easter experience of life in Jesus. As Lee writes, "God's fatherhood reveals itself, on the one hand, through the giving away of power. . . . On the other hand, God's fatherhood operates in the Gospel by drawing others into the filial relationship between God and Jesus, so that it becomes symbolic of God's relationship to the world."[45] Ultimately, the challenge to the reader is not so much to see divinity in terms of fatherhood, but to re-vision fatherhood in the light of the gospel.

The Post-Easter Perspective

In 1965 a German scholar, Franz Mussner,[46] presented a new hermeneutical approach for reading the Fourth Gospel, based on the interpretation

---

[44] Lee, "Divine Fatherhood," 181.

[45] Lee, *Flesh and Glory*, 126.

[46] Franz Mussner, *Die johanneische Sehweise und die Frage nach dem historischen Jesus.* QD 28 (Freiburg: Herder, 1965), translated by W. J. O'Hara as Franz Mussner, *The Historical Jesus in the Gospel of John.* QD 19 (New York: Herder, 1967).

theory of Gadamer. In his study he used the term *johanneische Sehweise,* which I translate as a Johannine way of seeing, or Johannine perspective. This perspective merges the pre-Easter history of Jesus and the post-Easter experience of Jesus as the risen and glorified Lord—Gadamer's "fusion of horizons." The present experience of the risen Jesus, mediated through the Paraclete, brings to this gospel its particular first-person character, which at times is made explicit: "we have seen his glory" (1:14) and at times is implied: "He who saw this has testified" (19:35). As well as its first-person character as a witness, this gospel offers a self-conscious post-Easter recollection of events: "After he was raised from the dead, his disciples remembered that he had said this" (2:22); "when Jesus was glorified, then they remembered that this had been written of him and had been done to him" (12:16).[47] Mussner's initial work has been most comprehensively developed by another German scholar, C. Hoegen-Rohls,[48] who argues that the Johannine perspective is governed by the activity of the Spirit enabling believers to look back on the life and death of Jesus and to see and recognize in him the presence of the divine Word. In other words, the Spirit enables a symbolic way of interpreting the Jesus event, and this is the foundation of the Fourth Gospel's theology, which is then given expression in the narrative. The present Spirit-mediated experience of the risen and glorified Lord permeates the narrative vision of the evangelist, giving this gospel its unique quality when compared with the Synoptics. While Mussner developed his argument by examining the terms used in the gospel by which people came to knowledge of Jesus, Hoegen-Rohls takes as her starting point the final discourse and Jesus' promises regarding the Paraclete (14:16-17, 26; 15:26; 16:13-14). Hoegen-Rohls' work articulates the underlying premise of this study, that a careful and sensitive reading of the narrative will reveal not only the theology of the evangelist but also the gospel's post-Easter spirituality.

---

[47] Mussner summarizes his findings in these words: "The Johannine mode of vision deepened the early Church's knowledge of Christ, by rendering present in the Gospel through the Paraclete the 'remembrance' of the Christ-event and so maintaining the 'situation' of Jesus in the church and the world" (*The Historical Jesus,* 93).

[48] Christina Hoegen-Rohls, *Der nachösterliche Johannes: Die Abschiedsreden als hermeneutischer Schlüssel zum vierten Evangelium.* WUNT 2nd ser. 84 (Tübingen: Mohr, 1996) 309–10.

John as Witness and Friend

The gospel narrative opens with the person of John. On this point the Fourth Gospel is in agreement with the Synoptics, but thereafter the similarities end. In the Synoptics, John is the herald, the precursor. He is the one who comes before, "to prepare the way of the Lord," where "the Lord" is Jesus of Nazareth. So strong is this tradition of John's role as the forerunner that it is regularly taken to reflect the historical and sequential reality that John baptized Jesus, then John was arrested, then Jesus began his ministry of preaching in Galilee. This is the sequence we find in the first chapter of Mark, with its parallel in Matthew 3–4. Luke follows a similar temporal scheme, but this is shown predominantly in the birth narrative, where John precedes Jesus; in Luke's gospel narrative John is in prison prior to Jesus' baptism (3:20), and this change to Mark's order is seen as an attempt by Luke to downplay the significance of John in comparison with Jesus.[1] The single voice dissenting from this picture is that of the Fourth Gospel, which in the past has been too readily dismissed as "unhistorical" and "spiritual" because of its symbolic language. In this gospel, however, history and symbol are not mutually exclusive realities, for it proclaims that history is now the locus of the divine presence. In the flesh of Jesus we have the eternal Word of God, and therefore history is now radiant with the glory of God. "The Word became flesh and dwelt among us, and we have seen his glory, glory as of a Father's only son" (1:14). The event of the incarnation undergirds the principle that will govern the telling of this gospel's story.[2] Words

---

[1] Walter Wink, *John the Baptist in the Gospel Tradition* (Cambridge: Cambridge University Press, 1968) 83, 91.

[2] This description of the uniquely Johannine way of recounting the tradition of Jesus was termed the "Sacramental Principle" by Sandra Schneiders, and her article, "Symbolism and the Sacramental Principle in the Fourth Gospel" remains one of the clearest

and deeds, places and times will be both mundane, in that they refer to things of this world, and symbolic, in that they at the same time look to the transcendent to find their fuller meaning. There is a reality in the gospel narrative that is fully historical and at the same time transcends the historical. Where this gospel stands apart from the Synoptics is in its way of recounting the tradition it has received. Whereas the Synoptics invite the reader into a symbolic world in the many parables of Jesus recounted as part of the narrative, the Fourth Gospel uses the narrative itself to invite the reader into its symbolizing dynamic.[3] Sandra Schneiders writes: "Symbolism in John is not an element in the Gospel but a dimension of the Gospel as a whole, namely, its characteristic revelatory mode."[4] The story of Jesus is, from the beginning, the history of the Word-made-flesh. Nowhere is this more evident than in the portrayal of John, where history and symbol are juxtaposed. This chapter will not attempt a reconstruction of the historical Baptizer; for those wanting a historical assessment of what evidence we have, I recommend the excellent study by John Meier in the second volume of his work on Jesus, *A Marginal Jew.*[5] There is also a short study of the Baptizer material from a historical perspective in an article by Frank Moloney, "The Fourth Gospel and the Jesus of History."[6] My interest is to take up two images from the early tradition and see how the fourth evangelist has used this traditional material for his christological and ecclesial purposes, for John is the reader's introduction to the household of God.

The Prologue

John appears first in the Prologue, where he is described as "a man sent from God" (1:6). His God-ordained role is "as a witness to testify to the light, that all might believe through him" (v. 7). This verse clearly names

---

expositions of the symbolic character of the Fourth Gospel as a theological strategy. See there especially pp. 221–35.

[3] Brown, *Introduction to the Gospel of John* (see ch. 1, n. 13 above), 289, compares Johannine symbolism to the Synoptic parables.

[4] Schneiders, "History and Symbolism in the Fourth Gospel" (see ch. 1, n. 34 above), 376.

[5] John P. Meier, *A Marginal Jew: Rethinking the Historical Jesus.* 3 vols. ABRL 2: *Mentor, Message, and Miracles* (New York: Doubleday, 1994–) chs. 12 and 13, especially 101–105. This chapter will not repeat the details of Meier's arguments, but will draw on many of his conclusions. More recently Catherine Murphy's work provides a helpful introduction to redaction criticism in its evaluation of Baptist material; see Catherine M. Murphy, *John the Baptist: Prophet of Purity for a New Age.* Interfaces (Collegeville: Liturgical Press, 2003).

[6] Francis J. Moloney, "The Fourth Gospel and the Jesus of History," *NTS* 46 (2000) 42–58.

who John is in this gospel, not John the Baptizer but simply John, the witness. The Fourth Gospel never gives John the title "the Baptist" from the Synoptics, nor do we ever see John baptizing anyone. His ministry of baptism is obviously known and referred to (1:25-28; 3:23) and is a reason why he was sent (1:33), but this aspect of his ministry is downplayed so that his role as witness can be emphasized.

Still within the Prologue, John witnesses directly and says, "This was he of whom I said, 'the one coming after me ranks ahead of me, for he existed before me'" (v. 15). This brief verse raises a number of critical issues:

- Who is John referring to by this expression?

- What is meant by the expression "coming after me"? Does it mean discipleship?

In the context of the Christian proclamation of Jesus and the Fourth Gospel's theology of the pre-existent Word, the verse as it now stands is a reference to Jesus, who ranks higher than John and whose existence has already been situated "in the beginning."[7] However, the statement is more complex than this. This verse is one of very few in the Fourth Gospel that has a close parallel in the Synoptics, as the following table shows.

John	Mark	Matthew	Luke
1:15 (John witnessed to him, and proclaimed, "This was he of whom I said, **'the one coming after me ranks ahead of me, for he existed before me.'"** **1:27** ". . . **the one coming after me,** the thong of whose sandal I am not worthy to untie."	**1:7** He proclaimed, **"One more powerful than I is coming after me;** I am not worthy to stoop down and untie the thong of his sandals."	**3:11** "I baptize you with water for repentance, **but one coming after me is more powerful than I am;** I am not worthy to carry his sandals. He will baptize you with the Holy Spirit and fire."	**3:16** John answered all of them saying, "I baptize you with water, **but one more powerful than I is coming;** I am not worthy to untie the thong of his sandals. He will baptize you with the Holy Spirit and fire."

The Fourth Gospel shares with Mark and Matthew a statement placed on the lips of John about "one who is coming after me" (in Luke this sequence is implied), a statement of unworthiness to untie his sandals (all

---

[7] Raymond E. Brown discusses the understanding of this expression in a temporal sense as referring to the pre-existent *logos*; see his *The Gospel According to John: Introduction, Translation, and Notes.* 2 vols. AB 29, 29a (New York: Doubleday, 1966, 1970) 1:56, 63–65.

Synoptics), and a comparison indicating that the coming one is more deserving of honor (ranks before [John]; is mightier [Synoptics]). In assessing the evidence, on the grounds of multiple attestation John Meier concludes that "we have good reason to accept this as substantially the Baptist's own teaching."[8] But what would John have meant by this in its original setting? Again, drawing on Meier's work, we can say that this statement probably indicates John's expectation of the dawn of the eschatological age, and that he realized that there was one coming who would have a greater role in bringing this about.[9] According to the prophet Malachi, Elijah was to return before the Day of the Lord. "Lo I will send you the prophet Elijah before the great and terrible day of the LORD comes" (Mal 4:6). It is possible that during John's ministry he considered that such an Elijah figure was soon to come and that his own ministry was in preparation for that day.[10] Read in this light, his statement in 1:15 would have had a temporal sense of "the one who comes after me (Elijah *redivivus*) is more important than I, for he was before me."[11] Taken by itself, as far as we can hypothesize, these words "coming after me," as spoken by John, do not suggest discipleship, but rather a statement about the temporal order: John first, then the coming one. Meier will use other material in order to propose that there was a time when Jesus followed John, in the sense that he shared John's view that Israel's end-time was approaching and Israel needed to undergo a radical change of heart if it was not to experience God's judgment.[12] The question of whether Jesus stayed within John's circle of disciples meets with varying responses. Only the Fourth Gospel depicts Jesus carrying out a ministry of

---

[8] Meier, *A Marginal Jew* 2:33; Murphy, *John the Baptist,* 57.

[9] Meier, *A Marginal Jew* 2:35.

[10] There has been considerable debate about whether the expectation of Elijah was part of Second Temple Judaism or owes its origin to early Christian teaching. A brief summary of this debate can be found in Joan E. Taylor, *The Immerser: John the Baptist within Second Temple Judaism* (Grand Rapids: Eerdmans, 1997) 281–88. Taylor draws the following conclusion based on evidence from Qumran and other intertestamental writings: "The main point to be derived from this brief survey of texts is that Elijah was expected by some Jews to come before the end, but how one imagined the end depended on many factors. There was no one, fully supported scenario among Jews of this time" (p. 285).

[11] The same temporal sense would apply to any apocalyptic figure such as Elijah, Moses, or Son of Man. As Meier notes, John would not have considered any of these figures his disciple (*A Marginal Jew* 2:118).

[12] Meier, *A Marginal Jew* 2:106–109. Moloney ("The Fourth Gospel and the Jesus of History," 48–49) goes further in suggesting that Jesus was a follower of John in the sense of a disciple, without John being aware of his identity as "the one coming after me."

baptizing (3:22), and while there is no corroborating evidence, the principle of embarrassment argues for the historicity of this information.[13] However, this activity alone does not indicate that Jesus is or was one of John's disciples in a formal sense. He may well have begun a ministry of preaching and baptizing independent of John. Weighing the evidence, I think there is a strong possibility that Jesus was a disciple of John for some period, but I speak of this as possibility rather than probability.

Day 1. John and the Jewish Delegation

When the gospel narrative begins, John appears in dispute with priests and Levites from Jerusalem regarding his identity. John does not identify the "one coming after" him explicitly as Elijah or the Son of Man, but leaves this identity vague.[14] What is clear, though, is that John, along with other Jews, is still expecting another figure to come, and is not seeing himself in the role of Elijah *redivivus*. In fact, in the Fourth Gospel he explicitly denies this title when asked by the delegation from Jerusalem, "Are you Elijah?" John replies, "I am not" (1:21). Given such a clear and resounding "I am not" (*ouk eimi*), why has the Christian tradition so strongly identified John as the forerunner, the Elijah?

The association of John with Elijah comes as part of the post-Easter proclamation of Jesus as the Christ. In looking back at these two figures and attempting to clarify their roles and relationships, Christians concluded that if Jesus was the Christ, then John must have been the Elijah promised in the prophet Malachi.[15] Therefore we must distinguish between the historical John, as far as he can be ascertained, and John as a character created in the Synoptic texts. From the above discussion of the phrase about "the mightier one" coming after John, which we have argued was part of John's own teaching, it is clear that the historical John did not consider himself to be that figure. In fact, in Mark's Gospel Jesus is the one who is first considered to be Elijah (Mark 6:15; 8:28).[16] It is likely that an early form of

[13] Meier, *A Marginal Jew* 2:122. That Jesus' baptizing activity was embarrassing can be seen in the correction of this information in John 4:2: "Although Jesus himself did not baptize, but only his disciples."

[14] Meier suggests that this vagueness may have been intentional on John's part; see *A Marginal Jew* 2:35.

[15] On the association of Elijah and John in the early Christian community see Ferdinand Hahn, *The Titles of Jesus in Christology: Their History in Early Christianity*, trans. Harold Knight and George Ogg (London: Lutterworth, 1969) 365–72.

[16] There are passages in the Synoptics in which Jesus identifies John and Elijah (Mark 9:11-13; Matt 11:9-10; Luke 7:24-27), but Meier (*A Marginal Jew* 2:141–42) argues that these sayings are "probably a Christian reflection added to an authentic logion of Jesus

Mark introduced John simply as "the voice of one crying in the wilderness: 'Prepare the way of the Lord, make straight his paths'" (Mark 1:3).[17] This is almost identical to the way John is introduced in the Fourth Gospel. At a later stage the lines from Malachi were added, "See, I am sending my messenger to prepare the way before me" (Mal 3:1). This verse from Malachi, which does not directly follow its introduction, "as it is written in Isaiah the prophet," expresses the post-Easter association of John with the apocalyptic messenger of Malachi, who is like a refiner's fire and whose task is to purify the sons of Levi, refining them like silver and gold (Mal 3:2-3). These images of purification by fire sit well with Elijah, the prophet of Mount Carmel (1 Kgs 18:30-39), but since John's ministry was with water it is unlikely he saw himself in that role.[18] Matthew and Luke develop these images of purification by fire and link them with one coming after John (Matt 3:11-12//Luke 3:16-17). The presentation of John simply as the voice in the wilderness preparing for another greater one still to come, which is found in the pre-Markan tradition and in the Fourth Gospel, is therefore more likely to be historical than the later, clearly Christian, association of John and Elijah. As C. K. Barrett states, "John sharply contradicts the earlier, and apparently growing, tradition, returning perhaps to a pre-synoptic stage of Christian belief, before apocalyptic necessity called for the discovery of Elijah in some forerunner of Christ."[19]

---

concerning the Baptist (Matt 11:7-9 *par.*)." For more details on the Markan redaction see Josef Ernst, *Johannes der Täufer: Interpretation—Geschichte—Wirkungsgeschichte.* BZNW 53 (Berlin: de Gruyter, 1989) 30–34.

[17] The quotation from Malachi is an awkward insertion, suggesting a later revision. Because of the form of the quotation, which is identical to that found in Matt 11:10//Luke 7:27, Mark may have relied on a source such as Q. In their introduction of John the Baptist, Matthew and Luke omit the lines from Malachi since they do not follow Mark's introductory phrase, and a later copyist corrected the introduction to read "As it is written in the prophets" (A K P W); see John A. T. Robinson, "Elijah, John and Jesus: An Essay in Detection," *NTS* 4 (1957–58) 267 n. 1; Bruce Metzger, *A Textual Commentary on the Greek New Testament: A Companion Volume to the United Bible Societies' Greek New Testament* (3rd ed. London: United Bible Societies, 1971) 73. For a further discussion of this verse, with the suggestion that the Malachi citation is editorial, see Ernst, *Johannes der Täufer,* 11–12. Even the description of Mark's clothing, which is often read as a direct allusion to Elijah, is now being questioned. The NRSV translates 2 Kgs 1:8 describing Elijah as a "hairy man," following the LXX, and not as a man "who wore a garment of haircloth" (RSV); see Robinson, "Elijah, John and Jesus," 261 n. 1; Meier, *A Marginal Jew* 2:47.

[18] So Robinson, "Elijah, John and Jesus," 265.

[19] C. K. Barrett, *The Gospel According to St. John* (2nd ed. London: S.P.C.K., 1978) 144; also Raymond E. Brown, *New Testament Essays* (Milwaukee: Bruce, 1965) 139:

Once the tradition made the John/Elijah association in order to affirm its identification of Jesus as the Christ, this colored its presentation of both John and Jesus and their respective ministries. John/Elijah is the forerunner who prepares the way and then withdraws, which is essentially the picture of John presented in the Synoptics. However, this sequence of John-then-Jesus, with John as the precursor, must be seen as a Synoptic interpretation and not taken uncritically to represent historical events.

After denying the titles the delegation from Jerusalem presented to him (John 1:20-21), John describes himself with the quotation from Isaiah referred to above, but with a significant change.

Isaiah	Mark	Matthew//Luke	John
40:3 A voice cries (*phōnē boōntos*): "In the wilderness prepare the way of the Lord, make straight in the desert a highway for our God."	**1:2** As it is written in the prophet Isaiah, "See, I am sending my messenger ahead of you, who will prepare your way; **3** a voice of one crying in the wilderness: 'Prepare the way of the Lord, make his paths straight.'"	**3:3** For this is the one of whom the prophet Isaiah spoke when he said, "The voice of one crying in the wilderness: 'Prepare the way of the Lord, make his paths straight.'"	**1:23** He said, "I am a voice of one crying (*phōnē boōntos*) in the wilderness, 'Make straight the way of the Lord,'" as the prophet Isaiah said.

The Fourth Gospel follows the LXX reading, as indicated by the use of the verb *boan*, when this gospel usually uses *krazein* (1:15; 7:28, 37; 12:44) or *kraugazein* (11:43; 12:13; 18:40; 19:6, 12, 15), but does not use the verb "prepare." Instead it conflates the two clauses found in Isaiah to read "make straight the way of the Lord." In discussing this change, Maarten Menken notes that the verb "prepare" is used to describe the task of someone preparing something for another who is absent, and only when it has been accomplished does the other arrive.[20] With the task of preparation finished, the one doing the preparation can depart. While this describes the role of a forerunner, which is how the Synoptics present John, it is not an appropriate description of John's role as described in the Fourth Gospel. John is to bear witness, which means he must know the one about whom he testifies. Therefore in the Fourth Gospel John cannot depart the scene as soon as Jesus appears. Instead there is a series of encounters between Jesus and John

---

". . . JBap seems to have conceived of his role only in terms of the Isaiah voice in the desert (a text associated with him in all four Gospels)."

[20] Maarten J. J. Menken, *Old Testament Quotations in the Fourth Gospel: Studies in Textual Form.* CBET 15 (Kampen: Kok Pharos, 1996) 26–28.

(1:29-34, 35-37; 3:23, 27-30), and it is implied that there was a previous encounter when Jesus was baptized (1:32-34). The ministry of John and the early ministry of Jesus are contemporaneous, thus making it possible for John to bear witness. Menken concludes: "John the Baptist is not so much Jesus' precursor as a witness who appears next to Jesus."[21]

The change in the wording of the Isaiah prophecy, along with John's explicit denial of the role of Elijah, indicates to the reader that the Fourth Gospel need not follow the temporal sequence of the Synoptics. In breaking the John/Elijah nexus the Fourth Evangelist is free to develop his own portrait of the relationship between the two men and free also to draw on earlier, pre-Markan traditions regarding them. In other words, the Fourth Gospel is free to bypass the Synoptic theological interpretation of John's role as the forerunner and can draw upon more historical memories; of course, the evangelist may also shape and present these memories in a way to augment his particular christology. Further evidence will be needed to decide on the historical reliability of John's characterization, but at least this evaluation can be freed from the assumption that the Synoptic sequence is necessarily historical, thus making the Synoptics the measure of historicity.

Days 2 and 3: John's Witness

On the following day Jesus is introduced into the narrative for the first time. At this point John witnesses to an event that had previously taken place, when Jesus' identity was revealed to him (1:32-34). Until that time John was unaware of Jesus' identity (1:31). The Fourth Gospel does not indicate when this revelation to John had occurred, other than that it was related to Jesus' baptism on some prior occasion. The next day John is with his disciples when he sees Jesus again and, following his identification of Jesus as "the Lamb of God," these two disciples follow Jesus (vv. 35-39).[22] From this point we hear nothing further of John until he returns in chapter 3, in the narrative of Jesus' early ministry. What I wish to emphasize is that John does not disappear completely from the gospel when Jesus appears and begins his own ministry. It is not said that John has been imprisoned. Furthermore, at some indefinite time before the start of the narrative, John and Jesus have already met at Jesus' baptism. Jesus invites two of John's

---

[21] Ibid. 31.

[22] It is beyond the scope of this study to discuss the possible meaning of the phrase "Lamb of God." At the 2005 Colloquium in Leuven a consensus was forming that this must be understood as a messianic title, placed as it is between John's denial that he is the Messiah (1:20, 25) and Andrew's statement to Simon, "We have found the Messiah" (1:42).

disciples to follow him, then begins his own ministry while John continues his. The Fourth Gospel therefore differs from the Synoptics in two significant ways: first, the ministries of Jesus and John overlap; second, some of Jesus' first disciples came from a group around John, a possibility that Moloney suggests "does not strain the imagination."[23] It was Raymond Brown who first proposed that some of the early members of the Johannine community might have been disciples of John, including the anonymous Beloved Disciple.[24] His hypothetical reconstruction of the Johannine community offers a way of understanding the high esteem accorded John in this gospel, while at the same time Jesus' superiority over John is consistently affirmed: John is a burning lamp (5:35), Jesus is the light (8:12); John is the witness (1:15), Jesus is the coming one (1:30); John is the bridegroom's friend (3:29), Jesus is the bridegroom (3:29); John must decrease while Jesus must increase (3:30).

Once we realize that the "John-then-Jesus" sequence of the Synoptics may be theologically driven, as an explanation of the relationship between the two men in terms of Elijah the forerunner, followed by the Christ, it is possible to weigh the evidence of the Fourth Gospel on its own merit. The chronology of all the gospels places John before Jesus. In Mark and Matthew, John baptizes Jesus (Mark 1:9-11; Matt 3:13-17), and the criterion of embarrassment suggests that this scene is recounted because it has a basis in history. It is unlikely that an early Christian community would invent this episode.[25] But the Fourth Gospel depicts Jesus in the ambit of John for at least three days, and then carrying out an independent ministry of baptism. How can this be evaluated?

John Meier addresses these questions by looking at the polemical nature of the Fourth Gospel's rhetoric in the description of John. He concludes that this rhetoric is necessary because the Fourth Evangelist seems to have had some opposition from some Baptizer followers still claiming the superiority of John over Jesus.[26] While John himself is presented very positively,

---

[23] Moloney, "The Fourth Gospel and the Jesus of History," 50.

[24] Raymond E. Brown, *The Community of the Beloved Disciple* (New York: Paulist, 1979) 29, 32. For a recent review of Brown's hypothesis on the historical development of the Johannine community and a survey of other reconstructions see Brown, *Introduction to the Gospel of John*, 69–78. See also W. Barnes Tatum, *John the Baptist and Jesus: A report of the Jesus Seminar* (Sonoma, CA: Polebridge Press, 1994) 163; Moloney, "The Fourth Gospel and the Jesus of History," 50–51, 57–58.

[25] Meier, *A Marginal Jew* 2:100–105; Murphy, *John the Baptist,* 59.

[26] Meier, *A Marginal Jew* 2:119. See also Brown's comments (*Introduction to the Gospel of John,* 156): "The cautions uttered against exaggerating the role of JBap and placing him on the level of Jesus may have arisen in Johannine history out of conflict

the view that John could be greater is strongly corrected at every opportunity. It is in the interest of the Evangelist therefore to minimize the significance of John compared to Jesus. If such were his pastoral situation, it would be thwarting his own goals were he to create a narrative suggesting that in any way Jesus was a follower of John. It would suit his christological purpose to follow the Synoptic lead and have John disappear from the scene before Jesus begins his ministry. That he does not do this, but allows the potentially embarrassing scenario of John and Jesus carrying out similar ministries at the same time, argues for the historical plausibility of the Fourth Gospel's account. A similar argument from embarrassment argues for the probable historicity of some of John's disciples becoming disciples of Jesus. "Granted the theological program of the Fourth Evangelist, it is difficult to imagine him making up the story that some of the most important disciples of Jesus had first chosen the Baptist as their master."[27]

I am not arguing here that every aspect of the Fourth Gospel's presentation of John is historical, but that his overall schema of John and Jesus engaging in similar and contemporary baptizing ministries is quite probable, as is his description of Jesus' first disciples coming from the ambit of John.[28] I think the Fourth Gospel is correct that John did not see himself as an Elijah figure, but thought there was another coming soon who would fit this role. John's task was to ready the people for this coming one by being the "voice in the wilderness" as prophesied by Isaiah. That the historical John clearly identified Jesus as this coming one is highly questionable. In Matthew and Luke John sends disciples from his prison to ask this question, and Meier argues for the historicity of this scene, using the criteria of embarrassment and discontinuity with later Christian apologetic.[29] Moloney considers that John most likely "went to his death not certain that his former follower, now exercising a ministry of his own, was ὁ ἰσχυρότερος [the mightier]."[30] It is also reasonable to suppose that had John recognized in Jesus the one he was awaiting, he himself would have become Jesus' disciple rather than simply sending two of his followers.

---

with the sectarians of JBap, but in the final Gospel they are not addressed to such sectarians. They have a Christological function of deepening the faith of John's Christian readers."

[27] Meier, *A Marginal Jew* 2:120.

[28] Joan E. Taylor argues otherwise, and accepts the Synoptic chronology that John was imprisoned before Jesus began his baptizing ministry (*The Immerser*, 288–99), but while she recognizes the christological agenda of the Fourth Gospel, I do not think she pays sufficient attention to the christological agenda of the Synoptics in casting John in the role of Elijah, the forerunner.

[29] Meier, *A Marginal Jew* 2:130–37.

[30] Moloney, "The Fourth Gospel and the Jesus of History," 48.

The Bridegroom's Friend[31]

When John's disciples follow Jesus, the narrative focus shifts away from John to the opening account of Jesus' ministry. John returns to the narrative following the episode with Nicodemus when some of his disciples raise their concerns regarding Jesus' popularity. In this context John provides his second statement clarifying his identity and role.[32] He is the friend of the bridegroom.

All four gospels have sayings applying the image of the bridegroom to Jesus within a context of a comparison between Jesus and John. In the Synoptics Jesus is asked why John's disciples fast while his disciples do not. In the Fourth Gospel the discussion begins with the issue of purification, and John's disciples ask him about Jesus' baptizing ministry, which seems to be more effective than John's.

Mark	Matthew	Luke	John
2:18 Now John's disciples and the Pharisees were fasting; and some came and said to him, "Why do John's disciples and the disciples of the Pharisees fast, but your disciples do not fast?" **19** Jesus said to them, "The wedding guests cannot fast while the **bridegroom** is with them, can they? As long as they have the **bridegroom**	**9:14** Then the disciples of John came to him, saying, "Why do we and the Pharisees fast, but your disciples do not fast?" **15** And Jesus said to them, "The wedding guests cannot mourn as long as the **bridegroom** is with them, can they? The days will come when the **bridegroom** is taken away from them, and then they will fast."	**5:33** Then the Pharisees and their scribes said to him, "John's disciples, like the disciples of the Pharisees, frequently fast and pray, but your disciples eat and drink." **34** Jesus said to them, "You cannot make wedding guests fast while the **bridegroom** is with them, can you? **35** The days will come when the **bridegroom** will be	**3:25** Now a discussion arose between John's disciples and a Jew about purifying. **26** And they came to John, and said to him, "Rabbi, the one who was with you beyond the Jordan, to whom you bore witness, here he is, baptizing, and all are going to him." **27** John answered, "No one can receive anything unless it has been given from heaven.

---

[31] In discussing marriage customs at the time of Jesus we must recognize that there are few, if any, texts from this period providing conclusive evidence of the social customs. What follows draws on scholarship based on references to marriage found in the biblical literature over a range of centuries, and what was codified in the Mishnah in the post-biblical era. A law code from Sumerian times indicates that the role of the bridegroom's friend was a very ancient custom that extended beyond Israel and included other Middle Eastern nations. I am presuming here that some of the customs described were preserved during the period of the Second Temple. See Adrianus Van Selms, "The Best Man and Bride—From Sumer to St. John with a New Interpretation of Judges, Chapters 14 and 15," *Journal of Near Eastern Studies* 9 (1950) 65–75.

[32] His first identifying statement was "I am the voice of one crying in the wilderness, 'Make straight the way of the Lord'" (1:23).

Mark	Matthew	Luke	John
with them, they cannot fast. **20** The days will come when the **bridegroom** is taken away from them, and then they will fast on that day."		taken away from them, and then they will fast in those days."	**28** You yourselves bear me witness, that I said, I am not the Christ, but I have been sent before him. **29** The one who has the bride is the **bridegroom;** the friend of the **bridegroom,** who stands and hears him, rejoices greatly at the **bridegroom's** voice; therefore this joy of mine has been fulfilled. **30** He must increase, but I must decrease."

Meier argues for the authenticity of the bridegroom image within a saying of Jesus in response to questions about fasting. "The sharp antithetical metaphors of fasting and a wedding, compressed into a single rhetorical question, are typical of the forceful rhetoric and parabolic speech of Jesus."[33] Without going into the possible meaning this image may have had for Jesus as an oblique reference to his own identity and mission, I wish to focus on the way the image was developed in the post-Easter communities, particularly the community behind the Fourth Gospel. The image of Jesus as the bridegroom has its background in the spousal imagery used in the Old Testament to describe the relationship between God and Israel (Hos 1, 2; Jer 2:2; Isa 61:10). In the post-Easter preaching this image was one of many such images transferred by the Christian communities to describe the relationship between Jesus and the *ekklesia* (2 Cor 11:2; Eph 5:27). The Ephesian imagery draws on the marriage custom by which the young woman prepares for her wedding by bathing before being led in procession and presented to her husband.[34]

> Husbands, love your wives, just as Christ loved the church and gave himself
> up for her, in order to sanctify her by cleansing her with the washing of water

[33] Meier, *A Marginal Jew* 2:448. While arguing for the authenticity of an original core saying, Meier also shows how later tradition has made use of this saying for apologetic reasons.

[34] Marie-Émile Boismard, "L'ami de l'Époux (Jo. iii, 29)," in Henri de Lubac, ed., *A la rencontre de Dieu: Mémorial Albert Gelin.* Bibliothèque de la Faculté Catholique de Théologie de Lyon 8 (Le Puy: Xavier Mappus, 1961) 292.

by the word, so as to present the church to himself in glory, without a spot or wrinkle or any such thing—yes, so that she may be holy and without blemish. (Eph 5:25-27)

The washing "of water by the word" is a reference to baptism, indicating that this community at Ephesus linked baptism with the bridal bath and drew on the marital imagery so loved by the prophets of Israel to speak of Christ's love for his church. When turning to the bridegroom imagery in the Fourth Gospel, we find a similar baptismal context.[35] John's disciples are comparing Jesus and John and, if we can read a spoken tone into the printed word, they seem disgruntled that Jesus is attracting more people than their own master. A similar air of annoyance seems to be voiced by John's disciples in Matthew's account above, "Why do we fast . . . but your disciples do not" (Matt 9:14)? There appears to be a genuine memory behind this episode. It recalls some rivalry between the disciples of these two men, who, at least for some period, were involved in similar baptizing ministries and yet have different practices. The Fourth Gospel takes up the image of the bridegroom, which the evidence suggests was originally a saying of Jesus, but places this on the lips of John. Now it is John who makes the comparison between himself and Jesus, with Jesus as the bridegroom while John has the role of the bridegroom's friend.

The Role of the "Friend" in Betrothal and Marriage Customs

Marriage in biblical time was purely a social institution with no religious ceremonies, since there is nothing in the Torah stipulating how marriages are to be celebrated.[36] It was an arrangement entered into by two families. While each village no doubt had its own local variations, the following description provides a general pattern for this arrangement. Marriage involved,

[35] My study of the Baptizer material is leading me toward accepting Ephesus as the most likely place for the final stages of this gospel's production. According to Acts 19:1-7, disciples of John were baptizing in Ephesus before Paul arrived there some time in the early fifties. Ephesus could therefore provide a location where a community needed to clarify the respective roles of John and Jesus. Since the bridal imagery was part of the community's understanding of baptism, this could have been influential in the Johannine development of the image of Jesus as the bridegroom in the narrative, particularly in relation to John.

[36] John J. Collins, "Marriage, Divorce and Family in Second Temple Judaism," in Leo J. Perdue, et al., *Families in Ancient Israel* (Louisville: Westminster John Knox, 1997) 107; Edmond Stapfer, *Palestine in the Time of Christ*, trans. Annie Harwood Holmden (New York: Armstrong and Son, 1885) 159, 165.

first, a formal betrothal, with the wedding following after a period of at least a year. Arrangements for the betrothal were made by the heads of the families of the young man and the young woman (Gen 24:1-4; Judg 14:1-3); if the father was absent, the arrangements became the duty of the mother or the elder brother (Gen 21:14-21).[37] In these negotiations the two fathers did not deal directly with each other but acted through deputies, probably to avoid any loss of honor if the negotiations broke down.[38] This was one of the tasks of the bridegroom's friend.[39] The deputy would be informed of the dowry and how much of it would be paid at the time of betrothal and how much at the actual wedding. The father of the groom and this friend/deputy went formally to the house of the intended bride to begin discussions about the appropriate dowry, which the bridegroom would pay, and which would revert to the wife in case of divorce.[40] When the purpose of the visit was explained, the bride's father would send for a deputy to speak for him. When the two deputies were present, the negotiations began and continued until there was consent about the marriage and the dowry. While the arrangements were made between the parents, the young couple seem to have had some choice in these affairs; Rebekah and Saul's daughter Michal were consulted to see if they agreed to go with Isaac and David respectively (Gen 24:53-58; 1 Sam 18:20). When consent was reached, the deputies and the fathers drank together as a sign of the covenant now agreed upon. At this point the couple was considered engaged until a more formal betrothal ceremony could take place. In earlier times the betrothal was a spoken pledge before witnesses (Ezek 16:8; Mal 2:14), but after the Exile a written document was drawn up in the presence of the families of the bride and groom and of other witnesses. According to H. Clay Turnbull[41] it was the deputies who drew up the formal contract, which was signed by the two fathers, and this was then "committed into the trusty hands of the best

---

[37] H. Clay Trumbull, *Studies in Oriental Social Life* (Philadelphia: The Sunday School Times Co., 1894) 12. Trumbull describes customs among Arabs in the Middle East in the nineteenth century C.E. His description seems to accord with customs found in the biblical literature.

[38] "Few events held more potential for the transfer of honor than marriage. Conversely, for a father, especially of the bride, few events would have been as laden with anxiety as marriage . . . every juncture presented a possibility for shame and social disaster. In such an environment it is a miracle that anyone would want to enter the process of negotiating a marriage." See Michael L. Satlow, *Jewish Marriage in Antiquity* (Princeton: Princeton University Press, 2001) 104.

[39] Fred H. Wight, *Manners and Customs of Bible Lands* (Chicago: Moody Press, 1953) 127.

[40] Collins, "Marriage, Divorce and Family," 109.

[41] Trumbull, *Oriental Social Life*, 20.

man."[42] During this ceremony the young man would give the young woman a ring, or some other valuable article, or a written promise of marriage as an initial sign of commitment; part of the dowry could also be given at this stage with the promise of the rest at the time of the wedding.[43] At this time a pledge would be spoken.[44] A typical pledge was "She is my wife and I am her husband." The betrothal was a very formal and binding agreement that could only be broken by divorce or death. From this description it is clear that the bridegroom's friend had a very significant role in the proceedings even before the wedding. As friend, he was the one who dealt directly with the family of the young woman. His negotiations played a crucial part in the father's consent. It is for this reason that there were ancient laws forbidding the father, should he refuse the request of the intended bridegroom, to give his daughter to the bridegroom's friend.

> If a son-in-law [intended] has entered the house of his [intended] father-in-law and has performed the betrothal gift, and afterwards they have made him go out and have given his wife to his companion—they shall present to him the betrothal gift which he has brought and that wife may not marry his companion.[45]

The term "companion" in this passage refers to the formal role called today in western cultures, "the best man," or in the Fourth Gospel, the friend of the bridegroom (3:29). By virtue of the friend's role in the pre-betrothal arrangements he could never be the husband, even if the proposal was turned down. The bride could never be his.[46]

The wedding ceremony began with the joyous procession of the young woman from her father's house to the home of the bridegroom, which was his ancestral home since the young man usually stayed within the patriarchal

---

[42] Joachim Jeremias, "νυμφή, νυμφίος," *TDNT* 4 (1967) 1101 n. 20.

[43] The account of the betrothal of Isaac and Rebecca is similar to this description. Abraham's servant acts as the go-between and gives Rebecca a gold ring and bracelets. When her father has agreed to the betrothal, the servant produces more jewels of silver and gold as gifts to Rebecca and her family (Genesis 24).

[44] Samples of written pledges from the fifth century B.C.E. have been found in Egypt; see E. M. Yamauchi, "Cultural Aspects of Marriage in the Ancient World," *Bibliotheca Sacra* 135 (1978) 246. Collins ("Marriage, Divorce and Family," 111–12) also describes contracts from the early second century C.E.

[45] van Selms, "The Best Man," 65–70.

[46] This is the situation described in Judges 14, when the woman Samson claims for his wife is given instead to the best man; thus Samson considers himself blameless for his actions against the Philistines (Judges 14–15). See also van Selms, "The Best Man," 71–74.

household. She was conducted to her new home by her relatives with songs and dancing. This ceremonial procession traveled slowly so that the entire village could see the finery and wealth of the young bride and would usually arrive late in the day for the wedding ceremony, which "was always in the evening at sunset."[47] Sometimes the groom himself would come to lead the bride, and sometimes this role would again be given to the bridegroom's friend.[48] While the procession was a public feature of the wedding, the most solemn moment came when the bride entered into the home of the bridegroom.[49] Here she prepared herself and waited with her attendants while festivities continued outside. Throughout the procession her face was veiled, for now only her husband could see her face within his house. Often the bridegroom would also travel in his own procession, arriving at the home some hours later in the evening. The best man then led him into the bridal chamber, and it would appear that the best man awaited the call of the bridegroom to fetch the nuptial sheet to testify to the virginity of the bride.[50]

John, Witness and Friend of the Bridegroom

These details of the customs surrounding marriage and betrothal shed light on the Fourth Gospel's presentation of John. John identifies himself using two images, "the voice" (1:23) and "the friend of the bridegroom" (3:29), while the narrative calls him a "witness." Evidence about marriages in the Second Temple period is primarily legal in character, and, within the legal formalities of the betrothal, witnesses are a necessary part of the contractual arrangements, which stipulated the dowry and inheritance rights. During the wedding the bridegroom's friend then witnesses that the marriage has been consummated. When we look at John's role through the lens of social customs surrounding marriage, his roles as witness and friend of the bridegroom come together.

---

[47] Stapfer, *Palestine in the Time of Christ*, 163; Trumbull, *Oriental Social Life*, 39–44.

[48] Boismard, "L'ami de l'Époux," 292. Boismard refers also to a number of Rabbinic texts where God is considered to have had the role of the friend of the bridegroom when, following the creation of Eve, God presented her to Adam.

[49] Wight, *Manners and Customs of Bible Lands*, 133; Stapfer, *Palestine in the Time of Christ*, 163. Also Boismard, "L'ami de l'Époux," 292: "on la conduisait procession-nellement chez l'époux et c'est à partir de ce moment qu'elle était considerée comme effectivement mariée" ("she was taken in procession to the home of the bridegroom, and it was from that moment that she was considered finally married").

[50] Jeremias, "νυμφή, νυμφίος," 1101; Satlow, *Jewish Marriage*, 175–77.

John is the first to arrive on the scene, and he has been sent by God (1:6). In initiating marriage arrangements, the deputy/friend is the one who approaches the bride's father. He is the one to speak for his friend, to reveal his identity and desires, and to conduct the negotiations, which it is hoped will lead to a marriage. He is the voice of the friend in these matters and is expected to present his friend's suit in the best possible manner. He is not speaking for himself.

Jesus is first introduced into the narrative through John's voice (1:26-27, 29-30). John describes what he experienced at the baptism and reveals Jesus as the one who outranks him. He then reveals Jesus' identity as "the Son of God" (vv. 31-34). John acts in this narrative in the traditional manner of a deputy or friend of the bridegroom sent by the groom's father to initiate proceedings that will lead, it is hoped, to betrothal and marriage. He then, as friend of the groom, directs disciples to Jesus (1:35-36), as the friend would direct or lead the young bride to the bridegroom's place. We are told that the disciples saw where Jesus was and stayed with him (1:39). The time detail is given, "about the tenth hour," i.e., late afternoon, which would be the traditional time for a wedding celebration. The time detail, which seems to have no other narrative purpose, is one indicator to the reader that the evangelist may be working with symbolism; that is to say, the meaning of this detail is to be found beyond the actual narrative.[51] Once the disciples and Jesus have been brought together, John withdraws from the narrative, which now shifts its focus from John to Jesus.

Andrew, one of John's disciples, takes over John's role as he finds his brother Simon and leads him to Jesus (1:41-42). Then Philip, the only disciple directly invited by Jesus, finds Nathanael and leads him to Jesus (1:45). In this scene an initial group of disciples is being gathered, and all except Philip come to Jesus through the words of an intermediary. First John, then Andrew, then Philip all act as the friend of the bridegroom to mediate a relationship between Jesus and another. The meeting with Nathanael also appears to draw on the customs of the betrothal ceremony, for in this initial encounter a small sign is given when Jesus reveals surprising knowledge of Nathanael, "an Israelite in whom there is no deceit!" (1:47), and Nathanael

---

[51] In an article on Johannine symbolism Juan Leal offers four criteria that can indicate when the narrative has a symbolic as well as a literal meaning: (1) the presence of inconsequential details that seem to play no part in the narrative, (2) a discourse set within the narrative of an event such that they are mutually illuminating, (3) the evangelist's accentuating the importance of a person who has no significant role in context, (4) the use of later liturgical and Christian expressions. See Juan Leal, "El simbolismo histórico del IV Evangelio," *EstB* 19 (1960) 344-46.

responds with a confession of faith (1:49). This sign is followed by a promise of even greater things in the future, when Nathanael will see what his ancestor Jacob/Israel once saw (Gen 28:12). Nathanael will experience Bethel, the house of God. As mentioned above, at the betrothal a part of the dowry would be given by the groom with the promise of the rest to follow at the wedding.

Without going into details in this chapter, I draw the reader's attention to the overall movement of the narrative, beginning with John's witness and concluding with his self-identification as the bridegroom's friend.[52] Through John, disciples are introduced to Jesus; they then participate in a wedding where Jesus acts as the bridegroom in providing the wine for the festivities.[53] The Cana pericope concludes with an affirmation of faith: "his disciples believed in him" (2:11). The following narrative comment should not be overlooked. "After this he went down to Capernaum, with his mother, his brothers and sisters (*adelphoi*)[54] and his disciples; and they remained there for a few days" (2:12). The disciples have now been drawn into the family of Jesus. Trumbull notes that a distinctive feature of family life in the East was the idea that the bride belonged to the mother of the bridegroom.[55] The bridegroom's mother was the woman in the household who had greatest authority. Seen in this light, the narrative comment in v. 12 may be more than a simple conclusion to the Cana episode; it may be continuing the nuptial theme that, I am suggesting, shapes these early chapters.

The narrative so far has followed the customs of a Middle Eastern marriage. It has taken us from the initial witness of John, to disciples being directed and led to Jesus, to a first meeting with a small sign offered and a promise of more to come, a confession of faith, a wedding celebration, and the inclusion of disciples in Jesus' household. These are the preparatory stages for the final solemn moment in a wedding when the bride enters the home of the bridegroom, which is his father's house. Following the festivities, the groom also enters the bridal chamber, and that in some cases is the first time when the groom actually sees his new wife. The moment when

---

[52] Chapter 3 will provide a more detailed analysis of the early narrative events in which Jesus is with his disciples; this present chapter focuses on John's role in initiating these events.

[53] At Cana, Jesus' role as the bridegroom is implied when the head steward goes to the bridegroom to congratulate him on producing good wine late in the festivities. This would indicate that the bridegroom has the task of providing wine, and in this case it is Jesus who has provided the good wine. See Moloney, *John*, 68–69, 72–73.

[54] *Adelphoi* is an inclusive plural meaning both brothers and sisters. See ἀδελφός in Henry G. Liddell and Robert Scott, *A Greek–English Lexicon* (Oxford: Clarendon Press, 1971).

[55] Trumbull, *Oriental Social Life*, 33.

the bride's veil is lifted is a key moment for their relationship.[56] He will see her face for the first time, and she will read his response to her in his face. It is a revelatory moment for them both.

From Capernaum, Jesus and his disciples travel to Jerusalem and enter his "Father's house" (2:16), the Temple. Here, in his Father's house, Jesus reveals his identity explicitly for the first time and confirms the testimony of John that he is "the Son of God" and that God's Spirit dwells in him (1:34). The Temple that had been called "the LORD's House"[57] can be called by Jesus, "my Father's house" because he is Son (1:14, 18). As the Son in whom the Spirit dwells, Jesus is now the locus for God's presence in history, so that by the end of the pericope the meaning of the Temple shifts from a building to his own person. The reader has known from the Prologue that Jesus is the tabernacling presence of God (1:14), and a veiled reference was given to Nathanael with the allusion to Jacob's dream at Beth-el (1:51).[58] These allusions are made explicit in this scene when the disciples hear for the first time Jesus' identity as the Temple of God's presence (2:19), a new house of God.[59] The encounter within the Father's house has been a decisive moment of revelation. The nuptial imagery does not dominate this scene as it did at Cana, but in a number of ways the narrative indicates that this imagery is still operative: the Temple is named as "my Father's house"; inside this "house" Jesus reveals his identity. The placement of the Temple incident directly after the wedding festivities at Cana reflects the usual custom of the bridegroom taking his bride to his father's house. The nuptial imagery will come to the forefront again in the next two chapters.

Following these events within the Temple, the marital imagery continues in the encounter with Nicodemus, where Jesus teaches the necessity of being "born anew" and Nicodemus ponders the impossibility of returning to the mother's womb (3:3-5). The language of birth dominates the first part of the pericope, where the setting is a conversation between two people (3:1-10),[60] while the second part, which can be called discourse (vv. 13-21),

---

[56] Trumbull (*Oriental Social Life*, 43, 58) notes that in many parts of the East the "specific celebration of the marriage rite is called today 'the lifting of the veil,' or 'the uncovering of the face.'"

[57] "YHWH's house" is the most frequent name of the Temple in the Old Testament, occurring over two hundred times.

[58] Beth-el means "house of God."

[59] A detailed treatment of the Temple pericope can be found in Coloe, *God Dwells with Us*, 65–84.

[60] The conversational tone ends after v. 10, where there is a shift from singular to plural.

introduces the theme of eternal life (3:15, 16). Birth and new life are the final testimony to a complex social process that began with an initial approach by the bridegroom's friend to the home of the intended bride. The birth of a child fulfills the marriage blessing that the bride would bear many children (Gen 24:60; Ruth 4:11).[61] A childless marriage is cause for divorce, according to the school of Hillel,[62] and so a marriage is not considered complete until the birth of a child. The gospel narrative has taken us through all the stages in the process of a first-century marriage: a first meeting initiated by John, with initial signs and the promise of greater things to come, a wedding, entry into the Father's house, and finally birth. After the episode with Nicodemus John returns to the narrative for the last time and concludes his testimony by identifying himself as the friend of the bridegroom, a friend whose role is now complete; "he must increase, but I must decrease" (3:30). The narrative has moved from John as witness to John as friend, and in between, it has drawn on nuptial imagery, which can be shown schematically as follows:

1:19-34	John (witness)
1:35-51	disciples of John/Jesus
2:1-12	wedding
2:13-25	my Father's house
3:1-21	birth
3:22-24	disciples of John/Jesus
3:25-36	John (friend of the bridegroom)

Conclusion

The Fourth Gospel has drawn on historical memories in its characterization of John. Rather than interpret John as Elijah, this gospel has used what is probably a pre-Synoptic designation of John as "a voice crying in the wilderness," an expression that probably goes back to John's own testimony. In its interpretation of the relationship between John and Jesus, the Fourth Gospel uses another remembered saying, this time from Jesus, in which he applied the metaphor of the bridegroom. These sayings have

---

[61] Yamauchi, "Cultural Aspects of Marriage," 247. By Rabbinic times the blessing, called "the groom's blessing," was a major feature of the wedding celebration and was recited several times over the days of the feasting; see Satlow, *Jewish Marriage in Antiquity*, 178.

[62] R. W. Wall, "Divorce," *ABD* 2 (1992) 218.

provided the evangelist with two images that he develops in an extended metaphor of Jesus as the bridegroom and John as the witnessing "voice" of the bridegroom's friend. Using this nuptial imagery rather than that of the Synoptic forerunner, the evangelist is able to incorporate into his narrative further historical reminiscences that the Synoptic Gospels must omit if they are to maintain the Elijah/Christ model. The Fourth Gospel therefore is able to show that John and Jesus were both involved in baptizing ministries at the same time, that this was a cause of tension between their disciples, and that some disciples of John left him to become followers of Jesus.

History and symbol have joined in a narrative that not only tells a story *about* what happened, but also offers insight into the *meaning* of what happened. Jesus, the divine Word incarnate, enacts the prophetic words of the Old Testament describing God's betrothal to and love of Israel. Within the sequence under consideration (1:1–3:36), the nuptial symbolism is explicit only in the wedding at Cana and in John's concluding words. Its presence is felt, however, from the moment John is introduced as the man sent by God as witness (1:6-7), and I suggest that a first-century audience/reader familiar with Jewish marital customs would pick up the allusion. The marital imagery makes apparent the underlying narrative logic of the events across these chapters beginning and ending with John. Paul Ricoeur speaks of the need to link together the action kernels that constitute a narrative's structural continuity;[63] symbols hold the actions of a narrative together in a particular way by providing a deeper network of associations than simple chronology. Reading a narrative while being alert to its historical and symbolic potential enriches the reading experience by offering a second dimension.

John, as witness and friend of the bridegroom, reveals the identity of Jesus as the incarnation of God's nuptial love of Israel, a love that desires espousal and fecundity. John sets the scene for the initial betrothal and formation of God's household, which will be depicted in the first gathering of disciples and the events that follow, as briefly described above. It is now time to examine these events in greater detail.

---

[63] Ricoeur, *Interpretation Theory* (see ch. 1, n. 10 above) 85.

Gathering the Household

JOHN 1:19-51

Following the witness of John, the gospel enumerates a sequence of days in which the first disciples gather to Jesus (1:35-51). While these verses provide some parallel with the Synoptics in the gathering of an initial group of disciples at the start of Jesus' ministry, there are remarkable differences. The names of the first disciples are different (Andrew and an unnamed disciple); the first two who approach Jesus are disciples of John (1:35), and only Philip is called directly by Jesus (1:43). Unlike the Synoptics, there is no admonition to leave everything behind, nor are there any indications of a ministry. Discipleship in the Fourth Gospel appears to be simply being and remaining (*menein*) with Jesus (1:39).

The pericope can be divided by means of the indications of different days, and this raises issues of where this initial pericope concludes and what theological purpose there is in this sequence; these are not two separate issues, but are related. How one interprets the meaning of the daily sequence will determine where one concludes this first discipleship pericope, at 1:51 with the promise of seeing greater things, or at 2:12 following the Cana miracle. Some scholars suggest that the gospel begins with a seven-day week, with the theological purpose of presenting Jesus' ministry as the start of a new creation.[1] While this is attractive, the sequence is not a full week,

---

[1] A helpful summary and table of the scholars who divide 1:19–2:12(13) into a seven-day week can be found in Harold Saxby, "The Time-Scheme in the Gospel of John," *ExpT* 104 (1992) 13.

but six days.[2] An alternative to the creation sequence has been suggested by Francis J. Moloney, who proposes that the background for 1:19–2:12 is to be sought in the description of the Sinai covenant and how this came to be memorialized within the Feast of Weeks.[3] In what follows I will extend his suggestion and show how the Feast of Weeks links the events of 1:19–2:12 and provides a rich theological and liturgical insight into the gathering of the first disciples.[4]

The Sinai Background

The Cana narrative begins with the words *"On the third day"* (2:1), and concludes with a statement that this was the first sign by which Jesus *"revealed his glory"* (*doxa*) (2:11). In the course of the narrative the mother of Jesus says to the servants, "Do whatever he tells you" (2:5). These three expressions suggest a deliberate allusion to the revelation of God's glory on the third day at Sinai (Exodus 19–24), during which the Israelites affirm, "Everything that the LORD has spoken we will do" (Exod 19:8; 24:3, 7). Moses is instructed that the people are to be consecrated and prepared "for the third day; because on the third day the LORD will come down upon Mount Sinai in the sight of all the people" (Exod 19:10-11). Moses then instructs the people: "Prepare for the third day" (Exod 19:15). The narrative continues: "On the morning of the third day there was thunder and lightning, as well as a thick cloud upon the mountain" (Exod 19:16). Following the covenant ceremony in chapter 24, Moses ascends the mountain and God's

---

[2] There is a textual variant in v. 41, found in the Old Latin and Old Syriac, giving *prōi* (early in the morning) where the majority of manuscripts (including א, B, 𝔓⁶⁶ and 𝔓⁷⁵) give *prōton* (first). This minority reading gives a total of seven days. For a discussion of all four variant readings in this verse see Rekha M. Chennattu, "On Becoming Disciples (John 1:35-51): Insights from the Fourth Gospel," *Salesianum* 63 (2001) 479 n. 55; also Bruce Metzger, *A Textual Commentary on the Greek New Testament: A Companion Volume to the United Bible Societies' Greek New Testament* (3rd ed. London: United Bible Societies, 1971) 200.

[3] Francis J. Moloney develops this Sinai theme in his interpretation of the Cana miracle; see Moloney, *John*, 50–51, 66.

[4] Even on textual grounds there are arguments for linking the events from 1:19–2:12, indicated by the temporal markers in 1:29, 35, 43; 2:1. John Painter concludes: "The temporal markers show that the evangelist wished to bind together the sequence of events from 1:19–2:11." See Painter, *The Quest for the Messiah: The History, Literature and Theology of the Johannine Community* (2nd ed. Nashville: Abingdon, 1993) 185–86 n. 65. I include v. 12 within the Cana pericope for reasons that will be clarified in the discussion below.

glory settles on the mountain (Exod 24:16, 17).[5] The juxtaposition of the revelation of God's glory on the third day and the people's faith acclamation that they will do "everything that the LORD has spoken," associated with the Sinai covenant in Exodus, provides an Old Testament parallel for the revelation of Jesus' glory on the third day.

Sinai and Pentecost

By New Testament times the Sinai event was linked to the annual pilgrim festival of Weeks, which is also known as "First Fruits" and in the later Greek books as "Pentecost."[6] In its origins this was simply a harvest festival, a day of thanksgiving for God's care and bounty in the harvest. In response to God's gifts of grain the people brought offerings of their firstfruits. For most of the Old Testament period there is no indication that this is linked to an event in Israel's history, but by the time of the book of *Jubilees* (ca. 150 B.C.E.), First Fruits is associated with a series of covenant rituals (Noah, *Jub.* 6:1, 18; Abraham and the Sinai covenant, *Jub* 15:1; 6:11).[7] According to *Jubilees*, all the covenants were made in the third month, which is when the Israelites arrive at Sinai (Exod 19:1). The community at Qumran also kept this feast in the third month, and this may have been the occasion for admitting new members to the community.[8] The emphasis in the Qumran literature is on the covenant as a creation of a new people attentive to the

---

[5] Within the Greek Old Testament the term glory (*doxa*) is a technical expression reserved to translate the Hebrew word *kabod*, which is associated with weightiness in the sense of a person's honor. In English this becomes "glory." Within the OT the term *doxa* comes to mean the divine revelation of God's essential nature in the created world. See Robert G. Bratcher, "What does 'glory' mean in relation to Jesus? Translating *doxa* and *doxazō* in John," *BT* 42 (1991) 401–408; Ceslas Spicq, "Δόχα, Δοχάζω, Συνδοχάζω," *TLNT* (Peabody, MA: Hendrickson, 1994) 362–79; Gerhard von Rad and Gerhard Kittel, "Δόχα," *TDNT* 2 (1964), especially 238–46.

[6] Feast of the Harvest (Exod 23:16), Feast of Weeks (Deut 16:10), day of the First Fruits (Num 28:26; Exod 23:16; 34:22; Lev 23:17), Pentecost (Tob 2:1; 2 Macc 12:32). See J. C. Vander Kam, "Weeks, Festival of," *ABD* 6 (1992) 895. "Feast of the Harvest" may have been its original title; see John C. Rylaarsdam, "Weeks, Feast of," *IDB* 4 (1962) 827.

[7] Vander Kam, "Weeks, Festival of," 896.

[8] Ibid. "D'après des manuscrits inédits de Qumrân, on sait maintenant qu'en ce jour se célébraient l'entrée des nouveaux membres dans la communauté et le renouvellement de l'alliance" ("From the unedited manuscripts at Qumran we now know that the entry of new members into the community and the renewal of the covenant were celebrated on that day"). See Jean Potin, *La Fête Juive de la Pentecôte: Étude des Textes Liturgiques.* LD 65 (Paris: Cerf, 1971) 124.

word of God.[9] For these sectarians the festival marked them as a people set apart from the Temple and from the other Israelites, whom they judged as no longer living as God's holy convocation. Following the destruction of the Temple the rabbis shifted the focus from the celebration of the covenants to the celebration of the gift of the Law on Sinai. The earliest reference to this association with Torah is attributed to Rabbi Eleazar ben Pedath (ca. 270 C.E.): "Pentecost is the day on which Torah was given."[10] The festival during biblical times was never assigned a precise day, since it was calculated in relation to the day of the "wave offering" at Passover time (Lev 23:15-16). According to Deuteronomy, "You shall count seven weeks; begin to count the seven weeks from the time the sickle is first put to the standing grain. Then you shall keep the festival of weeks for the LORD your God" (Deut 16:9-10).

In the celebration of Weeks the three days of Exodus 19 were prefaced by four days of remote preparation.[11] The fourth day of this remote preparation is also the first of three days of immediate preparation, according to the Exodus account. These preparations culminate, therefore, on the "third day," or the sixth from the beginning of the sequence. Moloney, correctly in my opinion, concludes that "This time-scheme shapes the order of the events reported in John 1:19–2:12."[12]

Structure: 1:19–2:12

Day 1 (vv. 19-28): John's testimony to the Jerusalem delegation

Day 2 (vv. 29-34): John's testimony to Jesus' baptism

Day 3 (vv. 35-42): Two of John's disciples follow Jesus. Andrew brings Peter to Jesus.

Day 4 (vv. 43-51): Day One of the Exodus three days of preparation. Philip and Nathanael.

Day 5/2

Day 6/3 (2:1-12) The revelation of Jesus' glory in Cana.[13]

---

[9] Ibid. 131.

[10] Rylaarsdam, "Weeks, Feast of," 827; for a study of the feast in the Rabbinic tradition see Potin, *La Fête Juive de la Pentecôte*, 131–40.

[11] Moloney, *John*, 50.

[12] Ibid.

[13] The *Mekhilta on Exodus* 19:10-11 describes the giving of the Torah on the sixth day. "Und der Ewige sprach zu Mose: Geh zu dem Volke und heilige sie heute, d.i. der 4. Tag. Und morgen, d.i. der 5. Tag. Und sie sollen bereit sein für den dritten Tag, d.i. der 6.

This naming of days in a sequence is similar to the Targum version of the Sinai revelation (*Ps-Jon. Exodus* 19:1-24), which gives the following:[14]

On the first day of the month, they came to the wilderness of Sinai (19:1).

On the second day Moses went up to the top of the mountain (19:3).

On the third day the Lord said to Moses, "Behold, I will reveal myself to you in the thickness of the cloud of glory (19:9).

On the fourth day the Lord said to Moses, "Go to the people and prepare them today and tomorrow. . . . Let them be ready for the third day; for on the third day the Lord will reveal himself" (19:10-11).

On the third day, on the sixth of the month . . . the Lord was revealed on Mount Sinai (19:16, 20).

When considering the likelihood that John 1:19–2:12 is shaped by the festival of First Fruits, I have given attention to the similarities between words found in the Cana pericope and the Sinai covenant found in Exodus 19–24. From the evidence of the book of *Jubilees* and the Dead Sea Scrolls, the Sinai covenant was memorialized in the Pentecost Festival by the first century. The Targums offer support to this thesis, and add the possibility that in the synagogue liturgy the Exodus account had six enumerated days.

Tag, an welchem die Thora gegeben wurde" ("And the Eternal spoke to Moses: Go to the people and sanctify them today, that is, the 4th day. And tomorrow, that is, the 5th day. And they must be prepared for the third day, that is, the 6th day, when the Torah was given"): see Jakob Winter and August Wünsche, *Mechiltha: Ein tannaitischer Midrasch zu Exodus* (Leipzig: J. C. Hinrichs, 1909) 198. It goes on to say that the fifth day was given to the building of an altar and the sealing of the covenant with the blood ritual described in Exodus 24. The *Mekhilta* then repeats that it was on the third day, i.e., Day Six, that the Torah was given (199). The *Mekhilta* attributed to R. Ishmael is dated by many scholars ca. 250 C.E.; see Jacob Neusner, "*Mekhilta* Attributed to R. Ishmael (Exodus)," in Jacob Neusner, Alan J. Avery Peck, and William Scott Green eds., *The Encyclopedia of Judaism* (New York: Continuum, 1999–2003) 1161–63.

[14] Since a similar numbering of days is found in the *Mekhilta* (Potin, *La Fête Juive,* 132), we can conclude that such a detailed ordering was part of early rabbinic Judaism. One significant difference between the Targum and the *Mekhilta* is that on the sixth day the Targum emphasizes the revelation of God, whereas the *Mekhilta* places the emphasis on the giving of the Law. This suggests that the Targum tradition is closer to the traditions found in the first century, prior to the destruction of the Temple, since in rabbinic times the focus shifts to the Torah.

First Fruits

The Nathanael episode provides further considerations supporting the Festival of First Fruits as the likely background for this passage. The Hebrew word for First Fruits (*bikkurim*)[15] means literally "early figs." In Hebrew, various terms describe the fig at different stages of its development. The early fig is called the בִּכּוּרָה (*bikkûrā*) (Isa 28:4 etc.), which usually ripens in June,[16] the third month according to biblical calculations, coinciding with the festival of First Fruits. Jesus tells Nathanael that he saw him under the fig tree (1:48). This apparently trivial detail has been interpreted in various ways: Nathanael was studying the Torah;[17] Jesus' extraordinary knowledge indicates his ability as a wonderworker.[18] Notwithstanding these other interpretations, the naming of the fig tree may be alluding to the festival of First Fruits, which takes its name from the early fig. A second possible allusion is found in the name Nathanael, which means *God's gift*. The feast of First Fruits celebrates *God's gifts* of the cereal harvest of the past seven weeks and involves *giving to God* the first fruits. Whether speaking of God's gifts to Israel or God's gifts offered by Israel, the name Nathanael, found only here and in 21:2,[19] possibly has a symbolic purpose indicating this feast. Third, following the dialogue between Jesus and Nathanael, Jesus promises that the disciples will see greater things and alludes to the vision of Jacob in Genesis 28. According to the book of *Jubilees* it was in the third month, i.e., at the time of First Fruits, that Jacob recalled his dream at Bethel and experienced a further vision of God.

> And Israel took his journey from Haran from his house on the new moon of the third month . . . and he offered a sacrifice to the God of his father Isaac on the seventh of this month. And Jacob remembered the dream that he had seen at Bethel, and he feared to go down into Egypt. And while he was thinking of sending word to Joseph to come to him, and that he would not go down, he remained there seven days, if perchance he could see a vision as to whether he should remain or go down. And he celebrated the harvest festival of the

---

[15] Matitiahu Tsevat, *bᵉkhôr*, *TDOT* 2 (1975) 122–23.

[16] John C. Trever, "Fig Tree, Fig," *IDB* 2 (1962) 267.

[17] "Rabbinic sources say that the sages sometimes studied the Torah under a fig tree, suggesting that Nathanael was under the fig tree perusing scripture and its messianic prophecies." Craig Koester, "Messianic Exegesis and the Call of Nathanael (John 1.45-51)," *JSNT* 39 (1990) 23, 31 n. 3.

[18] Moloney, *John*, 56.

[19] Most scholars consider chapter 21 a supplement to the original gospel, possibly added following the death of the Beloved Disciple; for discussion on this issue see Moloney, *John*, 546.

first-fruits. . . . And on the sixteenth the Lord appeared unto him, and said unto him, "Jacob, Jacob"; and he said, "Here am I." And He said unto him: "I am the God of thy fathers, the God of Abraham and Isaac; fear not to go down into Egypt, for I will there make of thee a great nation. I will go down with thee, and I will bring thee up. . . . And Israel rose up from the Well of the Oath on the sixteenth of this third month. (*Jub.* 44:1-6)

This passage from the book of *Jubilees* makes quite explicit that the second vision of Jacob occurred during the festival of First Fruits and specifically on the day of its celebration, the sixteenth of the third month, which according to Jubilees is the date when the Law was given to Moses.

And it came to pass in the first year of the exodus of the children of Israel out of Egypt, in the third month, on the sixteenth day of the month, that God spake to Moses, saying: "Come up to me on the Mount, and I will give thee two tables of stone of the law and of the commandment, which I have written, that thou mayst teach them." (*Jub.* 1:1-2)

Nathanael, already identified by Jesus in terms of his eponymous ancestor Jacob/Israel, recognizes Jesus as "Son of God" and "King of Israel," and he is promised a further vision of greater things (1:50).

Can Anything Good Come from Nazareth?

Within this introductory scene Nathanael is given particular prominence, which may be explained in the light of my previous work on the Temple. The dialogue between Philip and Nathanael emphasizes the village of Nazareth, which is named twice (1:45, 46). This is the only place in the gospel where the village of Nazareth is named, and I draw attention to the fact that the Greek associates the *place* Nazareth with Joseph, "Jesus, son of Joseph of Nazareth" (v. 45).[20] The link between Jesus and Nazareth I believe is reserved until it can be used in a rich, symbolic manner within the Passion narrative, where Jesus is given the title "Jesus the Nazarene" (18: 5, 7; 19:19). "Nazareth" and "Nazarene" both come from the Hebrew root נצר (*nzr*). This was confirmed in 1962 when excavations at Caesara found a Hebrew inscription of a family from Nazareth clearly showing that this word was spelled with the Hebrew letter צ (*tz*) and not the simpler ז (*z*).[21]

The gospel narrative reaches its conclusion in the hour when Jesus dies under the title "the Nazarene." Where other gospels call this *an inscription*

---

[20] *Iēsoun huion tou Iōsēph ton apo Nazaret.*

[21] James F. Strange, "Nazareth," *ABD* 4 (1992) 1050–51.

(Mark 15:25; Luke 23:38) or *charge* (Matt 27:37), the Fourth Gospel calls it a title, *titlos* (19:19), and it is a title reserved for the Passion account, where it occurs twice in the garden of Gethsemane (18:5, 7) and here on the cross. What is so significant about this term "*the Nazarene,*" that the gospel adds it to the sign found in the Synoptics, which simply reads "King of the Jews"? Its significance I believe points to Jesus' role as the builder of the new Temple.

The book of Zechariah is the only place where the builder of the new Temple is named.

> Collect silver and gold from the exiles—from Heldai, Tobijah, and Jedaiah— who have arrived from Babylon; and go the same day to the house of Josiah son of Zephaniah. Take the silver and gold and make a crown, and set it on the head of the high priest Joshua (*Jēsou*) son of Jehozadak; say to him: Thus says the LORD of hosts: Behold a man (cf. John 19:5) whose name is the *Branch:* for he shall *branch* out in his place, and he shall build the temple of the LORD. It is he that shall build the temple of the LORD; he shall bear royal honor, and shall sit and rule on his throne. (Zech 6:10-13)

This term *Branch* is related to the Messianic branch found in Isaiah, "A shoot shall come out from the stump of Jesse and a branch shall grow out of his roots" (Isa 11:1).[22] While in the Hebrew text the word translated "Branch" in Zechariah (*tzamah*) is not the same Hebrew word we find in Isaiah (*netzer*), by first-century methods of exegesis it was possible to use these similar terms interchangeably, and the evidence from Qumran shows that not only was it possible, but it was happening.[23] I believe that this Johannine addition, *Jesus the Nazarene*, deliberately exploits the double meaning of the term *Nazarene* that is found three times in the Passion Narrative. When the soldiers come searching for Jesus in the garden, Jesus asks

---

[22] See Coloe, *God Dwells with Us*, 171–74, for a more detailed discussion of these texts. An article by Hans-Peter Rüger makes a similar case for linking "Nazareth" with Isa 11:1 when examining the Synoptic usage in Matt 2:23; 13:54, and Mark 6:1. He makes no mention of the Johannine usage. See Rüger, "ΝΑΖΑΡΕΘ / ΝΑΖΑΡΑ / ΝΑΖΑΡΗΝΟΣ / ΝΑΖΩΡΑΙΟΣ," *ZNW* 72 (1981) 257–63.

[23] In the scrolls (4 Q161 [4QpIsaᵃ line 11, 18]) we find an interpretation of Isa 11:1-5 in which, following the quotation from Isaiah, the text is given a sectarian explanation. The quotation of v. 1 follows the Hebrew text and uses *netzer* (branch). In the commentary on this verse, the term *netzer* is rendered "the shoot of David," but uses the expression *tzamah* from Zech 6:12. See Florentino García Martínez and Eibert J. C. Tigchelaar, *The Dead Sea Scrolls Study Edition, 1Qq-4Q273.* 2 vols. (New York: Brill, 1997) 1:316. For other examples of the interchange of *netzer* and *tzamah* see 4QFlor col 1:11, which comments on 2 Sam 7:11, and 4QpGen col 5:3-4. See also the discussion of the "Branch" in Koester, "Messianic Exegesis and the Call of Nathanael (John 1.45-51)," 23–24.

them twice, "Whom are you looking for?" (18:4, 7). On each occasion the response is "Jesus, the Nazarene" (18:5, 7), at which Jesus replies with the definitive theological expression of his identity, "I AM" (18:5, 8).[24] This is the last time Jesus uses this expression, and in its association with "the Nazarene" it gives this title a heightened significance. Not only is "the Nazarene" the final title applied to Jesus in the pre-Easter narrative by Pilate, it is also the final title Jesus accepts with the definitive "I AM." Where in the synoptic usage the title could simply mean "Jesus from Nazareth," by the meticulous usage found in the Fourth Gospel and the use of the definite article this title establishes Jesus as "the Nazarene"—the Temple-builder from Zechariah. In the crucifixion, while "the Jews" destroy one Temple, the temple of his body, Jesus, the Nazarene, is simultaneously raising another Temple, fulfilling the promise of Zechariah and his own words (2:21). I will discuss the Temple-building aspect of the crucifixion below; at this point I simply review the significance of the title "the Nazarene" in the context of Nathanael's question about Nazareth.

Jacob's Vision[25]

The final verse of chapter 1 is in fact directed to all the disciples and not simply Nathanael: "Amen, amen, I tell you [plural], you will see heaven opened and the angels of God ascending and descending upon the Son of Man" (1:51). The allusion is to Jacob's dream:

> He came to a certain place and stayed there for the night, because the sun had set. Taking one of the stones (*lithōn*) of the place, he put it under his head (*kephalēs*) and lay down in that place. And he dreamed that there was a ladder set up on the earth, the top (lit. head, *kephalē*) of it reaching to heaven; and the angels of God were ascending and descending upon it. And the LORD stood beside him" (Gen 28:11-13).

When Jacob awoke from his dream he took the stone he had used as a pillow, dedicated it, and called the name of that place Beth-el, i.e., the house of

---

[24] Jesus' use of "I AM" reflects the revelation of the divine name to Moses in Exod 3:14. David Ball examines the use of this expression across the gospel and its christological/theological significance; see his *'I AM' in John's Gospel: Literary Function, Background and Theological Implications*. JSNTSup 124 (Sheffield: Sheffield Academic Press, 1996).

[25] A number of scholars propose that this final verse is an addition to the Nathanael passage; see, for example, Jerome H. Neyrey, "The Jacob Allusions in John 1:51," *CBQ* 44 (1982) 586–89; Brown, *Gospel* 1:88–89. My proposal that the entire episode draws on the festival of First Fruits, and especially how this is linked to Jacob in the book of Jubilees, argues in support of this verse as part of the pericope and not an addition.

God. In this promise Jesus indicates to his disciples that they, like Jacob, will glimpse the divine world, and the place of this revelation is to be the mysterious figure, the Son of Man.[26] Following an extensive study of this Johannine title, Francis Moloney concludes that the title "Son of Man" in the Fourth Gospel directs the reader to the cross and to the ultimate revelation of Jesus in his hour.[27]

As I mentioned briefly above, my study of the Temple led me to conclude that one aspect of the revelation of the cross is the raising of the new house/hold of God in the community of disciples. Some scholars understand that Jesus' promise to the disciples that they will see greater things is fulfilled in the episode at Cana[28] or in the following ministry;[29] my understanding is that this promise is fulfilled at the cross. With the exception of 5:27 and 9:35, the Son of Man title is always used with the cross in view (3:13, 14; 6:27, 53, 62; 8:28; 12:23, 34; 13:31).[30] Therefore, in my opinion, the

---

[26] While there is general agreement that this verse alludes to Gen 28:12, there is much discussion about the particular reference of the imagery; for a discussion of the rather complex interpretations based on rabbinic traditions see William Loader, "John 1:50-51 and the 'Greater Things' of Johannine Christology," in Cilliers Breytenbach and Henning Paulsen, eds., *Anfänge der Christologie: Festschrift für Ferdinand Hahn zum 65. Geburtstag* (Göttingen: Vandenhoeck & Ruprecht, 1991) 257–60. For the purposes of this study it is sufficient to read the imagery as an indicator that Jesus is the new place of revelation, without pressing the details.

[27] "The Son of Man revealed God to men [sic] and brought judgement to men through his presence, as a man, among them. The high point of this revelation and judgment took place on the cross." Francis J. Moloney, *The Johannine Son of Man*. Biblioteca di Scienze Religiose 14 (2nd ed. Rome: LAS, 1978) 213. This interpretation of the Son of Man expression as a distinctly earthly revelatory figure was reiterated in a recent article in which Moloney engages with other interpretations that have appeared in the past twenty years. He concludes: "the Fathers correctly caught the link between the Johannine use of 'the Son of Man' for the presentation of the revelation of God in the human event of Jesus Christ, especially in his being 'lifted up' on a cross (cf. 3,14; 8,28; 12,32; 19,5? [sic])." See Moloney, "The Johannine Son of Man Revisited," in Gilbert van Belle, J. G. Van der Watt, and P. J. Maritz, eds., *Theology and Christology in the Fourth Gospel*. BETL 184 (Leuven: Peeters, 2005) 202.

[28] Brown, *Gospel* 1:83, 91; Painter, *The Quest for the Messiah*, 186; Rekha M. Chennattu, *Johannine Discipleship as a Covenant Relationship* (Peabody, MA: Hendrickson, 2005) 25.

[29] Rudolf Bultmann, *The Gospel of John: A Commentary*, trans. G. R. Beasley Murray et al. (Oxford: Blackwell, 1971) 106; C. H. Dodd, *The Interpretation of the Fourth Gospel* (Cambridge: Cambridge University Press, 1953) 294.

[30] But even these two Son of Man sayings, 5:27 and 9:35, are linked to the cross through the themes of judgment and revelation; see Moloney, *The Johannine Son of Man*, 214: "The use of 'the hour,' 'lifting up,' and 'the Son of Man'—themes which are closely

allusion to Beth-el, the house of God, is best fulfilled on the cross in the destruction and raising of the Temple, the House/hold of God (2:19). William Loader also argues that 1:50-51 is an internal prolepsis and that almost all of these refer to the event of Jesus' death.[31] Brown presents various interpretations of the "Son of Man" saying in this context of Jacob's dream and concludes: "whether it is as the ladder, the *shekinah*, the *merkabah*, Bethel, or the rock, the vision means that Jesus as Son of Man has become the locus of divine glory, the point of contact between heaven and earth. The disciples are promised figuratively that they will come to see this."[32] While Brown links this future vision to the revelation at Cana, I believe that the "Son of Man" saying links this vision more appropriately to the cross and to the building of a new Beth-el, House/hold of God, which will be seen by the disciples in the light of their Easter experience.[33]

In the discussion of the festival of First Fruits I made the association between the name of the feast in Hebrew (lit. "early figs") and Nathanael being seen by Jesus under a fig tree. Craig Koester's article on messianic exegesis offers a further association between the fig tree and the Old Testament, linking this to the prophecy of Zechariah and a messianic Branch. My work on the "Nazarene" and its christological significance in this gospel supports Koester's claim, which I now examine.

Koester begins with the statement by Jesus about seeing Nathanael under the fig tree. He proposes that this recalls the vision found in a number of Old Testament passages of "every man under his vine and under his fig tree" (1 Kgs 4:25; Mic 4:4; Zech 3:10; cf. 1 Macc 14:12). These passages "are associated with the coming of the messianic figure called the 'Branch' in Zechariah 3:8-10."[34] To support this claim he notes that there are a number of allusions to Jacob in the Johannine passage though Jacob is not actually

---

linked throughout John 1–13—points to a Christology in which the human Jesus is glorified in his being 'lifted up' upon the cross as the revelation of God to men. . . . Because of the revelation which took place in the *human* event of the cross, *men* can be judged by their reaction to it." See also Loader, "John 1:50-51 and the 'Greater Things' of Johannine Christology," 263–65.

[31] Ibid. 262.

[32] Brown, *Gospel* 1:91.

[33] Here I am in agreement with Neyrey, who writes, "The promise of 1:51, although not literally fulfilled, is realized in the vision of faith of the Johannine community which confessed Jesus as the divine Son of Man . . . and as Lord and God (1:1-2; 20:28)." See Neyrey, "The Jacob Allusions in John 1:51," 605. Where I differ from Neyrey is in locating this vision not in the heavens, but at the cross, in the crucified and glorified Son of Man.

[34] Koester, "Messianic Exegesis and the Call of Nathanael (John 1.45-51)," 24.

named. Nathanael is called an Israelite without guile, recalling that Jacob was noted for his "guile" (Gen 32:28) and is promised a vision of angels ascending and descending, such as the vision Jacob saw at Bethel. Without actually naming the reference to Jacob's story in Genesis 28, the parallels are made. "The evangelist expected readers to catch the allusion to the Jacob story in order to make sense of the narrative."[35] In a similar manner, by alluding to a passage but without giving a direct reference Koester claims that John 1:48 has as its background Zechariah 3:10.

> Now listen, Joshua, high priest, you and your colleagues who sit before you! For they are an omen of things to come: I am going to bring my servant the Branch. For on the stone that I have set before Joshua, on a single stone with seven facets, I will engrave its inscription, says the LORD of hosts, and I will remove the guilt of this land in a single day. On that day, says the LORD of hosts, *a man* will *call his neighbor* under a vine and *under a fig tree (hypokatō sukēs)* (Zech 3:8-10).[36]

This passage is echoed in the gospel when Jesus says "Before *Philip called* you, when you were *under the fig tree (hypo tēn sukēn)*, I saw you" (1:48). The context of the Zechariah passage "relates the image of one man calling another under a fig tree to the advent of a messianic 'Branch' (*tzamah*, 3:8), who was to build the temple and 'bear royal honor' (6:12-13)."[37] This is the same context found in the gospel. Philip calls Nathanael under a fig tree to announce the arrival of Jesus, whom the narrative will reveal as the Messianic Branch of Zechariah, the Nazarene Temple-builder. In addition to the similarities Koester notes between Zechariah 3:10 and John 1:48, the extended citation from Zechariah shows other points of contact in the light of my arguments about the relationship between Jesus the Nazarene/Branch and the "Branch" of Zechariah. The name Joshua (*Yēsou*) and Jesus (*Yēsous*) are almost identical, and it is at this point in the gospel that Peter is renamed "Cephas," the rock, with no explanation (1:42). It is possible that the change of name from Simon to Peter (*Kēphas*) is placed here in chapter 1 because of the allusion to Jacob's vision, when Jacob takes a stone (*lithos*) to place under his head (*kephalēs*), and also alluding to the above passage from Zechariah, which has two references to a stone. Not only do the two passages from Genesis and Zechariah have the word "stone" in common, but also the word "head" (*kephalēs*, Gen

[35] Ibid.
[36] I follow Koester's translation of v. 10 (ibid.).
[37] Ibid. 25.

28:11) is phonetically similar to *Kēphas*, the Aramaic equivalent of the Greek name *Petros*.[38] Koester's analysis of Zechariah 3 and my own work on the Nazarene title indicate that John's theology of the cross is already present and shaping this passage describing the gathering of Jesus' first disciples. The first-time reader of the gospel will not be aware of this and may simply be puzzled by the many differences between this passage and the call of the disciples in the Synoptic Gospels. A second-time reader, familiar with Johannine theology and style, can read this passage and marvel at its artistry and depth.

The Household as the First Fruits

One important feature of the Sinai covenant is the choice of Israel as God's special people. "Now therefore, if you obey my voice and keep my covenant, you shall be my treasured possession out of all the peoples" (Exod 19:5).[39] This choice gives Israel priority among the nations, so Israel is called the firstborn son of God (Exod 4:2; Jer 31:8). One of the Hebrew words for the firstborn (*bekhirah*) comes from the same root (*bkr*) as the word for firstfruits (*bikkurim*).[40] The prophet Jeremiah describes Israel as the first (*re'shith*) of YHWH's harvest (Jer 2:3), and this is translated as "the firstfruits" of the harvest.[41] In the New Testament the image of the firstfruits is applied to Jesus (1 Cor 15:20, 23), the Spirit (Rom 8:23), and also the Christian community (Jas 1:18; Rev 14:4). The Fourth Evangelist may have placed the gathering of the disciples in the context of Pentecost to exploit the imagery of the firstfruits, which can be understood in two ways. In the pre-Easter time this first discipleship group is the first indication of a harvest still to come (4:35-38) within the gospel's narrative and, more significantly, the post-Easter household of disciples is the firstfruit of the cross and resurrection of Jesus.

---

[38] In Matthew's gospel, Simon's name is changed following his confession of faith in Jesus as the Christ (Matt 16:18). Given the use of the Aramaic form of the name, some scholars see the Johannine version of the name-change as the earliest form of the tradition. On the significance of the name-change see also Chennattu, "On Becoming Disciples," 480 n. 57, also 494.

[39] Chennattu, *Johannine Discipleship as a Covenant Relationship*, 59–61. Chennattu develops the theology of John 1:19–2:12, focusing on the theme of covenant and giving particular attention to 1:35-51.

[40] Tsevat, *bᵉkhôr*, 122.

[41] There is a relationship between the terms firstborn (*re'shith*) and first fruits (*bikkurim*) that is not entirely clear, but the two terms are paired on occasion (Exod 23:19; 34:26; Ezek 44:30). See ibid. 122.

In telling the story of the original disciples seeking, finding, and remaining with Jesus, the narrative establishes a paradigm for all future disciples. Klaus Scholtissek describes the gradual stages of discipleship characterized in this pericope and uses the term "*mystagogic*."[42] He notes that many encounters with Jesus describe a process (*Wegcharakter*) through which there is a gradual self-revelation of Jesus leading to a lifegiving, rich relationship and intimate friendship.[43] Jesus initiates this process with the question "what do you seek?" (1:38), and this question is posed to disciples of all times. This question addresses the deep religious hunger within the human heart, and the disciples' reply, "where do you dwell (*menein*)?" needs to be read with the same depth of meaning posed by Jesus' initial question.[44] The disciples are not wondering about Jesus' accommodation! They seek more than this, and the word "dwell" hints at the depth of their seeking. For first-time readers the word "dwell" (*menein*) has yet to reveal its rich theological potential, which will become apparent particularly in the final discourse, but they may have noted its use twice in the witness of John concerning the Spirit descending and remaining/dwelling on Jesus (1:32, 33). The term "dwell" has thus been signaled as a descriptor of the abiding relationship of Jesus and the Spirit.[45] First-time readers/listeners have also just heard the Prologue describe Jesus being in the Father's heart (1:18), so they may realize that dwelling with Jesus will mediate the presence of the Father and the Spirit. Reading through the lens of Easter, a second-time reader realizes that Jesus dwells in the Father and in the believers, within the Father's house/hold (14:2). As Scholtissek notes, the use of dwell (*menein*) provides a spatial metaphor for the Johannine theology of immanence, which will be fully developed in the final discourse and only realized in the "hour" of Jesus' glorification and the outpouring of the Spirit.[46] The

---

[42] Klaus Scholtissek, "Mystagogische Christologie im Johannesevangelium?" *Geist und Leben* 68 (1995) 412–13. See also the study of the discipleship theme in Chennattu, "On Becoming Disciples," 465–96. Chennattu also emphasizes the *process* of discipleship and speaks of the call stories in ch. 1 as a "paradigm of discipleship," ibid. 489.

[43] Scholtissek, "Mystagogische Christologie," 413.

[44] "This question touches on the basic need of man [sic] that causes him to turn to God, and the answer of the disciples must be interpreted on the same theological level." See Brown, *Gospel* 1:78.

[45] Scholtissek understands the disciples' initial query as a question about Jesus' origins, which in this gospel is also a question of identity, as "sons" do as their "fathers" (for this principle see John 5:17, 19-20; 8:39-44). Klaus Scholtissek, *In Ihm sein und bleiben: Die Sprache der Immanenz in den johanneischen Schriften*. Herders Biblische Studien 21 (Freiburg: Herder, 2000) 240.

[46] Ibid.

disciples who seek, are invited into, and remain in the dwelling (place) of Jesus, mirror in the text the post-Easter experience of believers who seek, are invited, and come to dwell in the household of God.

On the Third Day: Cana

In his examination of the Cana miracle Moloney points out a number of differences between this and a typical miracle story.[47] The request by the mother of Jesus is not immediately followed by the miracle; instead, Jesus responds with what appears to be a rebuke, leading to his mother's order to the servants to "do whatever he tells you" (2:5). The miracle story does not lead to a response of wonder and awe on the part of the onlookers, and the miracle concludes with a statement that it is a "sign" and that in this sign Jesus manifested his glory. In departing from the standard form of a miracle story, the evangelist directs our attention elsewhere. The provision of abundant good wine is not the point of the narrative. It is a sign, an indicator of the identity of Jesus. The narrator also draws attention to the relationship between Jesus and his mother, albeit in a rebuke that appears to deny the relationship.[48] For the purposes of this study I draw attention to two aspects of the pericope: first, Jesus' action in providing wine for the wedding, and second, the role of the mother of Jesus.

The Bridegroom

In the previous chapter I looked at the role of John as friend of the bridegroom and the indications in the gospel that Jesus is the bridegroom. This is particularly clear in the Cana miracle. Following the miracle, when the steward discovers the miraculously provided wine, he goes to the bridegroom and comments, "you have kept the good wine until now" (2:10). His statement indicates that it was the role of the bridegroom to provide the wine, thus unwittingly revealing Jesus' identity as the bridegroom. When the narrator comments that this was the first of his signs, the word "sign" is not simply a synonym for miracle.[49] If the action is a sign, the reader may well ask, "a sign of what?" "What is being signified in this event?"

---

[47] Moloney, *John*, 70.

[48] So Dorothy Lee: "The effect of the rebuff is, at least in part, to direct the reader's attention to the mysterious 'hour' (*hōra*) which, as we will later discover, signifies Jesus' exaltation on the cross." See, Lee, *Flesh and Glory*, 144.

[49] "L'emploi du terme, *sēmeion* pour parler des miracles est un indice permetant de constater que le langage de Jean s'est enrichi d'un symbolisme présent dans tout l'Evangile." ("The use of the term *sēmeion* in speaking of miracles is an indication that permits us to say that John's language is enriched by a symbolism that is present through-

The sign of Cana points to the deeper identity of Jesus. The episode begins by situating this event "on the third day" and concludes with the statement that this was the first time Jesus "manifested his glory." The opening and closing phrases frame the pericope with allusions to Exodus 19, as discussed above. The covenanting God of Israel whose glory was once revealed at Sinai is now present in Jesus. In the prophetic literature one of the images of Israel's covenant relationship with God was that of a marriage, with God as Israel's bridegroom (Isa 62:5; Jer 2:2; Hos 2:16). Here at Cana, Jesus comes to Israel as the covenant/bridegroom providing abundant wine.

Mother and Son

One of the deeply puzzling aspects of the Cana episode is the sharp response Jesus makes to his mother when she indicates that the wine has run out; it reads literally, "What to me and to you?" (2:4). In all its uses in the LXX[50] this statement has a corrective, if not harsh, tone in a situation "in which two parties have nothing in common, or no relationship to each other."[51] The reply to his mother is strange, but then the puzzle deepens when Jesus acts in accordance with her wishes. The very strangeness of the expression draws the reader's attention to the relationship between Jesus and his mother and to the indication that this relationship is not significant now but will be in the future, when "the hour" arrives.[52] Considering Jesus' subsequent actions in changing the water into wine, his words to his mother must be understood primarily as a narrative strategy directing the reader's attention not so much to this Cana scene but to the future "hour." It is then

---

out the gospel.") See Frédéric Manns, *L'Evangile de Jean à la lumière du Judaïsme.* SBFA 33 (Jerusalem: Franciscan Printing Press, 1991) 111. On the significance of "signs" as a witness to divine authorization see M.-É. Boismard, *Moses or Jesus: An Essay in Johannine Christology,* trans. Benedict T. Viviano (Minneapolis: Fortress Press, 1993) 55–59.

[50] Judges 11:12; 2 Sam 16:10; 19:22; 1 Kgs 17:18; 2 Kgs 3:13; 2 Chr 35:21. Similarly in the New Testament it has the negative sense "leave me alone" (Matt 8:29; Mark 1:24; 5:7; Luke 4:34; 8:28).

[51] Arthur H. Maynard, *"TI EMOI KAI SOI,"* NTS 31 (1985) 584. For a discussion of its use in the LXX and the possible Semitism lying behind the expression see Jean-Paul Michaud, "Le signe de Cana dans son contexte johannique," *Laval Théologique et Philosophique* 18 (1962) 247–53.

[52] The theme of Jesus' "hour" will develop across the narrative and take on a meaning related to the Passion, as the "hour" of Jesus' death, exaltation, and glorification (7:30; 8:20; 12:23, 27; 13:1; 17:1). The presence of the woman/mother at Cana and at the cross links these two scenes and requires that the "hour" named here be understood in terms of the Passion.

that the relationship between Jesus and the woman, never named, but designated as "woman" and "mother" will be critical. The importance of her relationship as mother of Jesus, in this gospel, will only be revealed in "the hour." The Cana miracle happens, but in this harsh reprimand the first-time reader encounters a puzzle that will not be resolved until the Passion.

In addition to the unique title on the cross, "the Nazarene," discussed above, a second unique aspect of the Johannine crucifixion is the scene with the Beloved Disciple and the mother of Jesus.

> Standing near the cross of Jesus were his mother, and his mother's sister, Mary the wife of Clopas, and Mary Magdalene. When Jesus saw his mother and the disciple whom he loved standing beside her, he said to his mother, "Woman, behold your son." Then he said to the disciple, "Behold your mother." And from that hour the disciple took her to his own (*eis ta idia*). After this, knowing that now everything had been finished, that the Scriptures might be fulfilled, Jesus said, "I am thirsty." A jar full of sour wine was standing there. So they put a sponge full of the wine on a branch of hyssop and held it to his mouth. When Jesus had received the wine, he said, "It is finished." Then he bowed his head and gave down the spirit (*paredōken to pneuma*) (19:25b-30).

The significance of this scene has not been fully appreciated by most scholars who regularly interpret it in terms of Jesus' concern for his mother in handing her into the care of the Beloved Disciple. But this is the high point of the gospel! It is only after these words that Jesus' mission is finished and he announces, in words echoing those used when God completes the work of creation, "it is finished" (*tetelestai*). Verses 26 and 27, in my understanding, hold the key to the Johannine interpretation of the cross. They are the climax of the Passion and the resolution of so many puzzles that the reader has encountered in the narrative to this point.[53]

From the cross Jesus alters the relationship between his mother and the Beloved Disciple standing below. The woman, his mother, becomes "mother" to the Beloved Disciple, and the disciple becomes "son" to the mother of Jesus (19:26-27). In becoming "son" to the mother of Jesus, the disciple becomes brother/sister to Jesus and child of the one Jesus calls "Father." This is the moment when, through the gift of the Spirit, discipleship becomes divine filiation in the Johannine perspective. Following this scene, when the Risen One appears to Mary Magdalene, he tells her, "Go

---

[53] This scene, within its context in the Passion narrative, is discussed in more detail in my earlier works, which I summarize here as the critical lens through which I am undertaking this second reading of the gospel; see Mary L. Coloe, "Raising the Johannine Temple (Jn 19:19-37)," *ABR* 48 (2000) 47–58; also *God Dwells with Us*, 186–90.

to my *brothers and sisters (adelphoi)* and say to them, I am ascending to my Father and *your Father*, to my God and your God" (20:17). The Hour of Jesus draws disciples into the Father's house (Temple, 2:16), now properly termed the Father's household (14:2). Another way of saying this is that the new Temple/Household of God is the Johannine community, in whom the Risen Christ dwells through the mediation of the Spirit. The expression "to his own" (*eis ta idia*) forms an *inclusio* with the Prologue, which announced that Jesus "came to his own (*eis ta idia*), but his own did not receive him" (1:11). The Prologue then continues with the promise that those who did receive him would be given "the power to become children of God" (1:12). What was promised is now fulfilled. Disciples have become children and the action of the Beloved Disciple redresses the rejection by his own, as he takes Jesus' mother "into his own."

In the light of this scene at the cross, the apparent rebuke within the Cana episode can be understood as the narrative ploy to highlight the significance of the relationship between Jesus and his mother while directing the significance of this relationship away from Cana to the "hour." At Cana a miracle is performed and a sign is given; the true bridegroom is revealed and the disciples see Jesus' glory, but it is in "the hour" that disciples are born anew and become children of God. From the cross the Nazarene Temple-builder raises up the Father's house in the formation of the household of disciples/children of God.

A second-time reading of the gospel, knowing the significance of the title "Jesus the Nazarene," adds particular irony to Nathanael's disparaging response to Philip, "Can anything good come from Nazareth?" (1:46). In terms of this gospel, *everything* comes from the Nazarene. As the Nazarene Temple-builder, Jesus brings his mission to completion, and in his death the Spirit is released on a new creation. Jesus, the Nazarene, is the ultimate gift of God, (Nathana-el) for the salvation of the world (3:16).

At the conclusion of the Cana episode we read: "After this he went down to Capernaum, with his mother and his brothers and sisters and his disciples; and they dwelt (*emeinan*) there for a few days." In this short comment a household gathers around Jesus. As I noted in the previous chapter, after a marriage the bride belongs to the mother of the bridegroom; she is in her care. This verse therefore not only continues the nuptial theme introduced through John and made explicit at Cana, but in the form of a prolepsis anticipates the creation of the household at the cross, where the disciple is given to the Mother and the Mother is received by the disciple *eis ta idia*. With the arrival of the bridegroom and the completion of the wedding celebrations, the disciples are incorporated into the household of Jesus, dwelling with his mother and brothers and sisters (*adelphoi*).

Entering the Father's House[54]

In discussing marital customs in the previous chapter, I pointed out that the bridegroom would usually reside in his parents' house and become part of that household. The most solemn moment in the wedding is when the bride enters the home of the bridegroom, his father's house, as it would be termed. Within the house, in the bridal chamber, bride and groom would be revealed to each other, in some cases for the first time. Following the wedding at Cana, Jesus and his disciples go to Jerusalem and enter the Temple, which Jesus names "my father's house." Within this house Jesus reveals his identity to the disciples as the Temple that will be destroyed and as the Temple-builder who will raise it up (2:19, 21). The narrator comments that the disciples do not comprehend the significance of Jesus' words until after the resurrection (2:22). The narrative comment indicates that the gospel can only be fully understood retrospectively, and legitimates the hermeneutical approach taken in this study.

Conclusion

The introduction of John, the witness and friend of the bridegroom, sets in motion the divine process announced in the Prologue, that believers will become children of God (1:12). Through John a group of disciples gather to Jesus, at the tenth hour,[55] late in the afternoon, which is the usual time for a wedding; they see where he dwells and remain with him. The narrative structure and imagery suggest that these initial events occur within the liturgical context of Pentecost, which celebrates the firstfruits of the harvest. Within narrative time these disciples are the firstfruits of Jesus' mission, but their discipleship suggests a model of the process of discipleship for future believers beyond narrative time. The promise of future visions and the reference to the Son of Man point ahead to the Easter experience, thus drawing post-Easter disciples into the narrative. The story of Andrew, his unnamed companion, Peter, Philip, and Nathanael speaks to the gathering of future disciples as the firstfruits of Easter.[56]

---

[54] Since the Temple scene was discussed in some detail in *God Dwells with Us*, ch. 4, here I am noting one aspect of the scene as it relates to the image of the household.

[55] In Johannine chronology the day begins at dawn, making the tenth hour late afternoon. For a discussion of this chronology see Brown, *Gospel* 1:75.

[56] In her study of this scene Chennattu ("On Becoming Disciples," 489) notes the many verbs that are future oriented, that have the character of a promise: "you shall see: (v. 39), "you shall be called Peter" (v. 42), "you will see heaven opened" (v. 51).

Following this introductory movement, these disciples celebrate a wedding wherein Jesus is identified as the real bridegroom who provides abundantly. In this experience the disciples recognize the glory of God once revealed in the covenant of Sinai and now, in a festival celebrating that covenant, revealed in Jesus. The covenanting God of Sinai, whose relationship with Israel is often described in terms of a wedding, is now present in Jesus. The disciples move from the wedding feast and are gathered into Jesus' household with his mother and his siblings. They then enter his Father's house, where further revelations of his identity as the "Temple" occur.

The first-time reader may perceive some of the more explicit images across these chapters, such as the marriage as a symbol of the covenant, Jesus the provider of wine as the bridegroom, Jesus as the Temple. A second-time reader, who knows the gospel narrative and reads in the light of Easter under the guidance of the Paraclete (14:26), is invited to perceive not just the story of Jesus' disciples, but their own story of coming to dwell within the Father's household.

Life in the Household

NICODEMUS' STORY

The movement of the narrative, from John's initial witness (1:19-34), to the gathering of the first disciples (1:35-51), to a wedding (2:1-13), to the Father's house (2:14-21), may be understood as the natural progression in establishing a new household within the Jewish world of the first century. The birth of a child establishes the household within the ongoing history of Israel, as through birth comes the promise of life continuing into the future. Birth reassures that the national and ancestral line will live on beyond the death of an individual or a generation. The birth of a child is so critical that the biblical word for a childless man comes from the same root as the Hebrew word meaning "destroyed" (*arîrî*).[1] In this social context birth is essentially an eschatological event, pointing beyond the birth to future horizons now made possible, and so the reader should not be surprised that the Nicodemus passage leads from a discussion of birth to consideration of eternity life and judgment, which are usually presented as future eschatological realities. These are the themes that will be given emphasis in this chapter, necessarily leaving aside other issues not directly pertaining to the focus of this study.

Structuring the Passage

A question facing all interpreters is where to begin this pericope. Does the encounter with Nicodemus begin in 3:1, or has it already begun in 2:23?

---

[1] The adjective *arîrî* is used to describe childlessness when children were necessary for a sense of completeness. Abraham is described as *arîrî* (Gen 15:2) when he has no natural heir. See B. Seevers, ערה, in Willem A. VanGemeren, ed., *New International Dictionary of Old Testament Theology and Exegesis* (Grand Rapids: Zondervan, 1997) 3:527–31.

My own reading suggests that verses 2:23-25 are to be considered part of the Nicodemus pericope and not simply a conclusion to the Temple episode or a transition passage.[2] There are a number of key words repeated across 2:23–3:2, linking these verses into a unit: "person" (*anthrōpos*), "signs," as well as the theme of knowledge.[3]

> When he was in Jerusalem during the Passover festival, many believed in his name because they saw (*theōrountes*) the signs (*sēmeia*) that he was doing. But Jesus on his part would not entrust himself to them, because he knew (*gignōskein*) all people and needed no one to testify (*martyrēsē*) about any person (*anthrōpou*); for he himself knew (*egignōsken*) what was in a person (*anthrōpǭ*). (2:23-25)
>
> Now there was one (*anthrōpos*) of the Pharisees named Nicodemus, a leader of the Jews. He came to Jesus by night and said to him, "Rabbi, we know (*oidamen*) that you are a teacher who has come from God; for it is not possible for anyone to do these signs (*sēmeia*) that you do, unless God is with him." (3:1-2)

Repetition occurs also in 3:11 through the word "testify" and the themes of knowledge and seeing; "Amen, amen, I tell you, we speak of what *we know (oidamen)*, and testify (*martyroumen*) to what we *have seen (eōrakamen)*; but you (pl.) do not receive our testimony (*martyrian*)." These repetitions suggest that 2:23-25 is not just a bridge passage introducing Nicodemus, but is an introduction to the whole pericope (2:23–3:21).

Based on verbal and structural repetitions, I propose that the Nicodemus pericope develops in three major narrative blocks:

- *Section 1.* 2:23–3:10: A dialogue with Nicodemus.

- *Section 2.* 3:11-14: A discourse thematically and structurally related to Nicodemus but addressed to a wider audience, concluding with the theme of belief as a requirement for eternity life.

- *Section 3.* 3:16-21: A discourse that develops the theme of belief or unbelief and the consequences of eternity life or judgment.

Sections 1 and 2 show aspects of parallelism in the repetition of words and themes, and the structure of the argument develops from an initial polarity

---

[2] Brown (*Gospel* 1:126) names these verses as "Transition and Introduction to the Nicodemus Scene."

[3] By contrast to Brown, noted above, Schnackenburg ties 2:23-25 closely to the Nicodemus episode: "the verses are actually a necessary presupposition (cf. 2:23 with 3:2) or preparation for the dialogue with Nicodemus." See Rudolf Schnackenburg, *The Gospel according to St. John*, trans. Kevin Smyth et al. 3 vols. HTCNT (London: Burns & Oates, 1968–1982) 1:358.

(birth/rebirth, earth/heaven) to a statement of a principle followed by an example (the parable of the wind; Moses typology). The first section has a conclusion after which Nicodemus retires from the passage, while the conclusion to the second section is the developed discourse in Section 3. The structure of the first two sections is shown in the following table.

Section 1	Section 2
Dialogue: **The necessity of rebirth**	**Discourse:** **The Unique Heavenly Revealer**
Introduction When he was in Jerusalem during the Passover festival, many believed in his name because they saw (*theōrountes*) the signs (*sēmeia*) that he was doing. But Jesus on his part would not entrust himself to them, because he knew (*gignōskein*) all people and needed no one to testify (*martyrēsē*) about any person (*anthrōpou*); for he himself knew (*egignōsken*) what was in a person (*anthrōpǭ*). Now there was one (*anthrōpos*) of the Pharisees, named Nicodemus, a leader of the Jews. He came to Jesus by night and said to him, "Rabbi, we *know* (*oidamen*) that you are a **teacher who has come from God;** for it is not possible (*dynatai*) for anyone to do these *signs* (*sēmeia*) that you do, unless God is with him" (2:23–3:2).	*Introduction* 11 Amen, amen, I say to you, we speak of what *we know* (*oidamen*), and testify (*martyroumen*) to what we *have seen* (*eōrakamen*); but you do not receive our testimony (*martyrian*).
Birth/rebirth 3 Jesus answered him saying, "Amen, amen, I say to you, unless one is born anew (*anōthen*) it is not possible (*dynatai*) to see the kingdom of God." 4. Nicodemus said to him, "How is it possible (*dynatai*) for a person to be born when he is old? It is not possible (*dynatai*) to enter into the mother's womb a second time and be born."	*Earth/heaven* 12 If I have told you *earthly* things and you do not believe, how can you believe if I tell you *heavenly* things?

Section 1	Section 2
Dialogue: **The necessity of rebirth**	**Discourse:** **The Unique Heavenly Revealer**
5 Jesus answered, "Amen, amen, I say to you, unless one is born of water and the Spirit, it is not possible (*dynatai*) to enter into the kingdom of God.	
Principle 6 What is born of the flesh is flesh, and what is born of the Spirit (*pneuma*) is spirit.	*Principle* 13 No one has ascended into heaven but he who descended from heaven, the Son of Man.
Parable 7 Do not marvel that I said to you, 'You must be born from above (*anōthen*).'⁴ 8 The wind/spirit (*pneuma*) blows where it wills, and you hear the sound of it, but you do not know whence it comes or whither it goes; so it is (*houtōs*) with everyone who is **born of the Spirit.**"	*Typology* 14. And as Moses lifted up the serpent in the wilderness, so it is (*houtōs*) that the Son of Man must be lifted up, 15 that everyone who **believes in him may have eternity life.**"
Conclusion 9 Replying Nicodemus said to him, "How is this possible (*dynatai*)?" 10 Replying Jesus said to him "Are you a **teacher of Israel,** and yet you do not know this?"	*Conclusion* (Section 3, vv. 16-21)

Section 1 is defined by Nicodemus' description of Jesus as a "teacher who has come from God" (v. 2), and Jesus' description of Nicodemus as "a teacher of Israel" (v. 10). Apart from this *inclusio,* the section is held together by

---

⁴ In this context, speaking of the Spirit (*pneuma*), I translate the term *anōthen* as "from above"; similarly in the parable *pneuma* is best translated "wind." The evangelist is exploiting the double meaning of these Greek terms.

the repetition of the word *dynastai* (which I have translated using "possible" and its negative form "impossible"). Within this section, smaller units are also set in parallel form, e.g.:

3. "Amen, amen, I say to you,
    unless one is born anew (*anōthen*)   it is not possible to see the kingdom
                                             of God."
5. "Amen, amen, I say to you, unless
    one is born of water and the Spirit   it is not possible to enter into the
                                             kingdom of God."

The parallelism, typical of Hebrew poetry, establishes that seeing (v. 3) and entering (v. 5) the kingdom of God are synonymous; similarly, being born from above (v. 7) and being born of the Spirit (v. 9) are synonymous. The argument supporting Jesus' statements in verses 3-5 begins with a statement of a principle (v. 6), presumably one Nicodemus could agree with. The principle is then expanded upon in the form of a small parable about the wind and then related to Jesus' teaching about new birth. Section 2 begins with a brief introduction (v. 11), repeating words and themes in the introduction to the first section (2:23–3:2). The polarities of birth/new birth, water/Spirit from Section One are named in Section Two as earthly and heavenly realities. This leads into the principle that the only one who can reveal heavenly realities is the one who has come from heaven, the Son of Man. This principle is developed through the typology drawn from Numbers 21:6-9 to explain further the figure of the Son of Man, who is not only a heavenly revealer but one who enables a believer to have a new quality of life described as "eternity life" (*zōēn aiōnion*).[5]

The final section takes up the themes of belief and eternity life introduced in verse 14 to explain how it is that humanity can access this life, and what can prevent access. This third section, with its themes of eternity life and judgment, needs to be read through the particular Johannine eschatological viewpoint, which will be developed below. This section also develops structurally through parallelism, both synthetic and antithetic, in its sequence of similarities and contrasts, as the following table shows:

---

[5] I am translating *zōēn aiōnion* as "eternity life" in order to emphasize that this is a distinctively different quality of life and not simply the current experience of life extended in time. This quality of life will be discussed further below.

16. For God so loved the world that s/he gave the only-born Son[6] that whoever believes in him should not perish but have eternity life.	17. For God sent the Son into the world not to judge the world but that through him the world might be saved.
18. Whoever believes in him is not judged; whoever does not believe has already been judged for having not believed in the name of God's only-born Son.	19. And this is the judgment that the light has come into the world and humanity loved darkness rather than light because their deeds were evil.
20. For all who do evil hate the light and do not come to the light lest their deeds should be exposed.	21. But all who do what is true come to the light that it may be clearly seen that their deeds have been done in God.

Nicodemus, the Pharisee

Nicodemus is introduced as a Pharisee and ruler of the Jews. Based on the signs he has seen, he has initial knowledge enabling him to understand Jesus as a teacher authorized by God in the manner of the prophets, particularly Moses, whose signs witnessed to their divine commission.[7] While Nicodemus speaks of Jesus as a teacher "who has come from God," he is not fully aware of the truth of his words; the reader knows that Jesus has come from God (John 1:1) in a way that Nicodemus has not yet grasped. Nicodemus comes to Jesus thinking of him as a sign-prophet. As a Pharisee, Nicodemus belongs to a group within Judaism that has considered the

---

[6] The passive of the verb *gennaō*, used in the earlier dialogue (vv. 3, 5, 6, 8), can mean either "begotten," as of a masculine principle, or "be born," as of a feminine principle; see Brown, *Gospel* 1:130. Since the fundamental symbol in the pericope relies on birth from the mother's womb it seems appropriate to continue the image of birth through the pericope and to speak of Jesus as "the only-born" Son of God in vv. 16 and 18. On the symbol of divine motherhood see Dorothy Lee, *Flesh and Glory*, 135–65. This chapter is the only one within the narrative where the expression "only-born" appears. Its purpose here is to signify the uniqueness of Jesus vis-à-vis the believers, who are also to be "born" of God and be called "children of God" (vv. 12-13). Marie-Émile Boismard situates this distinction in Jesus' identity in the incarnation of the *logos*. The *logos*, eternally with God in the beginning, becomes incarnate as the only-begotten (1:14) Jesus, who, as the only-begotten, rests in the heart of the Father (1:18). See Boismard, *Moses or Jesus: An Essay in Johannine Christology*, 98–111.

[7] "In the account of Exodus, the miracles which Moses must do are called 'signs,' in the Hebrew text (אוֹת) as well as in the Septuagint (*sēmeion*). They must, in effect, constitute the 'signs' that Moses had indeed been sent by God" (ibid. 56).

question of life beyond death and has moved to accepting the idea that God will not permit the just to remain in death forever, but will renew their lives at the end of time through bodily resurrection.[8] Here, then, there is already openness to the possibility of renewal of life. Jesus, in turn, introduces the concept of rebirth as the means of seeing and apprehending an even deeper reality in himself than simply a sign-prophet in the Mosaic tradition. Rebirth enables vision of the reign of God, the presence of God now incarnate in history. These few verses thrust Nicodemus and the reader into the heart of the Johannine understanding of Jesus' mission: to give life to the world (3:16). Before continuing the dialogue with Nicodemus, it is therefore necessary to examine the particular Johannine meaning of the terms "life," "eternity life," "rebirth," and "the reign of God."

From the opening verses of the Prologue the reader knows that Jesus, the incarnate Word, participates in a dynamic communion of shared life with God, so that "what God was, the Word was" (1:1).[9] This communion of life, when revealed in human experience, is described analogically as the loving relationship between Father and Son (1:18). The Son is sent into the world to draw humanity with him into the divine communion, that is, to participate in his own filial relationship with and in God, to empower believers to become "children of God" (1:13). In the words of C. H. Dodd, "The Father, the Son, and the disciples dwell in one another by virtue of a love which is the very life and the activity of God."[10] The communion of life enjoyed by the Son in all time is offered as a gift of love for all men and women. In the language of the gospel this communion of being in God is called "life" and "eternity life."[11] It is a gift offered by Jesus to those who desire it and can believe in him; as such it is a gift enjoyed already in this world that physical death cannot annul. The nature of this life as a participation in God's life, the life of eternity, blurs the distinction made between this age and the age to come, bringing eschatology into the present as

---

[8] "The real approach in Judaism and primitive Christianity to the Johannine doctrine of rebirth is by way of the eschatological conception of the transfiguration of the blessed into forms of heavenly glory in the Age to Come. This is called *hē paliggenesia* in Matt xix.28" (Dodd, *Interpretation*, 304).

[9] Moloney, *John*, 42.

[10] Dodd, *Interpretation*, 196.

[11] The expression *zoēn aiōnion ktl.* occurs in 3:14, 16, 36; 4:14, 36; 5:24, 39; 6:27, 40, 47, 54, 68; 10:28; 12:25, 50; 17:2; and *aiōnios zoē* in 17:3. Dodd understands this expression in the Fourth Gospel to mean "the life of the Age to Come, qualitatively as well as quantitatively different from this life" (ibid. 144–49). In this qualitative sense the adjective "eternity" describes a quality of the divine in the writings of Plato and Philo (Dodd, *Interpretation*, 149–50).

something already impinging on history. From where could this uniquely Johannine vision, usually named "realized eschatology," have come? Is there any precedent for this theological thinking in the religious world of first-century Judaism?

Jewish Eschatology

Jewish eschatology, while a late theological development, is grounded in the long experience of Israel's faith in God's promises. At first these promises were directed toward an immediate future, but in time, particularly after the exile, faith in the fulfilment of God's promises shifted to a more distant time. In the words of Craig Evans, "Over centuries, however, it became clear that Israel (and later Judah) could not bring about the perfect Kingdom of God. . . . Yet future expectations and the hope for a better world did not die; instead, the horizon shifted to the end times."[12] Evans goes on to speak of prophetic eschatology, in which the oppression of the Jews by other nations is interpreted as Israel's punishment for breaking the covenant (e.g., Amos 4–8; Hosea 4–10; Jeremiah 2–8), and apocalyptic eschatology, where the oppression is linked to a cosmic struggle between God and other powers (e.g., Isa 24:17-23; Dan 7:1-8).[13] It is important to state here that there is no single, unified doctrine of the end times. Some views allowed for an end-time resolution of this oppression within history while other lines of thought, particularly within the apocalyptic tradition, placed such resolution beyond history, when this world or this age is brought to an end and a new age comes into being.[14] What is consistent is the conviction "that human failure has so corrupted life on this earth that only a radical transformation initiated by God alone could make things right."[15] The radical inbreaking of the transforming power of God is called, in the Synoptic tradition, the kingdom of God.

[12] Craig A. Evans and Peter W. Flint, "Introduction," in *Eschatology, Messianism, and the Dead Sea Scrolls.* Studies in the Dead Sea Scrolls and Related Literature (Grand Rapids: Eerdmans, 1997) 1–2.

[13] Ibid. 2.

[14] Hultgren comments that eschatology concerns itself with "a future coming age, a period of transformed existence that God will bring about—either within history or beyond it." See Arland J. Hultgren, "Eschatology in the New Testament: The Current Debate," in Carl E. Braaten and Robert W. Jenson, eds., *The Last Things: Biblical and Theological Perspectives on Eschatology* (Grand Rapids: Eerdmans, 2002) 67.

[15] Donald E. Gowan, *Eschatology in the Old Testament* (Philadelphia: Fortress Press, 1986) 122.

Ideas of an "afterlife" developed within these theological consider-ations and under the influence of Hellenistic thinking.[16] To paraphrase the words of Daniel Harrington, at the heart of notions of an "afterlife" is the problem of theodicy: "How can the all-powerful and just God allow righteous people to suffer?"[17] Whether the justification of the righteous happens within this historical world or in the New Age, the problem still remains: how can those who have died, particularly through martyrdom for their Torah loyalty, be vindicated? One solution is found in the books of Daniel (12:2-3) and Maccabees (2 Macc 7:9, 14), where those who have died before the end will be raised.[18] In this scenario the afterlife involves a final judgment for the ultimate vindication of the just one before his/her enemies. The righteous then enjoy the blessings their behavior deserved but that were denied them in life, while the wicked receive condemnation for their evil deeds. In order to have such a final judgment the dead must first be raised to life in order to appear before the Divine Judge. Resurrection is therefore a necessary part of the afterlife and this schema is termed "resurrection eschatology" by

---

[16] Stanley Porter argues that ideas about an afterlife, particularly the concept of resurrection, only arose through contact with Hellenism. "The tenor of Jewish thought until the Hellenistic period seemed to accept a high degree of finality to death, even if there was continued existence in Sheol. It was not until the Hellenistic period that there was any thought of a bodily resurrection, and even here the evidence was never particu-larly strong. Greek thought, however, much earlier engaged in serious discussion about the afterlife, including the immortality of the soul and rewards and punishments for the good and wicked behavior of humans on earth. There was even a tradition of resurrection preceding the Hellenistic period. . . ." See Stanley E. Porter, "Resurrection, the Greeks and the New Testament," in Stanley E. Porter, Michael A. Hayes, and David Tombs, eds., *Resurrection.* JSNTSup 186 (Sheffield: Sheffield Academic Press, 1999) 80.

[17] Harrington continues with the statement: "Apocalyptic solves this problem by deferring the full manifestation of God's power and righteousness to the last judgment." See Daniel J. Harrington, "Afterlife Expectation in Pseudo-Philo, 4 Ezra, and 2 Baruch, and their Implications for the New Testament," in Reimund Bieringer, Veronica Koperski, and Bianca Lataire, eds., *Resurrection in the New Testament: Festschrift J. Lambrecht.* BETL 165 (Leuven: Leuven University Press, 2002) 32. See also M. O'Brien, "Theodicy and Eschatology: Old Testament Considerations," in D. Neville, ed., *Theodicy and Es-chatology.* Task of Theology Today 4 (Adelaide: Australian Theological Forum Press, 2005) 1–17.

[18] This eschatological understanding will not be developed here. For detailed discus-sion of the afterlife envisaged in Daniel and the books of the Maccabees see M.-É. Boismard, *Our Victory over Death: Resurrection?* trans. Madeleine Beaumont (College-ville: Liturgical Press, 1999) chs. 1–2.

Sandra Schneiders,[19] and is the schema we find in the writings of Paul and the Synoptic Gospels, illustrated especially in Matthew 25:31-46. The Pharisees held and taught a belief in resurrection such as this.

But this is not the only possible afterlife scenario. In the last century of the biblical period, perhaps as late as 50 C.E.,[20] an Alexandrian Jew writing within the Wisdom tradition presented an alternative understanding not only of the afterlife but of this life as well.[21] The sage was probably reflecting on the historical situation of conflict between the Torah-loyal Jew in the Diaspora and his more lax co-religionists who were succumbing to Hellenistic influences. So while the oppressive situation is no longer from outside, as in the situation of Daniel and the Maccabees, there is still the issue of theodicy. In this Hellenistic setting, the writer of Wisdom is influenced by Greek philosophy as well as Jewish theology; in fact, he may have drawn deliberately on philosophical ideas and terminology in order to "set forth a Judaism that was more attuned to Greek cultural ideas."[22] The writer seems acquainted with Plato's theory of a pre-existent soul (Wis 8:19-20; 9:15), but there is no sense in the book of Wisdom that an embodied soul

[19] Sandra M. Schneiders, "The Johannine Resurrection Narrative: An Exegetical Study of John 20 as a Synthesis of Johannine Spirituality" (D.S.T. [unpublished], Pontificia Universitas Gregoriana, 1975) 76. A very brief synopsis of Schneiders' work on Jewish eschatology can be found in Sandra M. Schneiders, "The Resurrection (of the Body) in the Fourth Gospel: A Key to Johannine Spirituality," in John R. Donahue, ed., *Life in Abundance: Studies of John's Gospel in Tribute to Raymond E. Brown.* (Collegeville: Liturgical Press, 2005) 173–77. Boismard (*Our Victory over Death*, viii) also distinguishes two different eschatological understandings that he calls "a resurrection current" and "an immortality current."

[20] John Collins suggests that the book of Wisdom was written in Alexandria between 30 B.C.E. and 70 C.E. See John J. Collins, *Jewish Wisdom in the Hellenistic Age* (Edinburgh: T&T Clark, 1997) 179. David Winston places it in Alexandria during the reign of Caligula (37–41 C.E.); see his *The Wisdom of Solomon.* AB 43 (New York: Doubleday, 1979) 23.

[21] There is debate over the composition of the Book of Wisdom, with some scholars suggesting multiple authors. The position taken here is that of Winston and Boismard, who propose one author working with earlier material, revising and editing over a period of time to form the final document. See Winston, *Wisdom of Solomon*, 12–18; Boismard, *Our Victory over Death*, 65–66.

[22] Leo G. Perdue, *Wisdom and Creation: The Theology of Wisdom Literature* (Nashville: Abingdon, 1994). "The author of the book of the Wisdom of Solomon sought to represent the teachings of Judaism in a fashion that would maintain the integrity of Jewish faith, but in a decidedly Hellenistic guise that would allow for adaptation to the dominant cultural and intellectual forms common to the period" (p. 292).

is a fall from a higher state.[23] The anthropology of Wisdom draws on both Semitic and Hellenistic understanding of the human person in a way that creates some tension, if not contradiction, in the text. In words echoing the creation of Adam in Genesis 2:7,[24] he describes those who fashion idols: "they failed to know the one who formed them and inspired (*empneusanta*) them with active souls (*psychēn*) and breathed (*emphysēsanta*) a living spirit (*pneuma*) into them" (Wis 15:11). Here the soul is the vital breath of life given by God. This breath of life is lent (Wis 15:8) to humans; at death it is withdrawn by God and the human person returns to the earth and ceases to live. There is no immortal soul existing independently of the human body. Body and soul together constitute the human person, and the wisdom teacher does not distinguish among "soul" (*psychē*), "mind" (*nous*), and "spirit" (*pneuma*).[25] "Both [*pneuma* and *psyche*] designate the vital breath lent by God to humans, and by God withdrawn at the moment of death."[26]

An alternative anthropology is proposed in Wis 9:15. While Wis 15:11 draws on Genesis and shows its traditional Semitic anthropology, Wis 9:15 reflects Platonic thinking: "for a perishable body weighs down the soul, and this earthy tent burdens the thoughtful mind."[27] The dualistic thinking evident in this verse, as well as the concept of the immortality of the soul, borrows from Hellenistic philosophy rather than Semitic anthropology.[28]

Epicurean philosophy held that the gods had material existence but lived forever because they were incorruptible.[29] They enjoyed this state of incorruptibility because they were able to feed on ambrosia, the nectar of the gods, which enabled them to overcome the usual forces that dissipate atoms, causing material things to decay.[30] Therefore incorruptibility, or

[23] Collins, *Jewish Wisdom in the Hellenistic Age*, 185.

[24] "And God formed the human from dust from the earth and breathed (*enephysēsen*) on its face a breath (*pnoēn*) of life and the human became a living being (*psychēn*)" (Gen 2:7).

[25] Perdue, *Wisdom and Creation*, 296.

[26] Boismard, *Our Victory over Death*, 67.

[27] Cf. *Phaedo* 81C: "such a soul is weighed down by this and is dragged back into the sensible world."

[28] Winston points out a number of critical differences between the book of Wisdom and Hellenistic philosophy: the pre-existence of the soul, the soul's fall, the transmigration of souls, the divisions within the soul, and particularly the immortality of the soul "by its nature," since Wisdom describes immortality as a gift to the righteous. See Winston, *Wisdom of Solomon*, 26–30.

[29] Collins, *Jewish Wisdom in the Hellenistic Age*, 186.

[30] J. M. Reese, *The Book of Wisdom; Song of Songs*. Old Testament Message 20 (Wilmington, DE: Michael Glazier, 1983) 42.

immortality, is a divine quality; only God is immortal. When considering human existence, the author of Wisdom presents an interpretation of the two creation accounts in Genesis 1–3. Because human beings are made in the image of God (Wis 2:23), they can participate in God's immortality if they choose the path of righteousness, "But the righteous live forever (*eis ton aiōna zōsin*), and their reward is with the Lord; the Most High takes care of them" (Wis 5:15).[31] God's own incorruptible Spirit (12:1) maintains life and is God's gift to the righteous (8:21), allowing them to enjoy life forever "in the hand of God" (3:1). Life, properly understood, is more than mere existence, but is communion with God enjoyed by the just (4:10-14), and physical death neither destroys nor interrupts this. In fact, for the righteous physical demise is not really death, since they only "seem to die" (Wis 3:2).

The book of Wisdom makes the claim that "God did not make death" (1:13), then offers two explanations about the origins of death. One draws on the popular Middle Eastern mythology of a kingdom of death, Hades/Sheol. In this tradition Death was a deity in his own right. Within monotheistic Judaism, death, while not considered a deity, still represents a mythical power.[32] The wicked invited this power of death into the kingdom of God's creation. "But the ungodly by their words and deeds summoned death; considering him a friend, they pined away and made a covenant with him, because they are fit to belong to his company" (Wis 1:16). The second explanation for the experience of death in a creation made for immortality (Wis 1:14) draws once again on the creation story of Adam and Eve. For the first time in the Scriptures the serpent of Gen 3:1 is identified with the devil, and it is the devil's envy for human immortality that leads to the temptation of Eve and Adam to eat of the forbidden fruit (Wis 2:24). Through human sin, death entered into the world.

Against this large horizon of the possibility of immortal life and the possibility of death, the Wisdom writer urges his audience to choose the way of righteousness as the choice for eternal life. Therefore human beings exist now, participating in either eternal life[33] or eternal death. The demise of the body in physical death simply confirms this choice. The just remain at peace in the hand of God, while the wicked become "ignominious carcasses."[34] The book of Wisdom does not make explicit whether the just pass from death immediately into heavenly existence with God or whether there is some intermediate state. While it is said that their souls live on in a place

---

[31] Winston, *Wisdom of Solomon*, 29–30.

[32] Collins, *Jewish Wisdom in the Hellenistic Age*, 189.

[33] Perdue, *Wisdom and Creation*, 301.

[34] Winston, *Wisdom of Solomon*, 32.

of peace (Wis 3:23), in the hand of God (Wis 3:1), it is not clear that this is "heaven," as this expression may simply mean they are protected by God (cf. Deut 33:3).[35] So while there still may be some time in Sheol for the just and the wicked, these souls are not mere shades without life;[36] they remain alive, awaiting the time when, for the righteous, they will "abide with him in love" (Wis 3:9). But there is no sense here of bodily resurrection. It is the soul, the center of one's personality, that will enjoy the blessings of heaven.

There are different opinions about whether the book of Wisdom envisages a final end-time judgment. There does seem to be something more to come in the future rather than the soul going to dwell with God immediately after death, for Wisdom 3:7 speaks of a future "visitation": "In the time of their visitation (*episkopē*) they will shine forth, and will run like sparks through the stubble." The verb *episkopeō* means "examine," and this verse suggests that there may be a future examination by God;[37] then the just "will abide with him in love" (Wis 3:9).[38] Chapter 5 seems to describe a final judgment, when the virtuous will judge peoples and nations, reigning as kings, but Collins suggests that this scene may be a literary fiction to dramatize the miscalculation of the wicked.[39] Whether this judgment is thought of as a future reality or a literary fiction, there is no suggestion of bodily resurrection. For the martyrs, death is a moment of exaltation, while for those who do not experience martyrdom, death is a "taking up" or assumption (Wis 4:10-14).

In summary, there are two major issues in the book of Wisdom that distinguish its theology from that of Daniel and Maccabees. The first issue is what is meant by the term "life." In the book of Wisdom this means more than mere existence but is a participation already in the eternity life that is the divine prerogative. This quality of life is a gift for those who embrace Wisdom, and physical death will not destroy or even interrupt it. Physical

[35] Boismard, *Our Victory over Death*, 72.

[36] Sheol is not a place of life. "Whatever trace of the individual may survive in Sheol, it is not a human being because it does not enjoy subjectivity, community, or union with God." See Schneiders, "The Resurrection (of the Body)," 172. See this place for further discussion on Semitic anthropology.

[37] Cf. 1:6, where God is called "the true *episkopos* of the heart."

[38] N. T. Wright argues from the use of the term *episkopē* that after death there is a time of rest and only at the end of time will there be a genuine revival when the just will receive their reward. He therefore sees the book of Wisdom in continuity with Daniel and Maccabees. See N. T. Wright, *The Resurrection of the Son of God*. Christian Origins and the Question of God 3 (London: SPCK, 2003) 169–70.

[39] Collins, *Jewish Wisdom in the Hellenistic Age*, 186.

death will be a transition for the immortal soul/spirit. In physical death there is the separation of spirit and body, but the spirit continues to participate in life or remains in its state of deadliness. The second issue is that this theology does not seem to require bodily resurrection, for the inner spirit/soul lives on. Bodily resurrection on the last day may happen, but it is not essential in this schema, according to which there is no need for a final judgment, as judgment is already made in the choices operating in a person's lifetime. The end-time will be a manifestation and confirmation of these choices. With no final judgment, and the spirit continuing to live on beyond the grave, there is no need of resurrection, understood as the reuniting of body and spirit. While there is no necessity for bodily resurrection, this eschatological framework does not rule out the possibility of resurrection. As Sandra Schneiders states:

> Bodily resurrection does not figure explicitly in this sapiential understanding of the destiny of the just and unjust because the judgment of the ungodly takes place in their very choice of evil by which they "summon death" (cf. Wis 1:16) and the just are exalted by and/or assumed to God in their seeming death. However, the assumption or exaltation of the just is not simply immortality of the soul in the Greek philosophical sense, that is, the natural indestructibility of a spiritual substance. It is life in the Jewish sense. . . . And life, even after death, in which the body did not participate in some way would have been inconceivable to the Jewish imagination. So while nothing is said of bodily resurrection in sapiential eschatology, it is fundamentally susceptible to it.[40]

We therefore find in the book of Wisdom a type of realized eschatology in which end-time realities impinge on life in this world. With this as background, where can we situate the Gospel of John? What eschatological framework operates in this text: resurrection eschatology or the immortality eschatology found in the book of Wisdom?[41]

Wisdom and the Fourth Gospel

There have been a number of studies on the influence of Wisdom literature on the Fourth Gospel. Some of these deal with specific themes or sections of the gospel,[42] while Michael Willett, Sharon Ringe, Ben Withering-

---

[40] Schneiders, "The Resurrection (of the Body)," 175.

[41] Schneiders calls the eschatological picture that emerges from the book of Wisdom "immortality-eschatology." See Schneiders, "Resurrection Narrative," 76.

[42] See for example, John Ashton, "The Transformation of Wisdom: A Study of the Prologue of John's Gospel," *NTS* 32 (1986) 161–86; Catherine Cory, "Wisdom's Rescue: A New Reading of the Tabernacles Discourse (John 7:1–8:59)," *JBL* 116 (1997) 95–116.

ton III, and Martin Scott present systematic studies of Wisdom across the entire gospel.[43] Here I will briefly outline some major points of contact.[44]

The Prologue offers the first clue that the gospel is influenced by Israel's Wisdom traditions in the close similarities drawn between the Johannine Word and the Old Testament personification of Wisdom.[45] In considering the possible background to the Prologue, Schnackenburg writes: "The closest parallels in thought are to be found in Jewish Wisdom speculation."[46] The Word, like Wisdom, pre-exists with God (Sir 1:1; Prov 8:23; John 1:1), is an active agent in creation (Prov 8:27-31; John 1:3), and has come to dwell in Israel (Sir 24:8-12; Bar 3:36–4:1; John 1:11a). As with Wisdom, there have been varied responses to the Word, both rejection and acceptance (*1 Enoch* 42:1-2; John 1:11b).[47] The gospel narrative continues to present similarities as the Word, like Wisdom, gathers disciples inviting them to dwell with her (Sir 51:23; John 1:35-51),[48] offering them nourishment (Sir 24:19-22; Prov 9:1-6; John 6) and salvation (Wis 9:18; John 3:16).[49] The disciples of Wisdom are called children/sons (Prov 2:1; Sir 2:1; 4:10-11; Wis 2:13; John 13:13) and friends (Wis 7:27; John 15:15). Wisdom lives with God and is loved by God (Prov 8:30-31; Wis 8:3; John 5:20; 10:17); she is an initiate in the knowledge of God and an associate in God's works (Wis 8:4; John 8:29, 38, 42, 55). I conclude this very brief overview with the words of Michael Willett: "Wisdom strides through the Gospel in the

---

[43] Michael E. Willett, *Wisdom Christology in the Fourth Gospel* (San Francisco: Mellen Research University Press, 1992); Martin Scott, *Sophia and the Johannine Jesus.* JSNTSup 71 (Sheffield: JSOT Press, 1992); Ben Witherington III, *John's Wisdom: A Commentary on the Fourth Gospel* (Louisville: Westminster John Knox, 1995); Sharon H. Ringe, *Wisdom's Friends: Community and Christology in the Fourth Gospel* (Louisville: Westminster John Knox, 1999).

[44] See also a summary of "Wisdom Motifs" in Brown, *Introduction to the Gospel of John*, 259–65.

[45] For a recent discussion of the distinction between "hypostatizing" and "personifying" see ibid., 260 n. 93. According to Brown, hypostatizing indicates an independent being, while personifying is "a representation in personal terms" of an attribute.

[46] Schnackenburg, *Gospel* 1:481. See also Dodd, *Interpretation*, 274–75, for a chart showing parallels between the Prologue and Wisdom.

[47] "Wisdom went out in order to dwell among the sons of men, but did not find a dwelling; Wisdom returned to her place and took her seat in the midst of the angels" (*1 Enoch* 42:1-2).

[48] André Feuillet notes the similarity between the disciples of Jesus and the disciples of Wisdom, even though the latter are never called "disciples." See André Feuillet, *Johannine Studies* (Staten Island: Alba House, 1965) 89–91.

[49] On Wisdom's role in salvation see Alice M. Sinnott, "Wisdom as Saviour," *ABR* 52 (2004) 19–31.

person of Jesus of Nazareth. He is Wisdom incarnate, God reaching out to humanity to the fullest extent, as a human being."[50]

Wisdom Eschatology in John

In his study on the Johannine concept of resurrection, Maarten Menken draws attention to the fact that in the Fourth Gospel, unlike the Synoptics, there is no prediction of death and resurrection.[51] There is a statement about death, described as a lifting up (3:14),[52] but this is not followed by a statement about being raised. Indeed, throughout the Johannine narrative the death of Jesus is presented as the culmination of Jesus' hour, his moment of exaltation and glorification. As Brown comments, " Thus, in John 'being lifted up' refers to one continuous action of ascent. . . . The first step in the ascent is when Jesus is lifted up on the cross; the second step is when he is raised up from death; the final step is when he is lifted up to heaven."[53]

The emphasis throughout the gospel on the cross as the exaltation and means of return to the Father leaves little need for resurrection. This is confirmed by Jesus himself when he declares from the cross, "It is finished" (19:30). Jesus' death is not presented as requiring any further vindication. These considerations suggest that the Fourth Gospel is not working from resurrection eschatology but from the type of immortality eschatology found in the book of Wisdom.

Born Anew

Returning to the Nicodemus pericope, we find one clear indication that we are dealing here with notions of life and eternity life similar to that of the book of Wisdom. The phrase "the kingdom of God" (vv. 3, 5) is found only once within the Old Testament, in the book of Wisdom.

> When a righteous man fled from his brother's wrath, she guided him on straight paths; she showed him the *kingdom of God*, and gave him knowledge of holy things; she prospered him in his labors, and increased the fruit of his toil. (Wis 10:10)

---

[50] Willett, *Wisdom Christology*, 127. See also the discussion of the Johannine sapiential voice and style in Witherington, *John's Wisdom*, 18–27.

[51] Maarten J. J. Menken, "Interpretation of the Old Testament and the Resurrection of Jesus in John's Gospel," in Bieringer, Koperski, and Lataire, eds., *Resurrection in the New Testament*, 197.

[52] There are three "lifting up" passages in the Fourth Gospel (3:14; 8:28; 12:32-34, which may be understood as the equivalent to the three passion-resurrection statements in the Synoptics (Mark 8:31; 9:31; 10:33-34 *par.*); see Brown, *Gospel* 1:146.

[53] Brown, *Gospel* 1:146.

While the phrase "kingdom of God" no doubt had its basis in the preaching of Jesus, it does not dominate the Fourth Gospel as it does the Synoptics, being found only in this Nicodemus pericope (vv. 3, 5). Rather than look to the Synoptics for the source of this phrase and its meaning in this passage, we should see the book of Wisdom as a more likely intertext. This section of the book (10:1–19:22) recalls the history of Israel, told now with divine Wisdom/Sophia as the savior. It is Wisdom who guides Israel's ancestors, who comes to their aid, who grants them visions and knowledge of the kingdom. The above passage recalls the story of Jacob's flight from Laban and his dream at Bethel, described here as a vision of the kingdom of God. For one familiar with the Fourth Gospel, the Wisdom passage also recalls Jesus' promise to Nathanael that he would see the opening of heaven and the angels ascending and descending on the Son of Man (John 1:51). That we are meant to hear the Jacob story, retold through the book of Wisdom, is confirmed in the second allusion to Jacob in John 3:13, with its language of "ascending," "descending," "heaven," and "Son of Man." Genesis 28, Wisdom 10:10, and John 1:51 provide the rich intertext for understanding the Nicodemus pericope. In Jesus, the Son of Man/divine Wisdom has descended from heaven and the heavens have been opened, enabling access to the kingdom of God for the one who is born anew.

The term *anōthen* can function as both an adverb of place and an adverb of time. It can mean "from above," and it can mean "from an earlier time," hence "again," or "anew";[54] the meaning here (v. 3) is probably "born anew" rather than "born from above."[55] Nicodemus understands *anōthen* in a

---

[54] Friedrich Büchsel, ἄνωθεν, *TDNT* 1 (1964–76) 378.

[55] As this journal may not be readily accessible, I note in full the reasons given by Linda L. Belleville, "'Born of Water and Spirit:' John 3:5," *Trinity Journal* 1 (1980) 138 n. 75. "'Again' or 'anew' as opposed to 'from above' is to be preferred for the following reasons: (1) Nicodemus took the term to mean as such (i.e., he speaks of entering the womb a second time in v. 4). (2) John's device of misunderstanding (where in conversation Jesus' interlocutor misunderstands something Jesus says) does not depend on verbal ambiguity (e.g., 2:20). (3) Nicodemus' failure to understand Jesus in 3:4 is more easily explained. (4) Since 'from above' denotes the sphere or source of birth, Nicodemus would have had to deliberately choose to misunderstand *anōthen* to mean 'from below' (i.e., an earthly sense). (5) We know of no Hebrew or Aramaic word that carries both spatial and temporal meanings if Jesus did not speak in Greek. [This is the one reason I would disregard, as I take this dialogue to be a creation of the evangelist rather than a report of an actual historical event]. (6) Nicodemus by his response in v. 4 does not fail to understand the necessary fact of a second birth but rather the appropriate sphere which Jesus in vv. 5-12 proceeds to define. Godet, Bultmann, Ladd, Westcott, Ringwald, Calvin, Justin Martyr, Clement of Alexander, Tertullian, Augustine, and Jerome all opt for 'born again.' Cf. Coptic and Syriac versions." This same article provides an excellent synopsis

temporal sense, for he speaks of being born a second time (*deuteron*). The misunderstanding between Jesus and Nicodemus is not so much about the meaning of *anōthen*, but about what Jesus means by birth.[56] Nicodemus understands Jesus literally and offers the impossible scenario of an adult reentering the mother's womb. Jesus is speaking of a different type of birth, a second birth by the agency of the Spirit, as he clarifies in the following verses.[57] I believe that in speaking of being born of water and the Spirit (v. 5), Jesus is referring to two types of birth;[58] the first is natural birth achieved with the release of the mother's amniotic fluid (birth by water);[59] the second is the spiritual birth of the believer brought about through the gift of the

---

of the variety of interpretations, which Belleville describes as ritualistic, symbolic, physiological, dualistic, cosmological, and figurative. Larry Paul Jones also supports this reading of "born anew," noting that: "misunderstandings based on 'misplaced literalness' characterize the Fourth Gospel." See Larry Paul Jones, *The Symbol of Water in the Gospel of John*, JSNTSup 145 (Sheffield: Sheffield Academic Press, 1997) 69.

[56] Scholars are divided on the issue of whether Nicodemus' misunderstanding is to be found in the two possible meanings of *anōthen* (from above, again), or on the meaning of rebirth. With Dodd (*Interpretation*, 304), Witherington ("The Waters of Birth: John 3.5 and 1 John 5.6-8," *NTS* 35 [1989] 159), and Schneiders (*Written That You May Believe*, 120), I place the confusion with the meaning of "born *anew*." As Schneiders notes, if Nicodemus had understood Jesus at this point to mean "born from above," he would not have responded with the grotesque image of re-entering the mother's womb. Nicodemus has understood the expression to mean born again, which he then takes literally. See also the reasons for this reading in the preceding footnote.

[57] Being born of the spirit (*ek pneumatos gennasthai*, 3:5, 6, 8) echoes the promise of the Prologue that believers would become children of God, being born of God (*ek theou gennasthai*, 1:13).

[58] Understanding "of water" to refer to physical birth means that this phrase need not be interpreted as a reference to baptism and thus seen as the work of a later redactor, as Bultmann proposes; see Bultmann, *Gospel of John*, 138–39 n. 3. This is not to say that a Christian community did not see in this text an allusion to their baptismal rituals, but that its first meaning is to be sought in the natural realm, as Dorothy Lee writes: "It is likely that water, as a symbol, evokes both birth and baptism in this passage, the text making no attempt to delimit the symbolic meaning. While Christian baptism is not the primary focus of the dialogue, John's symbolism is evocative in a number of directions and suggests a wider field of meaning." See Lee, *Flesh and Glory*, 71. See also Jones, *The Symbol of Water in the Gospel of John*, 76: "Although the practice of baptism may stand somewhere behind the text, nothing stated by the narrator or by Jesus makes an association with baptism concrete." For a discussion of criteria for reading passages sacramentally see Francis J. Moloney, "When is John talking about Sacraments?" *ABR* 30 (1982) 10–33.

[59] "One needs to be aware that in ancient Near Eastern literature the word 'water' can be and is used as a *terminus technicus*, or at least a well-known circumlocution, for matters involving procreation, child-bearing, child-bearing capacity, or the act of giving birth itself." Witherington, "The Waters of Birth," 156. See this article for further ex-

Spirit. The first birth gives access to human life, which is mortal (of the flesh).[60] The second birth draws one into the life of the Spirit. The principle stated in verse 6 shows clearly that Jesus distinguishes between two types of birth, natural and spiritual:

What is born of the flesh is flesh,
What is born of the spirit is Spirit.

The parable of the wind points to the sensible reality of birth in the Spirit, even though there is mystery surrounding it. Without clearly knowing the coming and going of the wind, one can hear it. The text actually reads "you hear the voice of it (v. 8)."[61] While Nicodemus, and a first-time reader, may continue to be puzzled by this explanation, a second-reading reader remembers another parabolic speech in which these same words are used of the sheep who hear and know the voice of the Shepherd (10:3, 4, 16).[62] For one born of the Spirit it is possible to hear the voice of the spirit/wind. Nicodemus responds with the question: "How can this possibly happen?" which leads into the following discourse where Jesus explains "how" this can happen, through belief in the Son of Man (v. 14).

As the discussion above indicates, the dialogue with Nicodemus is one of the richest and most densely packed narratives in the gospel, requiring that the reader be "in the know" about Johannine christology (who Jesus is, his origins in God, his purpose to give life) and eschatology (the Johannine meaning of life and eternity life). Nicodemus has come to Jesus in the context of Passover and its celebration of the Exodus, with all its accompanying signs and wonders. In this context he perceives Jesus as a sign-prophet, perhaps like Moses (Deut 18:15), but does not know Jesus' true origins in God and so cannot perceive his true identity. Jesus responds to his blindness by introducing the possibility of seeing more than just a sign-prophet, and of seeing in him the reign of God already present. For this spiritual insight another birth is required, birth in the Spirit. Life begun through the natural waters of childbirth is life of the flesh, destined to die. Life begun through birth of the Spirit is of a different quality, the quality

---

amples of "water" used as a reference to childbirth. See also Schneiders, *Written that You May Believe*, 120; and Lee, *Flesh and Glory*, 68–71.

[60] Flesh in this context refers to creatureliness, the mortal nature of the human person. "By becoming flesh, God enters the world in the thin garb of mortality, entering the darkness of creation clad only in the armor of skin and vein, sinew and bone: mortal, vulnerable, naked." For a rich examination of the Johannine use of the term "flesh" see Lee, *Flesh and Glory*, ch. 1. The quotation is from p. 50.

[61] *Tēn phōnēn autou* (3:8).

[62] *Tēn phōnēn autou* (10:4).

of life within the kingdom of God. As a Pharisee, Nicodemus can be presumed to be open to the concept of new life within the kingdom of God, but his eschatology locates this new life at the end of time, following the final judgment. The presence of Jesus brings these eschatological realities into the present, giving birth, and the life that follows, new meaning.

Belief in the Son of Man

In the second section (vv. 11-14), while the context is still an encounter with Nicodemus, he seems to have faded from the picture and Jesus speaks to a plurality. Even Jesus recedes as his words are reported sometimes in first person singular "I" (vv. 11, 12), sometimes first person plural "we" (v. 11), but mainly in the third person as he speaks of "the Son of Man" descended from heaven (v. 13) and lifted up (v. 14), and the Son given and sent to the world (vv. 16, 17, 18).[63] This section again seems to resound with themes and words from the book of Wisdom.

Wisdom	John
9:16 We can hardly guess at what is on *earth*, and what is at hand we find with labor; but who has traced out what is in the *heavens*? 9:17 Who has learned your counsel, unless you have given wisdom and sent your holy spirit from on high (*apo hypsistō*)? (Wis 9:16-17)	12 If I have told you *earthly* things and you do not believe, how can you believe if I tell you *heavenly* things? 13 No one has ascended into heaven but he who descended from heaven, the Son of Man. 14. And as Moses lifted up (*hypsōsen*) the serpent in the desert, so it is that the Son of Man must be lifted up (*hypsōthēnai*).

In both passages we find a contrast between what can be known on earth and what can be known about heaven. Wisdom asserts that the only one who can learn God's ways is one who has been given wisdom, one to whom God's Holy Spirit has been sent from on high. Earlier in the dialogue the parallelism of verses 7 and 8 in the Nicodemus passage establishes that being born *anōthen* is synonymous with being born "of the Spirit." The

---

[63] The change from singular to plural has led some scholars to suggest that the discourse with Nicodemus concludes at v. 12; I disagree with this view for the structural and thematic reasons presented above. The use of the plural opens this dialogue out, so that Nicodemus is now seen as representative of a wider group (Israel), and Jesus voices the faith of the Johannine community. On the unity of the entire discourse see Brown, *Gospel* 1:149; on the representative nature of the plural forms see Moloney, *John*, 94. On representative characters in the Fourth Gospel see Raymond F. Collins, *These Things Have Been Written: Studies on the Fourth Gospel.* Louvain Theological and Pastoral Monographs 2 (Louvain: Peeters, 1990) 1–45, 56–67.

context of verse 7 means that *anōthen* at that point probably has the spatial sense of being born "from above." Therefore the gospel and Wisdom assert that knowledge of God (seeing the kingdom) is only possible through the Spirit sent "from above" (John 3:7), "from on high" (Wis 9:17). The Nicodemus discourse will use the verb *hypsoō* (cf. *apo hypsistō*, Wis 9:17) to speak of "lifting up" the Son of Man (3:14),[64] and will go on to speak of God giving the only Son (John 3:16) and sending the Son into the world (3:17). These verses parallel the book of Wisdom as it speaks of giving Wisdom and sending the Spirit into the world (Wis 9:17).

Most significant is Wisdom's retelling of the story of the fiery serpents from Numbers 21:6-9.

Numbers 21:6-9	Wisdom 16:5-6	John 3:14
Then the LORD sent poisonous serpents among the people, and they bit the people, so that many Israelites died. The people came to Moses and said, "We have sinned by speaking against the LORD and against you; pray to the LORD to take away the serpents from us." So Moses prayed for the people. And the LORD said to Moses, "Make a poisonous serpent, and set it on a pole (*sēmeion*, LXX); and everyone who is bitten shall look at it and live." So Moses made a serpent of bronze, and put it upon a pole (*sēmeion*, LXX); and whenever a serpent bit someone, that person would look at the serpent of bronze and live.	For when the terrible rage of wild animals came upon your people and they were being destroyed by the bites of writhing serpents, your wrath did not continue to the end; they were troubled for a little while as a warning, and received a symbol of deliverance [salvation] (*symbolon echontes sōtērias*) to remind them of your law's command. 16:7 For the one who turned toward it was saved, not by the thing that was beheld, but by you, the Savior of all.	As Moses lifted up the serpent in the wilderness, so it is that the Son of Man must be lifted up, that everyone who believes in him may have eternity life.

[64] Against Jewish notions of revealers who ascended to heaven and then returned bearing heavenly revelation, the Fourth Gospel asserts that no one has ascended to heaven. The only one who can reveal God to humanity is the one who has come from God, Jesus, the incarnate Word who was with God "in the beginning" (1:1). This revelation will be most visible when the Son of Man is elevated on the cross. For a detailed examination of these two critical verses see Moloney, *The Johannine Son of Man*, 42–67.

The bronze serpent fashioned by Moses is called a "sign" (*sēmeion*, LXX) or "symbol of salvation" (Wisdom). In the book of Wisdom salvation came not in some magical way by simply looking at the bronze serpent, but through the agency of Wisdom, called here "the Savior of all."

The Fourth Gospel draws the parallel between the lifted-up serpent and the lifted-up Son of Man as a focus of salvation or, in Johannine terms, eternity life. The serpent is the type of a savior; Jesus is the antitype.[65] The serpent narrative, told through the lens of Wisdom, provides the most likely background for the theme of salvation introduced in the Nicodemus passage and rarely used in the Fourth Gospel. As the parallelism between verses 16 and 17 indicates, salvation in the Johannine language system is expressed as eternity life.

For God so loved the world that s/he gave the only-born Son, that whoever believes in him should not perish but have *eternity life.*	For God sent the Son into the world not to judge the world But that through him the world *might be saved.*

Jesus' opening remarks spoke of birth anew as the requirement for access to the reign of God. Against the background of the book of Wisdom, Jesus speaks of a Spirit-generated birth through which a believer enters into not simply ordinary, mortal life, but a quality of heavenly or eternity life. As a Pharisee Nicodemus could have been expected to have some perception of a renewal of life, but he understood this in terms of a future resurrection. The Johannine Jesus speaks as divine Sophia, whose children (Prov

---

[65] Barrett (*Gospel*, 214), Bultmann (*Gospel*, 152 n. 1), and Schnackenburg (*Gospel* 1:395–96) explain the typology not in terms of the comparison between the serpent and Jesus but in the action of "lifting up." I believe the typology is better understood in terms of the serpent-Son of Man comparison, in light of the book of Wisdom's emphasis on Wisdom as the real savior and the Wisdom christology of the Fourth Gospel discussed above. In my opinion the parallelism in the verse, as well as the conclusion to the comparison, that salvation is to be found through belief in him, focuses attention on the figure lifted up rather than the action. Moloney (*Johannine Son of Man*, 64) writes: "the point of comparison between the raised serpent and the elevated Christ is that all who believe may have eternal life in him." While this typology of the Serpent-Jesus is strange, it is found in the *Letter of Barnabas* 12:5-7: "Finally Moses . . . made them a symbol of Jesus. So Moses made a bronze serpent and set it up conspicuously." The serpent was considered a symbol of eternal life in its ability to slough its skin and in the Hellenistic world was associated with Asclepius, the god of healing.

2:1; Sir 2:1; 4:10-11; Wis 2:13) participate in the life of God, sharing God's own eternity life.[66] This new birth, and the life it makes possible, is not a future eschatological reality, but is now present in and through the person of Jesus. In words reminiscent of the Prologue, the discourse concludes with images of light and darkness to convey that judgment is already operative in the choices people make in response to Jesus.

Conclusion

Following the Nicodemus passage, the figure of John the Baptizer returns, reminding the reader that this sequence, beginning at 1:19, has been initiated by John and has followed the normal sequence in establishing a household. The bridegroom's friend initiates the process by being the voice and witness to the bridegroom in the pre-nuptial negotiations. He is the one through whom the bride is introduced to the groom, who often leads the bride to the wedding feast, who conducts the groom into the wedding chamber in the father's house, and who bears witness to the consummation of the marriage, which it is hoped would lead to the birth of a child. In a sense John has overseen the progression of the narrative so far, from the initial gathering of disciples, their participation in a wedding, then being included with the brothers and sisters of Jesus in going with his mother to Capernaum and then entering with Jesus into his Father's house. The Nicodemus episode concludes this sequence in its teaching that these disciples, who are believing in Jesus, are experiencing a process of new birth enabling them to see the reign of God and hear the voice of the Spirit (3:8) dwelling in Jesus (1:33). New life has begun in the household. John's role is now complete, as he states: "he must increase; I must decrease" (3:30).

The sequence describing the initial coming to life of the household of disciples is set within the world of Judaism. Chapter 4 shows that this same opportunity for life is available in the world beyond Judaism, and it reveals a similar progression of ideas.[67] Jesus comes to Jacob's well in Samaria (4:6). In the encounter with the Samaritan woman, which has echoes of Jacob's meeting with Rachel (e.g., "the sixth hour," 4:6; cf. "high day," Gen 29:7; the name "Jacob's well," v. 6), Jesus offers her living water (4:10)

---

[66] The concept of eternity life will be discussed in more detail in the following chapter in the context of the raising of Lazarus.

[67] I have dealt with the two pericopes in Chapter 4 elsewhere and so provide here a very brief sketch of their content as it relates to this theme of the household. On the episode with the Samaritan woman see Coloe, *God Dwells with Us*, 85–113; on the second miracle at Cana see eadem, "Households of Faith (Jn 4:46-54–11:1-44): A Metaphor for the Johannine Community," *Pacifica* 13 (2000) 326–33.

welling up to eternity life (4:14).[68] The episode, with rich symbolism, reveals Jesus as the true bridegroom of Samaria, drawing Samaritans into the covenant community (cf. Ezek 37:21-23),[69] then dwelling (*emeinen*) with the Samaritans for two days (cf. Ezek 37:26-28); they acknowledge him as savior of the world (4:40-43), recalling the language and imagery of the Nicodemus pericope (3:17). Jesus then continues to Galilee where life is given to a household whose child lay at the point of death (4:47). The sequence concludes with a household of faith and life (4:53).

Across these opening chapters there is a marked contrast between the faith response Jesus finds within the household and the rejection he experiences within the Temple. The explicit statements of belief come at the conclusion of the Cana episode (2:11), while Jesus dwells with the Samaritans (4:39-42), and from within the household at Capernaum (4:53). By contrast, "the Jews" who confront Jesus in the Temple literally throw his own words back at him (Jesus: "I will raise it up in three days"; "the Jews": "You will raise it up in three days?" 2:19, 20). Nicodemus lies somewhere in between. He is not included within the household, as is shown by there being no reference to the disciples being present in this scene, but he has moved from Herod's Temple in his act of coming to Jesus. His final words to Jesus are not an outright rejection but a question: "How is this possible?" (3:9), which leaves open the possibility of further development, as in fact the narrative will show later (7:50-52; 19:39). In the following chapters, set within the context of a series of Jewish feasts, Jesus will again confront "the Jews" within the Temple, and their opposition will be even more pronounced: "so they sought to arrest him" (7:30); "so they took up stones to throw at him" (8:59); "the Jews took up stones again to stone him" (10:31); "again they tried to arrest him" (10:39). These narrative episodes, contrasting faith within household settings and rejection by those within Judaism aligned with the Temple, reflect the post-Easter situation of the Johannine community as it makes the transition from the Jewish institutional centers of Synagogue and Temple to the Christian household as the place of the assembly (*ekklēsia*).[70]

---

[68] See Coloe, *God Dwells with Us*, 91–92, for the Targumic allusions behind the image of the waters "welling up."

[69] On the nuptial imagery and symbolic interpretation of this scene as the "wooing of Samaria" see Schneiders, *Written That You May Believe*, 139–41.

[70] Hakola (*Identity Matters*) offers a more nuanced understanding of the narrative presentation of conflict with "the Jews." He rejects J. Louis Martyn's hypothesis of a historic conflict with the synagogue and understands the conflict theme as a narrative ploy to affirm a new identity for the Johannine community that places them outside Jewish practices. It is a narrative strategy reflecting intra-community tensions. See esp. 41–86.

Death in the Household of God

JOHN 11

The dialogue with Nicodemus raised the issues of birth and life, qualified as eternity life (*zōēn aiōnion*). John 11 is the next major episode involving a household, and this chapter raises the question of death. How is it possible for death to occur within a community promised eternity life?[1] The household of Bethany—Martha, Mary, and Lazarus—dramatically portrays this question and the Johannine response. John 11, more than John 20, provides a clear Johannine understanding of the meaning of life, eternity life, death, and resurrection. Although John 11 is usually called the "raising of Lazarus," the focus of the narrative is on the other characters, with Lazarus having a brief, though dramatic, appearance at the end. In the dialogues with and responses by the disciples, Martha, Mary, and "the Jews," the episode articulates the challenge to full Johannine faith in Jesus' promise of life in the face of death. The chapter takes us inside a household of Jesus' friends, believers and disciples who are now struggling with the ultimate test to faith—the reality of death. A recent monograph by Wendy Sproston North argues that chapters 11 and 12 in the Fourth Gospel have been deliberately created by the evangelist to teach afresh that "to believe in Jesus is to possess eternal life that death cannot vanquish."[2]

---

[1] My reading of the Lazarus account as a reflection of the post-Easter situation of the community has been greatly influenced by an article by Sandra M. Schneiders, "Death in the Community of Eternal Life: History, Theology and Spirituality in John 11," *Int* 41 (1987) 44–56.

[2] Wendy E. Sproston North, *The Lazarus Story within the Johannine Tradition.* JSNTSup 212 (Sheffield: Sheffield Academic Press, 2001) 130. For a discussion of the

Structure[3]

The chapter follows the usual structure of a miracle story, with the additional Johannine feature of an initial refusal or rebuke to the request for healing.[4]

Introduction: vv. 1-2. Now a certain man was ill, Lazarus of Bethany.

Request: v. 3. So the sisters sent to him saying, "Lord the one whom you love is ill."

Refusal: vv. 4-6. He stayed two days longer in the place where he was.

[Insert: discourse, vv. 7-16, shaped by the *inclusio* "Let us go," v. 7; "Let us also go," v. 16]

Narrative resumes, vv. 17-20

Responses: vv. 21-32, shaped by the *inclusio*, "Lord, if you had been here my brother would not have died" (vv. 21 and 32)

[Insert: Jesus' response, vv. 33-38]

---

historical issues surrounding the narrative see Brendan Byrne, *Lazarus: A Contemporary Reading of John 11:1-46* (Homebush: St. Paul, 1991) 77–83. Byrne concludes that this episode is a theological development of a healing miracle, possibly influenced by traditional material such as found in the Lukan parable of Dives and Lazarus (Luke 16:19-31). For more on the development of the tradition and the evangelist's original shaping of it see Alain Marchadour, *Lazare: Histoire d'une Récit, Récit d'une Histoire.* LD 132 (Paris: Cerf, 1988) 33–63, 185–94.

[3] For a comparison of the Lazarus miracle and the second Cana miracle in John 4 see Coloe, "Households of Faith," 326–33. Some scholars (e.g., Francis J. Moloney, "Can Everyone be Wrong? A Reading of John 11:1–12:8," *NTS* 49 [2003] 509) continue the Lazarus episode to 12:8 because the anointing scene (12:1-8) continues the story of the Bethany characters and provides a closure to the narrative "gap" in John 11:2, which mentions the anointing. I am guided in my structure by the pattern in the gospel of naming a Jewish feast: "Now the Passover of the Jews was at hand" (11:55; cf. 6:4; 7:2). These comments consistently mark a new pericope, indicating that 11:55 is the start of a new section. The form of a miracle story and the verbal repetitions (vv. 7, 16, 21, 32) also guide my shaping of the narrative.

[4] Miracle stories have the following typical structure: (a) problem described; (b) request made; (c) the miracle performed, accompanied by a gesture, touch, word, or name; (d) the successful accomplishment is described; (e) the response by the onlookers of wonder. The recognition and naming of this fivefold pattern is based on the work of Bultmann and the description here follows the wording of Moloney; see Francis J. Moloney, *Belief in the Word: Reading John 1–4* (Minneapolis: Fortress Press, 1993) 90.

Life given: vv. 39-44. "Take away the stone" (v. 39).
"Lazarus, come out" (v. 42).

Reaction: v. 39. "Lord, by this time he smells."

Confirmation: v. 44. The dead man came out.

Responses: vv. 45-53   Many believed in him (v. 45).
Some went to Pharisees (v. 46).
Caiaphas' decision (v. 50).

Conclusion: v. 54. Jesus has to retire to the wilderness.

The Miracle

In accordance with the pattern of a miracle story, there is a request that
Jesus come so that healing can happen. The long introduction to the miracle
establishes that Jesus has deliberately delayed going to Bethany, since he
waits two days before making the journey into Judea (v. 6).[5] When Jesus
makes this decision he speaks of Lazarus as one who "has fallen asleep"
(v. 11). The association of death and sleep emerges late in Israel's Scriptures
and is more common within the post-exilic and Wisdom writings, possibly
reflecting the developing notion that death is not an end, but that there will
be a time when the "sleeper" will awaken (Deut 31:16; Ps 13:3; Jer 51:39,
57; Dan 12:2; 4 Ezra 2:31; 7:32, 35; Sir 46:19, 20; 2 Macc 12:45; Wis
17:14).[6] Jesus explains the purpose of the delay to his disciples: "This illness is not toward death but for the glory of God, so that through it the Son
of God may be glorified" (11:4).[7] Jesus' words introduce the faith perspective of God's glory in contrast to death. As the narrative develops, the
characters will be dominated by death, but the reader, even in the face of
anguish and grief, must not lose sight of this faith perspective. Jesus' delay
results in his absence from the household during Lazarus' illness, eventual
death, and burial, establishing the conflict between God's glory and death.

[5] See Sproston North (*The Lazarus Story*, 132) on the evangelist's motive for this
delay.

[6] For a discussion of the historical development of this idiom see Wright, *The Resurrection of the Son of God*, 108–15.

[7] Jesus' words of explanation reiterate that his movements are directed by the divine
purpose (see John 4:4; 7:6-9). Similarly Byrne, *Lazarus*, 43. Schneiders ("Death in the
Community," 47) interprets the delay as an expression of Jesus' sovereign independence
in relation to human initiative. Moloney (*Gospel*, 322) identifies v. 4 as "the rubric" that
determines the unfolding of the narrative, shifting the focus from death to God's glory.

When Jesus and the disciples arrive in Bethany, Martha professes faith in Jesus' ability to heal when she says, "Lord, if you had been here, my brother would not have died" (v. 21). Jesus replies simply, "your brother will rise again." Martha understands this as a reference to the end-time resurrection, following the understanding of resurrection references in Daniel and Maccabees as discussed in the previous chapter.[8] "I know that he will rise again in the resurrection on the last day" (v. 24). However, Jesus' reply directs her away from this model of "end-time" resurrection, as he makes the resurrection a present reality in his own person:[9] "I am the resurrection and the life" (v. 25). Jesus then elaborates on this realized eschatological claim when he speaks about believers who have died (Lazarus) and current believers (readers).

- "Whoever believes in me, even if they should die, will live" (v. 25). Jesus is here refuting the Jewish notion of death as going into some type of non-life in the underworld while awaiting the end-time resurrection back to life. Lazarus, even though dead, lives on, as the miracle will soon demonstrate. Lazarus can be called back into this earthly life prior to a final resurrection. He has not passed through death to nonexistence.

- "Everyone who lives and believes in me shall never die" (v. 26). The gospel has consistently linked belief in Jesus to eternity life, most recently in the parable of the Good Shepherd (10:28), so that for the believer "life" is not simply existence, it is a quality of life given by Jesus that will not perish.[10] This quality of life is a present reality made possible by faith in Jesus who is, in his own person, the creative power

---

[8] Martin Scott (*Sophia and the Johannine Jesus*, 201) comments that "she appears to be presenting a form of one particular Jewish theology of the resurrection, possibly that of Pharisaic origins." See also the comment by Moloney ("Can Everyone be Wrong?" 513) that Martha seems to accept the relatively new idea in Jewish thought about life after death. See also Moloney's judgment on Martha's faith confession (v. 27), where he argues, rightly in my opinion, that for all its lofty titles it is not correct Johannine faith; ibid. 513–14.

[9] This approach is also taken by Dodd, *Interpretation*, 147, and most recently by Jörg Frey, *Die johanneische Eschatologie*. Vol. 3: *Die eschatologische Verkündigung in den johanneischen Texten*. WUNT 96 (Tübingen: J.C.B. Mohr, 2000) 455.

[10] Jean Zumstein makes this same point that "eternal life" is not life without temporal limits, but it is a qualitatively different life, which is a gift of God. See Jean Zumstein, "Foi et vie éternelle selon Jean," in Odette Mainville and Daniel Marguerat, eds., *Résurrection: L'après-mort dans le monde ancien et le Nouveau Testament* (Geneva: Labor et Fides, 2001) 226 n. 24; 228.

of God. This is the understanding of life for the righteous that is found in the book of Wisdom. For the righteous, death has no final reality: "they only appear to die" (Wis 3:2).[11] "Because of her I shall have immortality" (Wis 8:13). The physical body undergoes normal corruption, but the spirit/soul lives on in the "hand of God" (Wis 3:1).

Mary then repeats Martha's words, the exact repetition indicating that she shares the faith perception of Martha in Jesus' ability to heal: "Lord, if you had been here my brother would not have died" (vv. 21, 32).[12] Commentators vary in their interpretations of the faith implied by the statements of Martha and Mary. Schneiders sees in Martha's words, "I have believed that you are the Christ, the Son of God," the highest expression of Johannine faith and the equivalent to the Petrine confession in Matt 16:15-19.[13] However, as Francis Moloney points out, these titles have all been applied to Jesus before (1:41, 49), Martha's words do not directly reply to Jesus' question about belief in him as "the resurrection and the life" (11:25), and they are also stated in the perfect tense (have believed), which therefore expresses a previously held belief, not a newfound faith in response to Jesus' immediate revelation.[14] For Moloney it is Mary, not Martha, who portrays full Johannine faith in her act of falling at Jesus' feet, which Moloney interprets as an act of worship similar to that of the blind man (9:38).[15] Here also I must disagree. The exact repetition of the words of Martha indicates no significant development or change in the faith of the two women. Mary's

---

[11] Wisdom is said to have power over life and death, "For you have power over life and death; you lead men down to the gates of Hades and back again" (Wis 16:13).

[12] In describing the repetition of Martha's words by Mary, Byrne (*Lazarus*, 69–70) writes, "Mary echoes her sister's word of remonstration. . . . The repetition, with its implication that the two sisters had extensively shared their disappointment, powerfully draws attention once more to the (as we know, deliberate) absence of Jesus."

[13] Schneiders, *Written That You May Believe*, 106. Similarly Turid Karlsen Seim, "Roles of Women in the Gospel of John," in Lars Hartman and Birger Olsson, eds., *Aspects on the Johannine Literature.* ConBNT 18 (Stockholm: Almqvist & Wiksell, 1987) 71, and Raymond E. Brown, "Roles of Women in the Fourth Gospel," *TS* 36 (1975) 693.

[14] Francis J. Moloney, *Signs and Shadows: Reading John 5–12* (Minneapolis: Fortress Press, 1996) 162. Dorothy Lee also reads Martha's confession as lacking full faith and sees the titles as ambiguous at this stage. See Lee, *The Symbolic Narratives of the Fourth Gospel: The Interplay of Form and Meaning.* JSNTSup 95 (Sheffield: JSOT Press, 1994) 206.

[15] Moloney, *Signs and Shadows*, 166. Moloney moves slightly from this positive appraisal in a later study ("Can Everyone be Wrong?" 516–19), but continues to interpret Mary's act of prostration as an act of "trust and worship" (p. 516).

act of falling at the feet of Jesus is not called an act of worship, as was the blind man's similar act (9:38 *prosekunēsen*; 11:32 *epesen autou pros tous podas*).[16] This action, accompanied by her weeping, suggests grief rather than worship.[17] Mary's act of faith at the feet of Jesus must wait until the anointing scene in chapter 12.

Even when Jesus gives his word, "I am the resurrection and the life" (11:25), and orders, "take away the stone" (11:39), the sisters remain within their previous conceptions of life after death and hesitate: "Lord, by now he smells, for it is the fourth day" (v. 39). The fact that Lazarus has been in the tomb for four days is significant, as this would be the time when the processes of physical decay become obvious. In Jewish tradition this process identifies when the soul has definitely left the body.[18] "Lazarus is dead" (11:14), but as a friend of Jesus and a believer, "even if he should die he will live." Jesus calls Lazarus by name and commands him to come forth. The individual person Lazarus, in the full Semitic sense of a whole body-self, must still be alive, able to hear the voice of Jesus and to respond as Jesus leads him out of apparent death to life.[19] The tomb of Lazarus, his "death," has not meant nonexistence as an impersonal "shade" in Sheol. The raising of Lazarus thus demonstrates immortality or the Wisdom perception of life after death.

Jesus' words challenge Martha and Mary to leave their limited understanding of life restored at the end of time with the resurrection from the dead, to believe in his promise of life beyond the grave even prior to the

---

[16] The Louw-Nida dictionary gives a number of meanings for the verb *piptō*, including "to prostrate oneself before someone, implying supplication." The word by itself does not suggest worship. Johannes P. Louw and Eugene A. Nida, eds., *Greek-English Lexicon of the New Testament based on Semantic Domains*. 2 vols. (New York: United Bible Societies, 1988) 17.22.

[17] So Byrne, *Lazarus*, 59.

[18] Lightfoot quotes *Genesis Rabba* 100 [64a]), "The very height of mourning is not till the third day. For three days the spirit wanders about the sepulchre, expecting if it may return into the body. But when it sees that the form or aspect of the face is changed, then it hovers no more, but leaves the body to itself." See John Lightfoot, *A Commentary on the New Testament from the Talmud and Hebraica*. 4 vols. (Peabody, MA: Hendrickson, 1979) 3:367. See also Hermann Strack and Paul Billerbeck, *Kommentar zum Neuen Testament aus Talmud und Midrasch*. 6 vols. (Munich: C. H. Beck, 1922–61) 2:544–45.

[19] Most commentators note that the raising of Lazarus dramatizes what was stated earlier in 5:28: "Those who are in the tombs will hear his voice and come out." Sproston North (*The Lazarus Story*, 91) argues even further that "the Lazarus story was produced as a second exposition of the tradition in 5:24, picking up on the positive elements in the first, and expressing the whole through the medium of narrative."

"end time" resurrection.[20] With Jesus' presence, the *eschaton* has entered history, with implications for those who have died and those still alive.

Those who have died.	Those still alive.
whoever believes in me,	and everyone who lives and believes
even if they should die will live. (v. 25)	in me shall never die. (v. 26)

In these statements Jesus brings traditional end-time expectations into the present. The dead will not remain in death until some future time; they are promised life beyond death. For those who are alive and will experience physical death, this death too will not be death forever. Time distinctions blur, as the narrative has already indicated in verse 2 with the proleptic description of Mary as one "who anointed the Lord with ointment and wiped his feet with her hair" (11:2)—an action that will happen in the following chapter (12:1-3). Future events impinge upon the present, even in the narrative art.

In response to Jesus' command, Lazarus emerges from the tomb wearing the trappings of death, which has no power to bind him. But this miracle leads to schism, with some of "the Jews" believing while others go to plot with the Pharisees (v. 45).

A Household of Life

The Bethany miracle and the earlier miracle at Cana (4:46-54), provide a household context for exploring the desire for Jesus' presence, the problematic issue of his absence, and the reliability of Jesus' word as a word of life. Cana was the first time Jesus revealed his power to heal. By the time the reader arrives at Bethany, Jesus has given further demonstrations of his lifegiving authority. He was able to cure a crippled man (5:1-9) and then to give sight to one who was born blind (9:1-7). The three healings escalate in their intensity: a boy who was ill, a man crippled for thirty-eight years, a man blind from birth. The miracle at Bethany continues this escalation, since the household of Bethany is plunged into the liminal situation of death. This situation presents, therefore, the supreme test of who Jesus is, and of the disciples' faith in him.

The extreme nature of the miracle and the obvious friendship between Jesus and the members of the Bethany household, who, however, lack full

---

[20] Jean Zumstein makes the point that faith is not simply belief in Jesus as a miracle worker or belief in the resurrection. What is critical for Johannine faith is belief in the person of Jesus as the bringer of eschatological life. There is ambiguity about the faith of both Martha and Mary. See Zumstein, "Foi et vie éternelle selon Jean," 222–24.

faith in him, may explain why the Bethany miracle is elaborated on with longer dialogues and greater insights into Jesus' motives and reactions. In response to the weeping of Mary and "the Jews" with her, Jesus "groaned in his spirit and was troubled (*enebrimēsato tō pneuma kai heauton*)" (v. 33). This same expression, "groaning in his spirit," is used to describe Jesus' response to "the Jews" in verse 38. Mary's words and the words of "the Jews" are accusatory. "Lord, if you had been here my brother would not have died" (v. 32); "Could not he who opened the eyes of the blind man have kept this man from dying?" (v. 37). Jesus' emotions at this point in the episode could hardly be described as grief. He knows that Lazarus is dead (11:14); in fact he had earlier said that he was "glad" not to have been there so that his disciples might believe (v. 15). Mary, as friend and believer, knows that Jesus is a source of life, and "the Jews," who know about the blind man (9:1–10:21), should also know that he has come to give abundant life (10:10), but no one has yet really understood what Jesus means by "life." Martha, Mary, and "the Jews" think only in terms of this life and have an expectation that Jesus' presence will prevent this life from ending. This is obviously not what Jesus means. Believers will die. They will experience death as surely as Jesus will, but physical death does not put an end to the life Jesus offers. There is a second-level meaning to his offer of "life," just as there have been deeper levels of meaning in other gifts such as "rebirth" (3:3), "living water" (4:10), "bread from heaven" (6:50). Jesus' groans and his troubled spirit indicate his immense distress and frustration that even now, as his ministry draws to a close, his friends still fail to understand him.[21] "Jesus is angered and deeply disturbed emotionally—even to the point of tears—by the universal lack of faith."[22]

When Jesus is invited to see the tomb of Lazarus, further emotions are described. "Jesus wept (*edakrusen*)" (v. 35), and this emotion is interpreted as grief in the face of his love for Lazarus: "See how he loved him" (v. 36). This is a different emotional response than his earlier reaction to Mary (v. 33)

---

[21] This approach is similar to Moloney, *Signs and Shadows*, 167–68. Byrne (*Lazarus*, 72–73) and Lee (*Symbolic Narratives*, 211) offer an alternative interpretation of Jesus' distress and suggest it arises from Jesus' own inner conflict between his love for Lazarus and his awareness that this miracle will lead to his own death. The immediate context favors Moloney on this point. Jesus' distress at this point is not grief. According to the Louw-Nida dictionary (*Greek-English Lexicon*, 25.56) the verb *embrimaomai* means "to have an intense, strong feeling of concern, often with the implication of indignation." For a detailed discussion of the term *embrimaomai* see Stephen Voorwinde, *Jesus' Emotions in the Fourth Gospel*. Library of New Testament Studies 284 (London: T&T Clark, 2005) 169–77.

[22] Moloney, "Can Everyone be Wrong?" 518.

and his later reaction to "the Jews" (v. 38).[23] Jesus' tears now express the appropriate response to the loss of one who is loved. When facing the starkness of the tomb of his friend, and surrounded by the grief of others, Jesus experiences the normal human response to such loss. The reality of Christian resurrection does not take away the pain of death and loss for those still in life.

> Jesus' tears are an honest sharing in Mary's grief and perhaps in her anger at death, the enemy of all life. . . . This episode roots the spirituality of the community in the realism of human experience. Christian faith is neither Gnosticism nor Stoicism. Death is real and so is the suffering it causes. Faith is not compatible with despair, but it is no stranger to tears.[24]

The Household as an Image of the Johannine Community

As I articulated in the opening chapter, my understanding of the gospel is that it reflects not only the traditions originating with the life of Jesus, but also the ongoing experience of a Christian community living now with the indwelling of the Father, Jesus, and the Spirit. Guided by the Spirit/Paraclete, the remembrance of the community impacts on their continued living in a creative dialectic. This dialectic has given rise to the community's faith articulation in the gospel, written in a new hermeneutical situation at the end of the first century. The lapse of time between the historical event of Jesus of Nazareth and the gospel provided a positive and creative possibility to write from, within the developing interpretive tradition where "the encounter with the past and with tradition is prompted by the questions of the present."[25] Influenced by the writings of Hans Gadamer, Franz Mussner states that the new hermeneutical situation "is characterized by a peculiar merging of the two horizons of present and past."[26] The unique Johannine vision draws together the life of Jesus and the life of the community in what J. Louis Martyn termed a "two level drama."[27] Again in Mussner's words,

---

[23] On Jesus' grief at this point see Voorwinde, *Jesus' Emotions in the Fourth Gospel*, 182–84.

[24] Schneiders, *Written That You May Believe*, 159.

[25] Franz Mussner, *The Historical Jesus in the Gospel of John* (New York: Herder, 1967) 15.

[26] Ibid.

[27] The expression "two level drama" was first coined by Martyn in his *History and Theology in the Fourth Gospel*. New Testament Library (3rd ed. Louisville: Westminster John Knox, 2003) 89. For a helpful review of Martyn's thesis and its impact on Johannine

"Jesus of Nazareth is so expressed by John in his act of vision that the history of Christ projected and presented by him simultaneously gives an answer to the Christological questions of the time of its composition."[28] One way this "merging of horizons" is expressed in the gospel is through its presentation of Jesus from the perspective of post-Easter faith. Jesus, in this gospel, is the incarnation of the pre-existent divine *logos*. The narrative never loses sight of his true identity and origin. There is continuity between the pre-existent *logos*, the incarnation, and the death and glorification of Jesus the Christ. "This is the ontological ground which ultimately permits the evangelist to cause the glorified Christ to speak in the pre-paschal Jesus. . . . Jesus' earthly life is represented as the epiphany of the *doxa* of the divine Logos."[29]

In John 11 this post-Easter hermeneutical perspective begins to operate more explicitly within the narrative. This is evident not only in the subject matter, a resurrection, but in the title "Lord" that is used across this chapter and becomes the preferred title throughout the rest of the gospel.

Theological sense of *Kyrios/Kyrie*

	Chapters 1–10	Chapters 11–19	Chapters 20 [21]
Lord = YHWH (OT citations)	1:23 (Isa 40:3)	12:13 (Ps 118:26) 12:38 (Isa 53:1)	
The Lord[30] *Ho Kyrios*	6:23	11:2	20:2, 13, 18, 20, 25, 28 21:7(2x), 12
Lord (vocative) *Kyrie*	6:68 9:38	11:3, 12, 21, 27, 32, 34, 39 13:6, 9, 25, 36, 37 14:5, 8, 22	21:15, 16, 17, 20, 21

In the earlier chapters Jesus was usually called Rabbi or teacher by his disciples and by some other characters (Nicodemus [3:2], "the Jews" [6:25]). When he is addressed as *Kyrie* in chapters 1–10, this should be seen as a polite form of address (i.e., "Sir"), rather than given any theological weight,

---

studies see Francis J. Moloney's comments in Brown, *Introduction to the Gospel of John*, 70–78. For a detailed critique of Martyn's hypothesis see Hakola, *Identity Matters*, 41–86.

[28] Mussner, *The Historical Jesus*, 46.

[29] Ibid. 87.

[30] Some manuscripts have "the Lord" in 4:1, but the strongest witnesses ℵ, D, omit this title. For a discussion of this variant see Metzger, *Textual Commentary*, 205–206, and Barrett, *Gospel According to St. John*, 230.

unless the context indicates its theological meaning as in 6:68 and 9:38, when Peter and the formerly blind man profess their belief in Jesus. Within the final discourse Jesus refers to himself as *Kyrios* in 13:13, 14, 16, and the servant/master context suggests that the term is best translated "master" rather than "Lord."

Mundane Titles of Jesus

	Chapters 1–10	Chapters 11–19	Chapters 20 [21]
Rabbi/teacher The disciples Nicodemus "The Jews"	1:38, 49; 4:31; 9:2 3:2 6:25	11:8, 28 (13:13, 14 Jesus speaks of himself)	20:16
Kyrie/Sir	4:11, 15, 19, 49 5:7 6:34 [8:11] 9:36		20:15 (Mary Magda- lene, thinking Jesus is a gardener)
Kyrios/master	Jesus speaks of him- self in these cases.	13:13, 14, 16[31] 15:15, 20	

As a title, "the Lord" is the Easter designation of Jesus and here it needs to be given its full theological sense, which Thomas makes explicit in 20:28, "my Lord and my God."[32] When this title is used in the pre-Easter narrative it is usually in a citation of Scripture referring to Israel's God Yhwh (1:23; 12:13, 38). On only two possible occasions is Jesus directly called "the Lord" prior to Easter, in 6:23 and 11:2.[33] In 6:23 the association with Eucharist and early Christian liturgical traditions may explain this proleptic

---

[31] George D. Kilpatrick only gives v. 16 the meaning of Master; see his "'*Kurios*' in the Gospels," in Faculté autonome de théologie de Genève, *L'Évangile Hier et Aujourd'hui: Mélanges Offerts au Professeur Frans-J. Leenhardt* (Geneva: Labor et Fides, 1968) 69.

[32] On the development of the title "Lord" in early Christianity see F. F. Bruce, "'Jesus is Lord,'" in J. McDowell Richards, ed., *Soli Deo Gloria: New Testament Studies in Honor of William Childs Robinson* (Richmond: John Knox, 1968) 27–36; Timothy Radcliffe, "'My Lord and my God': The locus of confession," *New Blackfriars* 65 (1984) 52–62. The title "Lord" will be discussed further when examining Thomas' faith confession in John 20.

[33] In his evaluation of the use of *Kyrios*, Kilpatrick dismisses John 4:1 and 6:23 as textually uncertain and writes: "In John there are only twelve certain examples, all connected with Holy Week." See Kilpatrick, "'*Kurios*' in the Gospels," 69. He includes 13:13 and 13:14, which I consider may be "Master" rather than "Lord" in the light of 13:16, where it is clearly "Master."

use of the post-Easter title, if it is original to the gospel text: "Boats from Tiberias came near the place where they ate the bread of the Lord's thanksgiving (*eucharistēsantos*)."[34] John 11:2 may also be explained as a prolepsis, as the event referred to has not yet occurred, and even this event, the anointing, anticipates the hour of Jesus' glorification.[35]

When Jesus is addressed as "Lord" in John 11 by the disciples, Martha, and Mary, they speak as friends and believers. Their faith may still need strengthening, but they have already made a commitment to Jesus. In John 6, Peter spoke on behalf of the disciples to affirm their following of him: "Lord, to whom shall we go? You have the words of eternal life; and we have believed, and have come to know, that you are the Holy One of God" (6:68-69). Similarly, Martha's words in 11:27 express a past belief in Jesus. Therefore, in John 11, the title *Kyrie* means more than "Sir," but is already influenced by faith. The use of this title is one indicator that the narrative of John 11 brings about the "fusion of horizons" referred to by Mussner.[36]

In the households at Bethany there is a concern that Jesus come to the household, for only his presence can guarantee life. The miracle speaks to the experience of the post-Easter Christian community that no longer has the physical presence of Jesus, and his absence poses a threat to faith. The heart-rending cry of the sisters of Bethany echoes the cry of many disciples across the centuries: "Lord, if you had been here." In the face of this anguish the miracle affirms the central message of the early chapters: that the word of Jesus is trustworthy. The believer can rely on Jesus' word, and there is no need to see signs and wonders, no need even to have his physical presence; the word given by Jesus is sufficient.

The efficacy of Jesus' word as experienced at Cana (chapter 4), was affirmed at the Sheep Pool (chapter 5) and then again in the Temple precincts (chapter 9), but in all these cases the person, however ill or handicapped, was alive. The situation in chapter 11 presents the community's concern when faced with actual death. Is death incompatible with Jesus' presence? Lazarus' sisters have faith that if Jesus were present there would be life, but can they, and the later community, believe that Jesus is present even

---

[34] The phrase I have translated "of the Lord's thanksgiving" may be a late variant, as the phrase is not found in Bezae OL and OS.

[35] Brown (*Gospel* 1:423) considers this verse to be an editorial addition: "John does not usually use [the term 'Lord'] of Jesus during the ministry."

[36] Jean Zumstein also notes the use of the title *kyrios* as an indicator of a post-Easter "*relecture*" in John 13; see Zumstein, *Kreative Erinnerung: Relecture und Auslegung im Johannesevangelium.* ATANT (2nd rev. and expanded ed. Zürich: Theologischer Verlag Zürich, 2004) 170. I argue that this same post-Easter perspective is also present in John 11.

where there is death, or does death create the impossible boundary for Jesus' presence? Is death equivalent to absence?

Martha expresses traditional Jewish faith that the dead will rise on the last day. In this perspective resurrection is an "end-time" event, something that will happen in the future. A consistent theology of this gospel has been the affirmation that in the presence of Jesus the "end-time" has dawned, "the hour is coming and now is" (4:23; 5:25). The believers who die do not go down into the shadowy non-life experience of Sheol.[37] In Jesus, life continues beyond the boundary of death, even while those who have died await the fullness of the "end-time" event and its promise of future bodily resurrection.[38] The all-too-human experience of death is not incompatible with one who has life in himself (1:4; 5:27).

While there is no final expression of faith on the part of Martha and Mary in chapter 11, there are some characters whose faith undergoes change through this event. Among "the Jews" there is a division, with many believing in Jesus but some going to the Pharisees (11:45-46). "The Jews" were earlier described as being with Mary "in the house" (*en tē oikia*, 11:31), and many of these believed in Jesus (v. 45). Like those in the household of the royal official at Capernaum (4:53), some of "the Jews" associated with the household of Bethany come to faith in response to Jesus' miraculous deed. The story of the household of faith at Bethany will continue in the next chapter (12:1-8). There is a caution here that will continue in the anointing scene. Being associated with the household, and even being a disciple, such as Judas, does not guarantee faith. Not all in the Bethany household came to faith; some went away to the Pharisees (v. 46). Believing in Jesus is an ongoing commitment to him, with the possibility that even friends and disciples can fail.

The miracle, which shows that death is not a "dead end," leads into the ironic statement of Caiaphas that one man should die for the people in order to preserve the Temple (the holy place) from destruction (11:48). In these stark words the contrast established by the narrative between the Temple and the household comes to its ultimate and tragic conclusion. The Temple has been the place of Jesus' conflicts, and Caiaphas' words posit concern for the Temple as the immediate cause of Jesus' death. Whereas in the

---

[37] For a description of the Hebrew notion of Sheol and the realm of the dead see Theodor H. Gaster, "Dead, Abode of the," *IDB* 1 (1962) 787–88.

[38] Schnackenburg expresses this idea as "The life given to men [sic] in faith reaches beyond earthly death"; see Schnackenburg, *Gospel* 2:361. Schnackenburg has two important excurses relevant to this issue, "The Idea of Life in the Fourth Gospel," ibid. 352–61, and "Eschatology in the Fourth Gospel," ibid. 426–37.

household of faith there is a journey from death to life, in the Temple and through its priesthood there is a journey toward death. The narrator's comment transforms Caiaphas' words from a death warrant to a prophecy of life, for although Jesus is about to die, the Lazarus story witnesses that life continues beyond death, and through his death Jesus passes into that time beyond death when he can gather into one "the scattered children of God" (11:52). This is the first time in the actual narrative that the expression "children of God" appears. The Prologue promised that those who believed in Jesus would be given the power to become children of God (1:12), while "the Jews" have claimed to be "children of Abraham" (8:39).[39] The filiation that Jesus will offer through his death far surpasses the claims of "the Jews"; believers will be gathered as children of God's household. Jesus' death will be procreative, bearing children in a post-resurrection household of faith.

Lazarus' death thrusts the household of Bethany into a struggle toward full faith in Jesus. This household and "the Jews" who join with Mary need to experience the resurrection before they can truly believe. So it is with the household of disciples. They, like Martha, Mary, and "the Jews" who share the household's grief must experience the resurrection before faith is possible (see 20:8). In the post-Easter time of the Johannine community, although Jesus is absent from sight, he lives on and his work of gathering the scattered children into one continues in the missionary work of the disciples. Trusting in the efficacious word of Jesus, the household of faith can believe that death, both the death of community members and the death of Jesus, does not annul life.

"Resurrection of the Body" Within Johannine Realized Eschatology[40]

Finally, what can we make of the times when Jesus and the gospel use resurrection language? Is this an inconsistency in the text, or is it evidence of "another hand" adding to the text?[41]

---

[39] For further treatment of the claim to be children of Abraham see Mary L. Coloe, "Like Father, Like Son: The Role of Abraham in Tabernacles—John 8:31-59," *Pacifica* 12 (1999) 5–7, 10.

[40] Rather surprisingly, a recent book on the resurrection of the body (Claudia Setzer, *Resurrection of the Body in Early Judaism and Early Christianity: Doctrine, Community and Self-Definition* [Boston and Leiden: Brill, 2004]) does not discuss passages in the Fourth Gospel.

[41] This is the position taken by Boismard, *Our Victory over Death*, 119; Bultmann, *Gospel of John*, 238; Schnackenburg, *Gospel* 2:116; and Brown, *Gospel* 1:221. Against this notion Barrett comments, "There is no reason whatever for regarding vv. 28f. as a

There are four main clusters of passages in the gospel where resurrection type language is employed: John 2:19, 20, 22, in association with the Temple; John 5:21, 25-29, linked to the Sabbath healing; John 6:39, 40, 44, 54, in the Bread of Life discourse; and Lazarus, 11:24, 25; 12:1, 9, 17. The rest of this chapter will examine John 5 and 6 to determine if bodily resurrection has any place in Johannine theology.

Jesus' discussion with "the Jews" following the healing of the crippled man on the Sabbath rests on the principle stated in 5:17, "My Father is still working, and I am working," followed by the short parable: "the son can do nothing of his own accord, but only what he sees the father doing; for whatever he does, that the son does likewise. For the father loves the son, and shows him all that he himself is doing" (vv. 19-20). C. H. Dodd drew attention to these verses as a parable reflecting the learning of a trade by a son in a Middle Eastern family.[42] A second theological principle operating in this chapter is that on the Sabbath day God is permitted two works: that of creating life (v. 21) and that of judgment (v. 22), since birth and death still occur on the Sabbath.[43] As the son authorized by the Father, Jesus claims that he also can do these two works on the Sabbath (vv. 26-27).

The two issues here, of giving life and of judgment, must not be subsumed into one "end-time" event. The giving of life is a present reality, not something still to come, as evidenced by the use of the present tense:[44] "For as the Father raises the dead and gives them life, so also the Son gives life to whom he will" (v. 21). In this expression "raises the dead" does not refer to physical death and end-time resurrection, but to those who are spiritually dead in the present because they have not heard or have rejected the word of Jesus. This verse and verse 24 must be read in concert. "Whoever hears

---

supplement to the original Johannine discourse." See Barrett, *Gospel According to St. John*, 263.

[42] Dodd, "A Hidden Parable in the Fourth Gospel," 30–40.

[43] Dodd (*Interpretation*, 320–21) lists a number of rabbinic authorities on God's Sabbath activity.

[44] Martin Asiedu-Peprah notes the use of present tense verbs and adds: "the implication is that these actions are continually carried out and can therefore not be seen as actions to be accomplished at the end-time." See Asiedu-Peprah, *Johannine Sabbath Conflicts as Juridical Controversy*, 85 n. 136; similarly when commenting on v. 24, "the term *thanatos* should not be understood in the sense of physical death," ibid. 89. This is also the position taken by Jörg Frey in his magisterial work on Johannine eschatology. He notes that when the evangelist refers to ordinary physical life he uses the term *psychē* (12:25); *zōē* is reserved for the life of God given through Jesus. See Frey, *Die johanneische Eschatologie* 3:375. For further clarifying comments on Johannine anthropology see Schneiders, "The Resurrection (of the Body)," 170–73.

my word and believes him who sent me has eternal life." The son's purpose in coming into the world was to give life, not physical life, but eternity life (3:16), life in abundance (10:10). "His [Jesus'] coming to reveal God in history has made it possible for man to move from the sphere of death into that of life and to achieve his true existence, the life that he was intended to lead."[45] Those who do not have this quality of life are said to be "dead" even though they exist. The Father's action of "raising the dead" metaphorically expresses accepting the word of Jesus.[46] This same sense of "the dead" as those spiritually dead recurs in verse 25: "The hour is coming and now is, when the dead will hear the voice of the Son of God and those who hear will live."[47] The present reality is emphasized by the phrase "and now is."[48] The Father, who has life in himself, has granted the Son life in himself,[49] and so the Son of God, now present in history, is able to give life to those previously "spiritually dead" (v. 26).[50] The expression "and now is" has a twofold temporal sense. It refers to the narrative time of Jesus and the possibility that those who hear his voice and believe will receive his gift of life. But the expression is also the proleptic experience of the post-Easter community who now, as they hear the gospel narrative, have the same opportunity to believe and come to life.[51]

Just as "raising the dead" and giving them life is a present reality, so too is judgment. Judgment is being made here and now by the stance one

---

[45] Schnackenburg, *Gospel* 2:99.

[46] For a discussion of "raising the dead" as a metaphor for belief see Xavier Léon-Dufour, *Lecture de l'Évangile selon Jean*. 4 vols. Parole de Dieu (Paris: Editions du Seuil, 1988, 1990, 1993, 1996) 2:48.

[47] Strangely, Barrett interprets "the dead" in v. 21 as physically dead and those in v. 25 as spiritually dead; see Barrett, *Gospel According to St. John*, 260–62; similarly Brown, *Gospel* 1:215. I see no need for this change and interpret "the dead" in both verses in the sense of spiritually dead.

[48] "The present tense of the verbs used in verse 21 ff. [is] very striking and point[s] clearly to the fact that Jesus' giving life and judgment take place here and now in the present . . . in our acceptance or rejection of the word spoken by the Son." See Schnackenburg, *Gospel* 2:106. For a similar interpretation of v. 25 as a present experience see ibid. 111.

[49] Urban C. von Wahlde discusses the background to the phrase "life in himself" and shows its association with Wis 15:16-17. His article adds further evidence of the influence of the book of Wisdom on the anthropology and eschatology of the Fourth Gospel. See von Wahlde, "He Has Given to the Son To Have Life in Himself (John 5, 26)," *Bib* 85 (2004) 409–12.

[50] On the use of the title "Son of God" within a Father-Son relationship see Francis J. Moloney, "The Johannine Son of God," *Salesianum* 38 (1976) 73–77.

[51] Frey, *Die johanneische Eschatologie* 3:378.

takes toward Jesus.[52] The word Jesus speaks is already judging each person or, in a sense, each person brings judgment on himself or herself by his or her choice of belief or unbelief in Jesus. "He who rejects me and does not receive my words has a judge; the word that I have spoken will be his judge on the last day" (12:48). As this verse makes explicit, there is a close relationship in the Fourth Gospel between revelation and judgment.

> Judgment in the Fourth Gospel is intimately linked with revelation (see 3:19; 8:16; 12:31; 16:8, 11), and the judgment spoken of in vv. 24-25 refers to this self-judgment of men [sic] in their reaction to the revelation of Jesus Christ. This is continued in v. 27: judgment *takes place* in the Son of Man. . . . "The Son of Man," then, appears to be a title used almost in a passive sense of a *"locus revelationis."*[53]

While judgment is already being made, the Fourth Gospel, in keeping with Christian tradition,[54] does not reject an end-time manifestation of that judgment. Here again we see evidence of the influence of the book of Wisdom, which combined immortality with a final cosmic revealing of the destinies of the just and the wicked. Where traditional eschatology required the end-time judgment as a way to reverse the fate of the just and grant them the reward of life with God, this is not the eschatology of John. There is no need for a final judgment or reversal of fate, since those who believe in Jesus already come into eternal life in the present and this will not be destroyed by physical death. Similarly, those who do not accept Jesus bring judgment on themselves and remain in a state of spiritual death.

> For an hour is coming in which all who are in the tombs will hear his voice and come forth, those having done good deeds unto a resurrection of life, those having done evil unto a resurrection of judgment (vv. 28-29).

This verse has clear echoes of Isa 26:19 (LXX), which reads, "The dead shall rise, and they that are in the tombs shall be raised." At this point the gospel addresses the future of those who have died physically.[55] On the last day all those "in the tombs," those who have passed from this earthly existence and continue to exist in eternity life or deadliness, will come forth, i.e., their state of life or death will be made manifest. The evangelist does not speak of "those in the tombs" being raised, as the language of *being*

---

[52] See Schnackenburg, *Gospel* 2:106.

[53] Moloney, *The Johannine Son of Man*, 84–85.

[54] See Rom 2:6-10; 2 Cor 5:10; Acts 17:31; 1 Pet 4:5; 2 Tim 4:1 for evidence of a Christian tradition of eschatological judgment.

[55] Frey, *Die johanneische Eschatologie* 3:382.

raised from death to life has just been used to describe the present transition into eternity life of those who come to believe in Jesus (5:21). Those who have done good deeds will *come forth* "to a resurrection of life." The present state of their participating in eternity life will be made manifest. The term "life" qualifies the type of resurrection existence for the good. Conversely, evildoers will come forth "to a resurrection of judgment." The judgment they brought upon themselves in their earthly existence will be manifest. The term "judgment" qualifies their experience of resurrection. To summarize: Chapter 5 introduces bodily resurrection (vv. 28-29)[56] into an eschatology that is essentially realized but allows for a final manifestation of the victory of good over evil and the manifestation of the destinies of the good and the evil as a consequence of judgment made by their choices during their earthly existence.

In John 6 the expression "and I will raise him up at the last day" occurs three times (vv. 40, 44, 54) and once with the impersonal "it" rather than "him" (v. 39). Since the major thrust of John 6 has been the present offer of eternity life, the introduction of "last day" resurrection seems out of context, contradictory, and for some commentators it is evidence of a later hand. Resorting to a "later hand" seems an act of desperation and not necessary. The eschatology of the Fourth Gospel brings into the present moment the choice of belief or unbelief, the judgment that follows this choice and the situation of life or death now, which will continue beyond the tomb. While these "end-time" realities are brought into the present, as in the book of Wisdom, the experience of Jesus has revealed bodily resurrection, which by the time of the Fourth Gospel has become part of the Christian story.[57] Adding a bodily resurrection to what is otherwise a realized eschatology is not a contradiction; rather, it is a completion, as it gives the human person corporeal participation in end-time realities. The addition of corporeality in this chapter is most fitting, given the emphasis on the incarnation of the Word. Wisdom/Word has become flesh and it is this flesh, the humanity of Jesus, that is given for the life of the world. The choice for or against God's ways is made in response to this fully enfleshed Jesus. Later believers will confront the same choice and make their response by eating the flesh and drinking the blood of the Crucified and Risen One in their Eucharistic celebrations. The bodiliness of Jesus is an essential feature of the discourse in

---

[56] Bodily resurrection from the dead may be assumed by the expression "in the tombs."

[57] Jörg Frey explains the presence of both present and future eschatology as a reflection of dual traditions already part of the Johannine community's story prior to the written form of the Gospel. See Frey, *Die johanneische Eschatologie* 3:464.

John 6, and so the bodiliness of participation in eternity-life should not come as a surprise or be thought of as a foreign intrusion. But bodiliness need no longer be configured to temporality, as Dorothy Lee eloquently states: "The one who lies in the Father's embrace (1:18) is gathered into flesh; God takes shape in human form, created from clay, subject to death, mortal, vulnerable—radiant with deity, yes, but radiant also with the promise of flesh renewed, refined, immortal."[58]

Conclusion

Influenced by the elements of realized eschatology in the Jewish wisdom literature, particularly the book of Wisdom, the eschatology of the Fourth Gospel is primarily realized, as Bultmann and Dodd maintained.[59] Not only is this eschatology realized, it is also realistic, for obviously believers in Jesus die, but this gospel insists that the life they have received through faith in Jesus will continue through death. Whether influenced by Jesus' own apocalyptic teaching[60] or the Christian revelation of resurrection, the Fourth Gospel also envisages a "last day" raising of the body so that the full corporeal experience of human existence can participate in the eternity-life of God.[61] As Sandra Schneiders writes:

> Bodily resurrection is compatible with, perhaps even implicit in, but not explicitly affirmed in sapiential eschatology. However, it could become explicit if the right pressures were brought to bear upon it, e.g., by the Easter experience of the first followers of Jesus.[62]

This futurist eschatology need not be interpreted as a later foreign addition, or even as an element of theological confusion on the part of the evangelist. Given his announcement that "the Word became flesh," an eschatology that

---

[58] Lee, *Flesh and Glory*, 49.

[59] ". . . the earlier naïve eschatology of Jewish Christianity and Gnosticism has been abandoned, certainly not in favor of a spiritualising of the eschatological process to become a process within man's soul, but in favor of a radical understanding of Jesus' appearance as the eschatological event. This event puts an end to the old course of the world." See Bultmann, *Gospel*, 155. "All through the Book of Signs Jesus is represented as conferring on men the light and life absolute which belong to the supernal world, or the Age to Come: in that sense the time which is to come has come—*erchetai hōra kai nun estin.*" See Dodd, *Interpretation*, 372.

[60] Boismard, *Our Victory over Death*, 100–20; Donald J. Goergen, *The Death and Resurrection of Jesus*. A Theology of Jesus 2 (Wilmington, DE: Michael Glazier, 1988) 111–16.

[61] Frey, *Die johanneische Eschatologie* 3:460.

[62] Schneiders, "The Resurrection (of the Body)," 175–76.

was thoroughly realized would come fittingly to its completion when "flesh" enters into that life with God enjoyed by the pre-existent Word.[63] In the flesh of the incarnate Word all flesh is offered a participation in the triune communion of divine life. This gift of becoming "children of God" is available in the here and now of human historical existence with the surety that this eternity life continues through death into God's unending "now."

> By becoming flesh, God enters the world in the thin garb of mortality, entering the darkness of creation clad only in the armor of skin and vein, sinew and bone: mortal, vulnerable, naked. . . . The new order of fleshly existence envisaged in the symbolic universe of the Fourth Gospel comes from within, transfigured by the habitation of divine glory in mortal flesh. The enfleshment of the Sophia-Word raises "all flesh" to the level of divine glory.[64]

This book began by proposing that the "household" provides the best living metaphor of the Johannine community. In their lived experience of Jesus' presence still with them, mediated through the Spirit, community members perceived themselves as the locus for God's dwelling. Where the physical body of Jesus could be called the Temple or House of God because of Jesus' unique relationship with his Father (1:1, 18; 2:16, 19, 21), in the post-Easter period they too experienced the indwelling presence of Father, Spirit, and Jesus (14:10, 27, 23, 25). They came to understand themselves as the raised-up Temple of Israel's eschatological hopes. This new Temple, though, is conceived primarily in terms of its relationship to God rather than as a place of cultic sacrifice. A community of believers becomes the dwelling place of God in becoming part of Jesus' "family" at the cross and so being drawn into his Father's household (19:25-30). Because such a self-understanding is a presupposition of the community, its "taken for granted" status means it is not obvious to readers who have lost touch with the initial experience of the community. It is a transparent image that would only be obvious to those with an insider's knowledge and experience.

---

[63] In attributing the "resurrection passages" in John to a foreign hand, Boismard (*Our Victory over Death*, 120) denies that there will be a future bodily resurrection, but then, in a somewhat confusing way, suggests that the soul does not enter into eternal life "completely disembodied." He then draws on Pauline ideas (2 Cor 5:1) to say: "The soul joins a 'heavenly body' at the very moment it leaves this 'earthly body.'" I have argued that these resurrection passages are not later insertions but are thoroughly Johannine, allowing a last-day resurrection within a realized, immortality eschatology. The incarnation principle (1:14), which is the basis for Johannine christology, would seem to require some type of bodily participation in eternity life beyond the grave.

[64] See Lee, *Flesh and Glory*, 50.

In my study so far I have offered an insider's reading of the text, making explicit the issues that reach behind the narrative into the spirituality of the Johannine community from which the gospel text emerged. The first chapters explored the formation of the household in the call of the disciples and in the context of John's witness to Jesus as the bridegroom. The household of Bethany is the first developed insight into a household of disciples within the narrative. The issues faced by Martha and Mary in the narrative are issues faced by disciples in the post-Easter time. Is Jesus absent from our lives? The death of Lazarus, a friend of Jesus, and one presumably promised "life" by Jesus, thrusts this household, and post-Easter households of disciples, into a faith crisis.

While perceiving themselves as the household of God now, members of the community were not immune from the pain of illness and death. Martha and Mary depict the vulnerability of faith in moments of human anguish. They have faith, of a sort, but when put to the test it falters. They want the physical presence of Jesus. The miracle affirms that Jesus' word is sufficient and trustworthy. The word of Jesus alone reaches into the dark tomb of death to call Lazarus to life. While no longer sharing the privileged experience of the first disciples, future households of Christians are invited to believe that even illness and death are open to the power of Jesus' word.

Anointing the Household of God

JOHN 12:1-8

The story of the household of Bethany continues into John 12 as Jesus gathers with his disciples at table with Martha, Mary and Lazarus. At this point in the narrative death and resurrection have made their presence felt. The raising of Lazarus has led to the gathering of the Sanhedrin and the decision by Caiaphas "that one person should die for the people" (11:50). The Johannine interpretation of Jesus' death is also recalled from the Prologue: "to gather into one the children of God" (11:52; cf. 1:12). The Lazarus narrative provides the immediate context for the start of the Passover week. As well as the immediate context, the entire gospel has been providing clues to shape the reading of the following events. Therefore, before examining the anointing in John 12:1-8, I must first spend some moments establishing the broader context that will provide the particular lens through which I examine this scene. In establishing the context I will briefly touch on the major points developed in my book *God Dwells With Us: Temple Symbolism in the Fourth Gospel.* This overview is necessary, as I will show that cultic symbolism offers one way of understanding some of the unique elements of the Johannine anointing. As I stated in the introductory chapter, the work on the symbolism of the Temple provided my entry point for this second reading of the gospel, and as this current book moves toward the "hour," the motifs of Temple and Household resonate with each other like different themes in a Bach Prelude.

Temple Symbolism: A Review

In the Prologue to the gospel, Jesus is introduced as the tabernacling (*eskēnōsen*) presence of the divine *Logos* (1:14). The use of the term *eskēnōsen*, with its allusion to the tabernacle (*skēnē*), is then made even more explicit in chapter 2, in the first "public" action of Jesus when he drives the dealers and moneychangers from the Temple. Standing within the monumental edifice of the recently extended and renovated Temple, Jesus lays claim to this building, his Father's house, as a symbol of his own identity. Because of the intimacy between *Logos* and *Theos* (1:1), Jesus is the new locus of God's dwelling (1:14) and so he can rightly say "Destroy this temple, and in three days I will raise it up" (2:19); the narrator then adds, "He spoke of the temple of his body" (2:21). In my earlier book I argued that this scene in John 2 is the hermeneutical key to understanding both Jesus' identity and his mission in the Fourth Gospel.[1] It is up to the rest of the narrative to show how a Temple is destroyed by "the Jews" and raised by Jesus. If the text does not show this, then its claim to truthfulness (19:35) has no foundation.

In the following chapters of my book I show how the narrative does in fact support and carry out these programmatic words. Not only is the Temple a major christological symbol, but this symbol is doubly transferred in its meaning:

   i. from a building to the person of Jesus in John 2 and continued in John 4;

   ii. then from the person of Jesus to the community of those who believe in him in John 7:37-39, and especially 14:2.

It is this second transferral to the community that I summarize below.

In the Festival of Tabernacles (John 7:1–10:21) Jesus appropriates the key symbols of the Feast. As once God cared for the Israelites in their wilderness wanderings by providing them with gifts of water from the rock (Exod 17:1-2) and a pillar of fire to light their way (Exod 13:21-22), Jesus announces that in his person God continues to offer guidance and sustenance to the people. He is a source of water for the thirsty (7:37) and light for the world (8:12). It is during this feast that the Temple symbolism begins a second transference of meaning from being "the temple of his body" to being a future temple of believers.

John 7:37 is a notoriously difficult verse to understand because the manuscripts vary in how they punctuate it and so lead to different ways of translating it. It can be read to say that Jesus is the single source of water, and that from the heart of Jesus streams of water will flow.[2] It can also be read to mean that Jesus is a source of water now, and that believers who

---

[1] Coloe, *God Dwells With Us*, 65–84.

[2] This *christological* interpretation is adopted by Raymond E. Brown, Rudolf Bultmann, Francis J. Moloney, Rudolf Schnackenburg, and others.

come to him will in the future be channels of living water.[3] I read the verse in this second way, that while Jesus is present he is the source of living water but there will be a future time, associated with a future gift of the Spirit (7:39), when believers will be channels of living water.[4]

> On the last day of the festival, the great day, while Jesus was standing there, he cried out, "Whoever thirsts, let them come to me and drink. Whoever believes in me, as the scripture said, 'Out of his (*autou*) [the believer's] heart shall flow rivers of living water.'" Now he said this about the Spirit, which believers in him were to receive; for as yet there was no Spirit, because Jesus was not yet glorified. (John 7:37-39)

The text I see behind this image of "streams of living water" is the eschatological Temple of Ezekiel 47. While some scholars suggest other possible passages, there are later rabbinic writings that link the water-libation rituals of Tabernacles with Ezekiel's Temple vision. Although firm conclusions cannot be based solely on these later writings, the prominence given to Temple and cultic imagery in the Fourth Gospel supports Ezekiel as a likely allusion for the Scripture Jesus cites. While Jesus is present, he is the Temple whose waters can provide life and healing, but the promise is given of a future time when, through the gift of the Spirit, believers will also be Temple-people, able to be sources of living water. During the festival of Tabernacles the reference to the believers must be understood as a promise to be fulfilled when Jesus is glorified.

The promise of 7:37-39 is elaborated further during Jesus' farewell meal with his disciples (John 13–17). Jesus is leaving them. The hour has come for his return to the Father, and the loving intimacy of this meal speaks poignantly into the pain of a future absence. These chapters deal most explicitly with a critical issue for later disciples: How can post-Easter believers continue to experience the presence of God? Is God still with us, or is it all just a beautiful memory?

At the heart of the final discourse lie two chapters, 14 and 15, that speak of Jesus' ongoing presence with the disciples in terms of mutual indwelling. The theology of mutual indwelling is introduced in both chapters

---

[3] This translation is the more traditional approach taken in Patristic writings and has the support of the oldest manuscript tradition, 𝔓[66]. Modern commentators who take this approach include C. K. Barrett, Robert H. Lightfoot, Xavier Léon-Dufour, Robert Kysar, and Barnabas Lindars.

[4] A detailed discussion of this verse and my arguments for this ecclesial interpretation can be found in *God Dwells with Us*, ch. 6.

with an image: the house of the Father and its many dwellings (14:2), and the vine and branches (15:1, 5).

> Let not your hearts be troubled; believe in God, believe also in me.
> In my Father's house are many dwellings; if it were not so, would I have told you that I go to prepare a place for you? (John 14:1-2)
>
> I am the true vine, and my Father is the vinedresser . . .
> I am the vine, you are the branches. Those who dwell in me, and I in them, they bear much fruit, for apart from me you can do nothing. (John 15:1, 5)

While the metaphor of the vine and branches is readily understood as a symbol, since it makes no sense to speak of dwelling or abiding *in* a vine, the metaphorical use of the term "my Father's house" is not so readily perceived, as it is possible to dwell or abide *in* a house. Even when the term is understood in a symbolic sense it is taken by most commentators to mean the heavenly house of God.[5] The reading about "my Father's house" and its "many dwellings" (usually translated "rooms") is used very often at Christian funerals, and is taken to mean Jesus' return to heaven and his preparation of a heavenly place for his disciples. But such an interpretation offers little consolation to disciples on the eve of Jesus' departure. It is not enough to promise them (and later believers), some future heavenly reunion. A gospel that announced Jesus dwelling among us in the flesh (1:14) needs to offer more than an otherworldly, spiritualized presence. So I raise the question: what and where is "my Father's house"?

My Father's House[6]

In chapter 14 the phrase "in my Father's house" must be interpreted in the light of a similar expression in chapter 2, where "my Father's house" referred to the Jerusalem Temple, the building (2:16). While the scene in chapter 2 begins in the physical Temple building, by the end of the chapter the Temple has been reinterpreted to mean the body of Jesus (2:21). In this Fourth Gospel the Temple means more than a physical building. Beginning

---

[5] The most complete analysis of John 14:2 is a work by James McCaffrey, *The House With Many Rooms: The Temple Theme of Jn 14, 2-3.* AnBib 114 (Rome: Biblical Institute Press, 1988). He identifies the Father's house with the heavenly Temple. "Jesus enters through his passion-resurrection into the heavenly temple of the Father's House by the sacrificial transformation of his body into the New Temple of his risen body in which believers have permanent and abiding at-one-ment with God" (p. 256).

[6] For a discussion of the use of this term "my Father's house" (14:2) see Coloe, *God Dwells with Us*, ch. 8.

with the announcement of the Word tabernacling with us (1:14), and reiterated in 2:21, the function of providing a place for the Divine Presence shifts from the Jerusalem Temple to the living flesh of Jesus.

The term "my father's house" is open to further levels of meaning. In the Hebrew Scriptures this phrase usually means the group of people who make up the household, such as the family and servants, even the future descendants. For example: "So Joseph said to his brothers and to his father's house, 'I will go and tell Pharaoh and say to him: My brothers and my father's house have come to me'" (Gen 46:31).[7] It is rarely used in the sense of a building. In speaking of the Temple with this phrase, in chapter 2, the evangelist began to move away from Temple-as-building to something more personal and relational. In chapter 2 the image of Temple shifted to a single person, Jesus: "the temple of his body" (2:21).

Chapter 14 develops this personal and relational understanding even further with the shift from the word house (*oikos*), the term used in chapter 2, to household (*oikia*). In the gospel the term *oikos* is used **only** with the sense of a building, namely, the Temple building (2:16, 17) and the house at Bethany (11:20). The term *oikia* is used with a more fluid range of meanings, in that it can mean a physical building (11:31; 12:3—both references to the house at Bethany) but it can also mean the household (4:53—"the father believed and all his household," and 8:35—"the slave does not continue in the household forever"). Whereas in 2:16 the initial reference was to the *oikos* in the sense of a building, here in chapter 14, through the change of the word to *oikia* and the possibility that this can mean household and not just a residence, there is a continuation of the movement begun in 2:21 to understand the phrase "my Father's house" as a quality of personal relationships.

Many Dwellings (*monai pollai*)

While dwellings (*monai*) can mean the physical chambers within a house, and so could at one level be understood as many rooms within a physical Temple building, the shift from building to personal relationships suggested by the phrase "in my Father's household" requires a similar shift in understanding what the evangelist means by "dwellings." What are these many dwellings? The chapter itself, with chapter 15, provides the best interpretive clue to the particular Johannine meaning of this phrase.

---

[7] For other examples of this phrase meaning the entire household see Gen 7:1; 12:1, 17; 18:19; 24:38; 28:21; Exod 12:4; Lev 16:6; Num 16:32; Deut 25:9; Josh 2:13; Judg 6:15; 9:18; 16:31; 1 Sam 2:35; 22:15; 2 Sam 14:9; 1 Kgs 2:24; 1 Chr 17:10, 25; 28:4. *Beth ʾabh* is frequently translated "family" or "household" in English translations.

Chapters 14 and 15 use derivatives of dwell (*menō*) and dwelling (*monē*) to describe a variety of interpersonal relationships among the Father, Jesus, the Paraclete, and believers. The relationships are usually described with the translation *abiding* or *dwelling*. These relationships are appropriately introduced by the phrase *many dwellings*. As stated earlier, chapter 14 focuses on a series of divine dwellings:

- the Father who dwells (*menōn*) in Jesus (v. 10)

- the Paraclete who dwells (*menei*) with believers, and in the future will be in them (v. 17)

- the Father and Jesus who will make their dwelling (*monēn*) with the believer (v. 23)

- Jesus who dwells (*menēn*) with the disciples (v. 25).[8]

Many commentators would see the metaphor as a reference to God's heavenly dwelling, where the believers will abide at some future time. But the subject of the verb *dwell* throughout chapter 14 is not the believer, but God. The action therefore is not the *believers* coming to dwell in God's heavenly abode, but the *Father*, the *Paraclete*, and *Jesus* coming to dwell with the believers. It is a "descending" movement from the divine realm to the human, not an "ascending" movement from the human to the divine. Given that the emphasis in chapter 14 is on the *divine dwellings* with the believers, it is not altogether surprising to find this theology introduced with an image that draws on Israel's symbol of the divine presence in its midst—the Temple, Israel's house of the Lord, which had been renamed by Jesus in chapter 2 as "my Father's house" (2:16).

From the above analysis, the phrase "in my Father's house are many dwellings" is best understood, within the context of this gospel, to mean a series of interpersonal relationships made possible because of the indwellings of the Father, Jesus, and the Paraclete with the believer. The divine indwelling in the midst of a believing community makes it appropriate to speak of the community as a living Temple, the sacred place where God can now be found. The community is the house (household) of God.[9] David

---

[8] The imagery of *many dwellings* continues into ch. 15, where the verb *dwell* is again used to describe the believers' dwelling in Jesus. The shift to the community of believers is reflected by a shift in the metaphor from "house" to "vine," since the vine was a common image for the community of Israel.

[9] To ensure that the term "house" has the more personal sense of family rather than building I will use the word household, which is the more frequent meaning of *oikia* in the Fourth Gospel.

Aune suggests that the term house/household as it is used here and in 8:35, speaking of the son remaining continually in the household, "reflects the self-designation of the Johannine community."[10]

Supporting the argument that the phrase refers to a "household" is the fact that the discourse uses various family terms: Jesus gathers his own (13:1); they are called children (13:33). The language of family relationships continues in 14:18 with the word "orphans" to describe a state of Jesus' absence, followed later by the allegory of the woman in childbirth (16:21).

To Prepare a Place for You

The second part of the metaphor also resonates with allusions to Israel's Temple. In the Hebrew text the terminology of a *prepared place* is used almost exclusively of the Ark of the Covenant,[11] and then by extension the Temple: "David . . . prepared a place for the ark of God and pitched a tent for it" (1 Chr 15:1; also 15:3, 12; 2 Chr 1:4). "And Solomon began to build the house of the LORD in Jerusalem in the mount of Moriah in the place which David had prepared" (2 Chr 3:1).

In the ancestral narratives there are two scenes associated with the future site of the Temple in which the word *place* features prominently. The first story is that of the sacrifice of Isaac (Gen 22:3-14). The Mount of Moriah, the future Temple Mount (2 Chr 3:1), is the place where Abraham is told to sacrifice his only son. "Place" occurs four times in this short episode (vv. 3, 4, 9, 14). The second scene from the ancestral narratives that emphasizes the word "place" is Jacob's dream at Bethel (Gen 28:11-19). "Surely the LORD is in this place. . . . This is none other than the house of God" (vv. 16-17). "He called the name of that place Beth-el" (v. 19). In these two narratives the term "place" has a cultic significance that receives its full meaning in the Jerusalem Temple.[12]

With the experience of the exile and the destruction of the Temple, hope shifted to a future eschatological temple that would be the "place" for the gathering of the nations (Mic 4:1-2; Isa 2:2-3). Such an understanding lies behind the prayer of Nehemiah, "Gather together our scattered

[10] David E. Aune, *The Cultic Setting of Realized Eschatology in Early Christianity*, 130. Other NT passages that reflect the use of *oikos* as an image of the community are 1 Pet 2:5; 4:17; 1 Tim 3:15; Heb 3:2-6.

[11] The only exception is a reference to the land (Exod 23:20). All other references are to the Ark.

[12] See McCaffrey, *The House with Many Rooms*, 98–109, for further discussion of the cultic significance of the term "to prepare a place."

people. . . . Plant your people in your holy place, as Moses promised" (2 Macc 1:27-29; see also 2:17-18). From this survey of the background to the words *prepare* and *place* it is possible to see in the phrase "*to prepare a place* for you" an allusion to the Jewish Temple traditions, including the later traditions of the Temple as the eschatological gathering place God will prepare for the people.

Taken together, the two key phrases of 14:2, *in my Father's house there are many dwellings* and *I go to prepare a place for you*, show a uniquely Johannine concern with the Temple. But the Temple is now reinterpreted in a radically new way as the household of God, where the Divine Presence dwells within the community of believers. When the disciples fail to understand Jesus' words, his explanation leads into the promise of the Paraclete and an indication that "the household of my Father" will be prepared through the indwellings of the Father, Jesus, and Paraclete within the believer (14:17, 23, 25). In some way the action of Jesus in "going" to the Father is simultaneously the action by which he "prepares/builds" the "place" (Temple) for the disciples. The Father's house will no longer be a construction of stones, but will be a household of many interpersonal relationships, *many dwellings*, where the Divine Presence can dwell within believers. In chapter 14, Jesus' words are a promise looking ahead to the culmination of his "hour," when they will be realized.

Building the Temple/Household of God

The promise is fulfilled in chapter 19 when the narrative reaches its conclusion at the cross. Jesus dies under the title "the Nazarene," and as I noted earlier in chapter 3, this title establishes him as the Temple-builder, the branch, of Zechariah. "Here is a man whose name is Branch, for he shall branch out from this place and he shall build the temple of the LORD" (Zech 6:12). This term *Branch* is related to the Messianic branch found in Isaiah, "A shoot springs from the stock of Jesse and a branch shall grow from his roots" (Isa 11:1).[13] In his death Jesus draws the Beloved Disciple into his own relationship with his mother:—"Behold your son. . . . Behold your mother" (19:26, 27)—and also into his filial relationship with God.[14] In this scene disciples become "children of God," as the Prologue promised

---

[13] See Coloe, *God Dwells with Us*, 171–74 for a more detailed discussion of these texts. An article by Hans-Peter Rüger makes a similar case for linking "Nazareth" with Isa 11:1 when examining the Synoptic usage in Matt 2:23; 13:54; and Mark 6:1. He makes no mention of the Johannine usage. See Rüger, "ΝΑΖΑΡΕΘ, ΝΑΖΑΡΑ, ΝΑΖΑΡΗΝΟΣ, ΝΑΖΩΡΑΙΟΣ," 257–63.

[14] See above, ch. 3, and also Coloe, *God Dwells with Us*, 186–90.

(1:12). Jesus' "hour" draws disciples into the Father's house, now properly termed the Father's household. Another way of saying this is that the new Temple/household of God is the Johannine community, in whom the Risen Christ dwells through the mediation of the Spirit.

This is a very brief review of the arguments in my previous book, where the community as the living household/house of God is the new Temple raised up in the Hour. So, with this as background, I now turn to John 12.

John 12:1-8

A comparison of the Johannine anointing with the scene as it is found in the Synoptics, especially Mark and Matthew, reveals four Johannine features:

i. a time frame is given: "six days before the Passover" (12:1);

ii. the unknown woman is named as Mary (12:3), sister to Martha and Lazarus, from John 11 (12:3);

iii. the evangelist comments: "the fragrance of the perfume filled the house" (12:3);

iv. Judas is named and described as the one to criticize her action (12:4-6).

The rest of this chapter will examine the significance of these Johannine features to discover what importance they have within the theological perspective of the gospel, as outlined above.

Six Days before Passover [15]

Naming such a specific time is not usual in the Fourth Gospel. Far more common is a general expression such as "Now the Passover, the Feast of the Jews, was at hand" (6:4; see also 7:2; 11:55). Scholars offer various interpretations for the naming of "six days." C. K. Barrett sees in this time frame and the use of perfume a reference to the *Habdalah* ceremony marking the end of the Sabbath on the Saturday night, with Passover beginning the following Friday evening.[16] Sandra Schneiders reckons the counting of days differently; she places this meal on the Sunday evening and thus links

---

[15] Both Robert Holst and Robert T. Fortna see this expression as part of the Johannine redaction of his source material; see R. Holst, "The one anointing of Jesus: Another application of the form-critical method," *JBL* 95 (1976) 439; Robert T. Fortna, *The Fourth Gospel and its Predecessor: From Narrative Source to Present Gospel*. Studies in the New Testament and its World (Edinburgh: T&T Clark, 1988) 144.

[16] Barrett, *The Gospel According to St. John*, 410–11.

it to the eucharistic experience of the early church.[17] Rudolf Schnackenburg also suggests the Sunday, but dismisses this time detail as having no "further meaning."[18] I agree with Barrett and Schneiders that the time detail, particularly the unusual way it is expressed, is significant.[19] I suggest two possible backgrounds for this detail of time, one liturgical and one christological, with each one building on and developing the other, as is so often the case in the Fourth Gospel.

I. LITURGICAL BACKGROUND

In the reckoning of days I agree with Barrett that the meal at Bethany took place on the Saturday night at the conclusion to the Sabbath, six days before the Passover, which in the Fourth Gospel began on the Friday evening coinciding with the next Sabbath day (19:31). In this case the *Habdalah* ceremony at the conclusion of the Sabbath provides a liturgical context for a scene involving a meal, sweet aromatic spices, and an anointing. According to Barrett, since the schools of Hillel and Shammai agree on the elements of meal, light, and spices, it is likely that this service was happening at the time of Jesus.[20] The Talmud dates the *Habdalah* back to men of the Great Synagogue between the sixth and fourth centuries B.C.E. (*Ber.* 33a), although the exact order and wording were not finalized until Talmudic times.[21] The ceremony to conclude the Sabbath began as late as possible, and it marked the separation of Sabbath from the rest of the week.[22] The *Habdalah* prayers made three distinctions, between sacred and profane, between light and dark, and between Israel and other nations.[23] A special blessing was prayed over the spices, since the close of Sabbath meant the departure of joy and

---

[17] Schneiders, *Written That You May Believe*, 107.

[18] Schnackenburg, *Gospel* 2:366. Similarly Bultmann, *Gospel of John*, 414 n. 5; Francis J. Moloney, *Signs and Shadows: Reading John 5–12* (Minneapolis: Fortress Press, 1996) 180 n. 4.

[19] That the anointing happened six days before Passover is one of the inconsequential details that seem to have no part in the narrative. Juan Leal understands such detail as an indicator that the narrative has a symbolic as well as a literal meaning; see Leal, "El simbolismo histórico del IV Evangelio," *EstB* 19 (1960) 329–48.

[20] Barrett notes that there was controversy over the *order* of these elements but not the elements themselves (*Gospel*, 342).

[21] Abraham E. Millgram, *Jewish Worship* (Philadelphia: Jewish Publication Society of America, 1971) 297.

[22] Rather than at sunset, the *Habdallah* service did not start until three small stars appeared in the sky together. Samuel M. Segal, *The Sabbath Book* (2nd ed. New York: Thomas Yoseloff, 1957) 127.

[23] Abraham Z. Idelsohn, *Jewish Liturgy and its Development* (New York: Schocken, 1932) 148.

of a second soul that was present with the individual only while the Sabbath lasted. According to Abraham Millgram, the "sweet smelling spices symbolize the spiritual farewell 'feast' for the departing 'additional soul' which the Jew figuratively possesses on the Sabbath," while for Abraham Idelsohn the perfume of the spices was meant to invigorate the worshipers in this soul's absence.[24] Both of these aspects, farewell and encouragement, fit well in the context of the gospel and may supply a liturgical background for the way in which the odor of the perfume is highlighted in this chapter (12:3). These themes of farewell and encouragement will be made more explicit in chapters 13–17.

The *Habdalah* marked a movement from sacred *time* to ordinary *time*, and within Judaism another way of demarcating the sacred from the secular was through a ritual of anointing. Holy objects, persons, and spaces were set aside for God's service through anointing with special spices.

> Then you shall take the anointing oil and anoint the tabernacle and all that is in it, and consecrate it and all its furniture; and it shall become holy. You shall also anoint the altar of burnt offering and all its utensils, and consecrate the altar; and the altar shall be most holy. You shall also anoint the laver and its base, and consecrate it. Then you shall bring Aaron and his sons to the door of the tent of meeting, and shall wash them with water, and put upon Aaron the holy garments, and you shall anoint him and consecrate him, that he may serve me as priest. (Exod 40:9-13)

While there was no specific anointing within the *Habdalah* ceremony, the odor of the spices and the blessings mark out in time what anointing does in space, namely, the separation between sacred and profane. Whatever the historical meaning behind the woman's act of anointing Jesus, by placing this episode in a meal, possibly marking the close of Sabbath when blessings are said to distinguish the sacred from the profane, this gospel highlights the sacredness of Jesus' body. While the narrative does not describe the blessings and rituals to bring the Sabbath to a close, it would be presumed that a Jewish audience/readership would be familiar with these rituals. Since they would be just as familiar with the Johannine dating of Jesus' death on the eve of both Passover and the Sabbath, the dating "six days before the Passover" would be sufficient, for this community, to evoke the liturgical context. This brings me to the second possible meaning behind the term "six days," namely its christological significance.

---

[24] Millgram, *Jewish Worship*, 300; Idelsohn, *Jewish Liturgy*, 149. For more on this additional soul see Segal, *Sabbath Book*, 184.

II. CHRISTOLOGICAL BACKGROUND

The beginning of Jesus' public ministry was introduced by a specific reference to time: "On the third day there was a marriage at Cana in Galilee" (2:1). Francis J. Moloney argues that the time reference in this pericope is very significant and even a key to its understanding. The "three days" echoes the description of the "three days" of preparation before the manifestation of God's glory on Sinai (Exodus 19).[25] As the public ministry draws to a close, I believe the evangelist again makes use of a specific time frame and the Exodus imagery to recapitulate his presentation of Jesus' identity and mission before the beginning of his Hour.

Exodus 35 introduces for a second time the instructions for building the tabernacle:

> "*Six days* shall work be done, but on the seventh day you shall have a holy *Sabbath* of solemn rest to the LORD; whoever does any work on it shall be put to death; you shall kindle no fire in all your habitations on the Sabbath day." Moses said to all the congregation of the people of Israel, "This is the thing which the LORD has commanded. Take from among you an offering to the LORD; whoever is of a *generous* heart, let him bring the LORD's offering: gold, silver, and bronze; blue and purple and scarlet stuff and fine twined linen; goats' hair, tanned rams' skins, and goatskins; acacia wood, oil for the light, spices for the *anointing oil* and for the *fragrant* incense." (Exod 35:2-8)

The rest of the book of Exodus is taken up with these instructions and the building of the tabernacle. All that has gone before—the plagues, the miracle at the Sea, the covenant—all lead to the culmination of the Exodus event in preparing a place so that God may have a dwelling with the people. By itself the mention of *six days* in 12:1 could have various other precedents, but the Johannine anointing episode links six days with an act of anointing and a "generous" amount of spices, so that the house is filled with the odor of the perfume and it is likely that this episode occurred on the Sabbath. It is when all these elements are taken together that the Exodus tabernacle background is suggested. If I am correct in making this Exodus link, we have here a further example of the Jesus/tabernacle/Temple motif this gospel uses to emphasize continuity with Israel's heritage while professing its fulfilment as promised in the Scriptures.

III. THE TARGUMS AND THE ANOINTING

The case for seeing the christological significance of the anointing may be strengthened by considering the Targumic evidence, while noting the difficulty in dating these passages. In Exodus 40, Moses is told: "you shall

[25] Moloney, *John*, 66–70.

take the anointing oil and anoint the tabernacle . . . you shall also anoint the altar of burnt offerings . . . you shall also anoint the laver and its base" (40:9-11). *Targum Pseudo-Jonathan*, elaborating on the triple command *to anoint*, has the following:

> Take anointing oil and anoint the tabernacle and consecrate it
> *For the sake of the royal crown of the house of Judah and of the King Messiah.*

> You shall anoint the altar . . .
> *For the sake of the crown of the priesthood of Aaron and his sons and Elijah the High Priest.*

> You shall anoint the laver
> *For the sake of Joshua your attendant, the head of the Sanhedrin of his people, by whom the land of Israel is to be divided, and (for the sake of) the Messiah, the son of Ephraim.*[26]

The mention of the two crowns of royalty and priesthood and the name "Joshua" bear striking resemblance to the words of Zechariah 6:12, a passage that, I have already noted, identifies the one who will build the new Temple.

> Take from them [the exiles Heldai, Tobijah, and Jedaiah] silver and gold and make **crowns** and set [them] upon the head of **Joshua** the son of Jehozadak the high priest; and say to him, "Thus says the LORD of Hosts, 'Behold the man whose name is the Branch: for he shall branch out from this place, and he shall build the temple of the LORD. It is he who shall build the Temple of the LORD and he shall bear **royal** honor, and shall sit and rule upon his throne and shall be a **priest** upon his throne.'" (Zech 6:10-13)[27]

Zechariah identifies Joshua, the Temple builder, as one who can rightly wear the crowns of kingship and priesthood. A. T. Hanson notes: "In Greek 'Joshua' is of course indistinguishable from 'Jesus,' so an early Christian might well believe . . . that this passage concerned Jesus Christ."[28] In the

---

[26] The Cairo Damascus document also speaks of dual Messiahs of Aaron and Israel: *CD* 12:22-23; 13:20-22; *CD* 19:34–20:1; *CD* 14:18-19; *CD* 19:9-11. The antiquity of the idea of dual Messiahs is attested to by these fragments.

[27] This is a confused text, and where the Hebrew has plural "crowns," the Greek reads a singular "crown" and does not associate the roles of king and priest with only one person.

[28] Hanson relates the anointing to Hag 2:6-9, where words are addressed to Zerubabel and Joshua; see Anthony T. Hanson, *The New Testament Interpretation of Scripture* (London: SPCK, 1980) 118–21.

Fourth Gospel these three roles will come together in the Hour of Jesus when, as the royal priest, he builds the new Temple of God.[29] It is possible that the Targum rendition of Exodus 40:9-13 has developed as a midrash on Zechariah 6:10-13. The crowns of kingship and priesthood set on the one to build the future Temple, according to Zechariah, may have led to the triple elaboration of the tabernacle's anointing in the Targum version. Even if the Targum is not pre-Christian, the Gospel of John and the Targum show signs of similar exegetical tendencies. Read in the light of these tendencies, Mary's anointing not only identifies Jesus as the anointed tabernacle/Temple of God but also points ahead to his Passion, when he will be revealed as both king and priest.

The House Is Filled with the Fragrance of the Perfume

When the tabernacle has been built, Moses is instructed: "And you shall take the anointing oil, and shall anoint the tabernacle" (LXX Exod 40:9). When Moses completes all the instructions of God, in words echoing back to Genesis (Gen 2:2) and picked up later in John (19:29), we read: "So Moses finished the work" (Exod 40:33).[30] The final scene in Exodus is the tabernacle being filled with the presence of God's glory.

> Then the cloud covered the tent of meeting, and the glory of the LORD filled the tabernacle. And Moses was not able to enter the tent of meeting, because the cloud abode upon it, and the glory of the LORD filled the tabernacle. (Exod 40:34-35)

A similar expression is used when Solomon builds the Jerusalem Temple:

> And when the priests came out of the holy place, a cloud filled the house of the LORD . . . for the glory of the LORD filled the house of the LORD. (1 Kgs 8:10-11)

Prior to the giving of instructions for the tabernacle, God's glory is present on Mount Sinai for six days (Exod 24:16). On the seventh day the revelation begins. Echoes of the building of the tabernacle and Temple pervade the episode in John 12. As "the hour" approaches, God's glory, now to be seen in the flesh of Jesus (1:14), will be present with the disciples for six days, leading up to the full manifestation of his glory on the cross.

---

[29] I have argued that the Passion account not only reveals Jesus as king but also as high priest (Coloe, *God Dwells with Us*, 201–206). See this place for further references to interpretations along similar lines.

[30] These three passages all use forms of the verb *teleō*.

As part of the preparation for this full manifestation, Mary repeats the actions of Moses. Just as Moses took specially prepared oil and anointed the tabernacle, Mary anoints Jesus, whose flesh is the tabernacle of God's presence. The wiping of the feet with Mary's hair also carries an allusion to Exodus. The tabernacle was covered with curtains made from goats' hair (Exod 26:7), given by those of "generous heart" (Exod 35:6) and made by women whose hearts were moved to use their skill (Exod 35:26). Mary covers Jesus' feet with her own hair as she wipes away the perfumed oil poured out in generous abundance. The extended discourse we find in John 13–16, when Jesus instructs his disciples who will be formed into the new dwelling place of God (19:25-27),[31] has some parallel with the extended instructions given for the building of the tabernacle (Exod 25–31).[32]

The description of the spices used to make the anointing oil for the tabernacle emphasizes their purity and abundance. "Take the finest spices: of liquid myrrh five hundred shekel, and of sweet smelling cinnamon half as much, that is, two hundred fifty and two hundred fifty of aromatic cane" (LXX Exod 30:23). John 12 similarly emphasizes the purity of the ointment ("pure nard"), the large amount, and its expense (12:3, 5). Finally, the expression unique to the Fourth Gospel, "and the household (*oikia*) was filled with the fragrance of the ointment,"[33] recalls the description of God's glory filling the tabernacle (Exod 40:35) and particularly the description of the Temple in Chronicles, where "the house of the LORD was filled with the cloud of glory."[34] These words also extend the anointing beyond the person of Jesus to include the entire household. The house and its household (*oikia*) are enveloped in the pervasive aroma of perfumed oils, in marked contrast with the pervasive odor of death feared when the tomb of Lazarus was opened (11:39). In these various echoes of Exodus, the scene of the anointing continues to allude to the christological imagery of tabernacle and Temple presented earlier in the gospel (1:14; 2:19-21).

The Johannine additions to this anointing scene draw upon these cultic images with great artistry and subtlety. As once God's glory was manifest in the anointed tabernacle and the Temple, this glory will now be manifested

---

[31] John 19:26-28 is the moment when Jesus' words in 2:19 are fulfilled, when he draws disciples into his own experience of divine filiation through his words to his mother and the Beloved Disciple. See Coloe, *God Dwells with Us*, 185–90.

[32] Hanson also views this passage in John 12 as a reference to Jesus as the Temple, but he sees v. 3 as an allusion to Hag 2:6-9, while I place more emphasis on the Exodus account of the tabernacle.

[33] *Hē de oikia eplērōthē ek tēs osmēs tou myrou* (John 12:3).

[34] *Kai ho oikos eneplēsthē nephelēs doxēs kyriou* (LXX 2 Chr 5:13).

in the anointed body of Jesus given over to death. If the interpretation of the six days is also accurate in placing this meal on the night of Sabbath, when the *Habdalah* service occurred, then a further liturgical meaning enriches and supports the christological approach taken above.

The Household of Bethany

There are a number of narrative reasons why this gospel may have linked this scene with that of the raising of Lazarus. The place "Bethany" seems to be historically associated with both incidents.[35] If the Fourth Evangelist already had a Passion Source in which the anointing was part of the overall Passion narrative, then this incident, when an anointing is related to Jesus' burial, has strong theological ties with the Lazarus story of a death, burial, and resurrection. For narrative reasons the addition of the names Lazarus, Martha, and Mary provides a smooth progression from a narrative of Jesus' miracles to a narrative of his Passion. There is also the need to resolve the unfulfilled statement of 11:2 that had already named Mary as "the one who anointed the LORD with her ointment."

The above are narrative reasons for linking this episode with the characters from the preceding chapter. At a theological level this scene is a proleptic experience of the post-Easter household of God. For the characters Lazarus, Martha, and Mary, the anointing of a body in death and a resurrection are past events. They have moved through the trauma of death and burial to the joy of resurrection. In anointing Jesus' feet Mary anticipates the post-resurrection model of discipleship that Jesus will enact and command in the next chapter when he washes the feet of his disciples (13:1-11). The fact that they are a household is not incidental to the theology of the narrative. Martha, Mary, and Lazarus are brother and sisters, imaging the post-Easter relationship between Jesus and his disciples, whom he will call "brothers and sisters" and who will be children of his Father (John 20:17).

Judas' Objections

Where the Markan and Matthean accounts have an unnamed objector, the Fourth Gospel names Judas as the one who criticizes Mary's abundant generosity. As the one who holds the money-purse, he claims first rights to her gift. "Why was this ointment not sold for three hundred denarii and given to the poor?" (12:5). Judas was introduced as the betrayer earlier in the gospel (6:71). Chapter 12 fills out the description of Judas by describing him as a thief (*kleptēs*). In adding the term "thief" to the usual designation

---

[35] See Holst's comments on Bethany ("One Anointing," 439).

of Judas as the betrayer, the evangelist associates Judas with the thieves and robbers who threaten the sheepfold, seeking to kill and destroy (10:1, 8, 10).

If my arguments above are correct, and the anointing is a proleptic image of the post-Easter community who form a new Temple/household of God, what place does the figure of Judas hold for this community? In other words, who does the figure of Judas represent for the Johannine group? In chapter 10 the parable of the sheepfold is used within a juridical conflict between Jesus and the Pharisees/Jews. In this context, where Jesus identifies himself as the shepherd (10:2), the door (10:7, 9), and the good shepherd (10:11, 14), "the Jews" must therefore be represented by the terms "thief and robber" (10:1, 8), "stranger" (10:5), and "hireling" (10:12, 13). Calling Judas a thief associates him with those among "the Jews" who oppose not only Jesus but also his disciples (9:34). In the words of Frédéric Manns, "Judas becomes a model for 'the Jews.'"[36] In narrative time the anointing shows the opposition and conflict between Mary and *Ioudas*, and in the post-Easter community this conflict is continued between the members of the Johannine community and the *Ioudaioi*. In dealing with the Fourth Gospel it is important to note that this association between Judas and "the Jews" is a narrative construct reflecting a very heated, possibly local polemical situation at the end of the first century as nascent Christianity and rabbinic Judaism each struggled for its own identity.[37]

Conclusion

Whatever the exact action and meaning of the historical anointing, the Johannine account shows signs of careful redaction in line with the Fourth

---

[36] "Judas devient le type des Juifs (*Ioudas-Ioudaioi*)"; see Manns, *L'Evangile de Jean à la lumière du Judaïsme*, 271.

[37] While noting the narrative and polemical strategies of the Fourth Gospel, we must also acknowledge that this gospel has contributed to the historical development of anti-Judaism and anti-Semitism in Christianity. Proclaiming Jesus as the savior of the world (4:42) has meant rejecting other saviors, and the text sets up a clear choice between light and darkness, children of God and children of the Devil (8:39-47), believers in Jesus and nonbelievers, who in this historical and narrative context are the *Ioudaioi*. For more on this issue see Reimund Bieringer, Didier Pollefeyt, and Frederique Vandecasteele-Vanneuville, eds., *Anti-Judaism and the Fourth Gospel* (Louisville: Westminster John Knox, 2001); Michael Labahn, Klaus Scholtissek, and Angelika Strotmann, eds., *Israel und seine Heilstraditionen im Johannesevangelium. Festgabe für Johannes Beutler SJ zum 70. Geburtstag* (Paderborn: Schöningh, 2004). The fact that Judas is one of the disciples adds support to Hakola's arguments that the conflicts with the *Ioudaioi* in the narrative reflect conflicts within the community with those believers still wanting to follow Jewish practices. See *Identity Matters*, 225–38.

Evangelist's overall christology of Jesus as the presence of God with us, perfecting Israel's former tabernacle and Temple. As part of the construction of the tabernacle, Moses is called aside into the presence of God's glory for six days (Exod 24:15). When the tabernacle is completed, he is instructed to anoint it with specially prepared oils (Exod 30:22-29). Six days before Passover, when the Temple of Jesus' body will be destroyed and a new Temple raised up, Mary anoints his feet in preparation for this final transcending moment. Her actions reach beyond the historical Jesus to the post-Easter time when the community of disciples is the new house/hold of God. Mary's oils touch the body of Jesus, and this gospel adds that their perfume pervades the entire house/hold. Not only Jesus is touched by her actions, but also the future Temple, the household that will be raised up in Jesus' hour. Significantly, the Johannine anointing follows immediately on the raising of Lazarus, which had led to the ironic prophecy by Caiaphas, "It is expedient for you that one man should die for the people, and that the whole nation should not perish" (11:50). In opening the tomb of Lazarus and calling forth life from death, Jesus has transgressed what is usually the ultimate boundary, death. He has already, in a sense, gone where no mere mortal dares, and will shortly enter into this ultimate experience in his own person. That Jesus has finally crossed a threshold from which there is no turning back is reflected in both Caiaphas' decision and the narrative comment that follows, "From that day on they took counsel how to put him to death" (11:53). For Caiaphas and "the Jews," Jesus no longer has any place among the living; for Jesus, the time has come for his return to the Father.

Boundary crossing is a hazardous movement. It is a time to pause before moving from what has been to what has not yet become. It is a liminal experience in time and space, where for a moment right order seems suspended. Within Israel's rhythms of prayer and festivals, one such boundary moment is ritualized every week in the passing of Sabbath and the beginning of a new week. Within the gospel narrative, chapters 11–12 present, in a highly symbolic narrative, the transition from Jesus' public ministry to his private gathering of friends in his final movement to his Father. The scene of the anointing, in its familial intimacy and cultic allusions, honors this moment of transition and anticipates its final outcome when both Jesus and his "brothers and sisters" are revealed as the new Temple of God's dwelling.

Welcome into the Household of God

JOHN 13[1]

The gospel narrative began with the disciples seeking Jesus—more precisely, seeking the place where he dwelt: "Rabbi, where do you dwell (*menō*)?" (1:38). In response to their question Jesus replied with an invitation: "Come and see" (1:39). Chapters 13 to 17 invite the reader to "come and see" the intimate life within the household of disciples gathered around Jesus. The dwelling of Jesus in the love of the Father and Spirit will be revealed, as well as the invitation to disciples to enter into this same intimate and mutual indwelling. Not only do we glimpse something of the discipleship group at the time of Jesus; a close reading of the text will enable a glimpse of a community of faith living some decades after the events narrated. In the Middle East one was welcomed into a house with the simple and necessary act of washing one's feet. John 13 introduces the reader to the inner dynamism of the household of Jesus and his disciples with the episode of the footwashing. This action, in its symbolism, is the fitting point of entry for the Johannine theology of the "hour."

There are many different views on the sources, history of development, and structure of John 13.[2] Alongside these differing views are opinions on

---

[1] An early form of this chapter was published in the *Catholic Biblical Quarterly* 66 (2004) 400–15. I am grateful to the editors for allowing me to use this article as the basis for this chapter.

[2] For a brief summary of the various approaches to John 13–17 within the past century see Fernando F. Segovia, *Love Relationships in the Johannine Tradition: Agape/Agapan in 1 John and the Fourth Gospel* (Missoula: Scholars Press, 1982) 82–96.

how to understand Jesus' act of footwashing. The text itself appears to offer two different interpretations:[3]

    i. vv. 6-11 promise understanding of the meaning later, a reference to a time after the events of Jesus' "hour" (see 2:22; 12:16). These verses also suggest that this act of footwashing enables the disciples to participate in Jesus' "hour."[4]

    ii. vv. 12-15 then appear to offer a second interpretation: that Jesus' action is a "model" of humble service that disciples are to emulate.

My aim here is to offer a way of reading the footwashing within the context of the farewell discourse and of the gospel as a whole.[5] This chapter continues the hermeneutical perspective governing this book, that the gospel has emerged from the living spirituality of the Johannine community, exploring its received traditions of Jesus in the context of their post-70 experience. I begin by establishing a structure for the chapter, then presenting a narrative reading of the text, and finally I offer an interpretation.[6]

Structuring the Narrative

The Prologue to the "Hour" (John 13:1-3)

The initial three verses of chapter 13 are a small prologue introducing the second part of the gospel, the "hour" of Jesus (chs. 13–20 [21]) and, more specifically, his final meal (13:1–17:26).[7] A number of key themes that appear in the Prologue of the gospel (1:1-18) are repeated here: Jesus' origins and destiny are clearly stated (1:1; 13:1, 3); mention is made of his

---

[3] Raymond E. Brown, *The Gospel According to John* 2:558–62; Francis J. Moloney, *Glory not Dishonor: Reading John 13–21* (Minneapolis: Fortress Press, 1998) 1–2. For a summary of the discussions on these two views see J. C. Thomas, *Footwashing in John 13 and the Johannine Community* (Sheffield: JSOT Press, 1991) 11–17.

[4] In R. Alan Culpepper's words, "The foot washing scene, therefore, functions metaphorically and proleptically in relation to Jesus' death." See Culpepper, "The Johannine *hypodeigma:* A Reading of John 13," *Semeia* 53 (1991) 133–52, at 139.

[5] For a discussion of the possible development of this passage from a pre-Johannine narrative to its current form see Jean Zumstein, *Kreative Erinnerung: Relecture und Auslegung im Johannesevangelium* (Zürich: Theologischer Verlag, 2004) 168–76.

[6] There is no agreement on the structure of this chapter. Although my proposal has been influenced by the work of Frédéric Manns, I differ from him in separating the action of the footwashing (vv. 4-5) from the subsequent discussion and about the final setting out of parallel units. See Manns, "Le Lavement des Pieds. Essai sur la structure et la signification de Jean 13," *RSR* 55 (1981) 149–69.

[7] So Manns, "Lavement," 151; R. Alan Culpepper, *The Gospel and Letters of John* (Nashville: Abingdon, 1998) 203.

own (*ta idia*, 1:11; *tous idious*, 13:1); the world of human existence is named (*kosmos*, 1:9, 10; 13:1) alongside the major adversaries, Jesus (13:1) and the devil (13:2), who were symbolized in the Prologue in the images of light and darkness (1:5). These verses, 13:1-3, are structurally united by the two references to time, namely, "before the feast of Passover" and "at a supper," by the theme of Jesus' knowledge, and by the parallelism between verse 1 and verse 3 in the theme of Jesus' departure to the Father/God (vv. 1, 3). The unit is as follows:

1. *Before the feast of the Passover*
   Jesus, *knowing* that his hour had come to depart from this *world to the Father*, having *loved* his own, who were in the *world, loved* them to the end.

2. *While at a supper*
   the devil had already made up his mind that Judas Iscariot, son of Simon, should betray him.[8] 3. [Jesus] *Knowing* that everything had been given into his hands by the Father and that he came from God and was going *to God . . .*

The meal ends with the prayer of Jesus, which echoes these same themes and establishes chapters 13–17 as a literary unit.[9]

O righteous *Father,* the *world* has not *known* thee, but I have *known* thee; and these *know* that thou hast sent me. I made *known* to them thy name, and I will make it *known,* that the *love* with which thou hast *loved* me may be in them and I in them (17:25-26).

The Footwashing

Following this "mini" prologue, the narrative proper starts with the action of Jesus washing the feet of his disciples. This action begins the description of Jesus' final meal and, in its symbolism, offers a theological

---

[8] The translation of this verse will be discussed below.

[9] Speaking of these chapters as a literary unit does not deny the complex development of the text. This development allows the author to write an initial draft or even drafts before achieving the final form of the narrative. A recent detailed study of the possible historical development of individual units can be found in Fernando F. Segovia, *The Farewell of the Word: The Johannine Call to Abide* (Minneapolis: Fortress Press, 1991), especially 283–329. John Painter, "The Farewell Discourses and the History of Johannine Christianity," *NTS* 27 (1981) 525–43, at 526, argues for three separate strata within the discourse material written in response to different crises faced by the community, 13:31–14:31; 15:1–16:4a; 16:4b-33. Whatever the historical origins of the material, the final form shows a unified literary structure that needs to include all of chapter 13.

introduction to the discussion and prayer that follow (13:6–17:26). The scene is described very sparsely in two parallel clauses:

[Jesus]

> (v. 4) rose from the supper *and* laid aside his garments *and* taking a *towel girded* himself;

> (v. 5) poured water into a bowl *and* began to wash the feet of his disciples *and* to dry them with the *towel* with which he was *girded*.

The rhythm of the two verses, each having three verbs joined by "and" (*kai*), and the use of "girded" (*diazōnnumi*) to conclude both verses, indicates that this is a unit, entire in itself.[10] The brevity of the description of the action is not unusual in this gospel, in which Jesus' deeds are termed *sēmeia* (2:11; 4:34), and a discourse follows the action to interpret the meaning of the *sēmeia*.[11] This pattern continues in chapter 13, where, following the footwashing, the rest of the chapter is primarily discourse and dialogue, showing a structure of reverse parallelism.

There are two major sections in chapter 13: verses 6-20 and verses 21-38; the first section moves from Peter to Judas, and the second moves in reverse from Judas to Peter. Central to both sections are Jesus' teaching and "gifts" of a model and a new commandment. The diagram below shows this structure:

a. Dialogue with Peter, vv. 6-11	a'. Dialogue with Peter, vv. 36-38
b. Teaching and "gift," vv. 12-15	b'. Teaching and "gift," vv. 31-35
c. The betrayer, vv. 16-20	c'. The betrayer, vv. 21-30

Although most commentators conclude the footwashing at verse 30, following the departure of Judas, there are sound structural and thematic reasons for including verses 31-38 within the footwashing pericope.[12] The departure of Judas makes a break between vv. 21-30 and what follows, but this break simply concludes the unit. Judas' departure sets in motion Jesus' arrest and crucifixion, which are presented in this gospel as the "hour" of Jesus' glorification (12:23). Judas' departure is the catalyst for Jesus' exultant

---

[10] Manns ("Lavement," 153) notes this parallelism and also that there is an *inclusio* formed by the verb *niptō* in vv. 6 and 10, but he considers vv. 4–11 a single unit.

[11] John 5 and 9 show a similar brief description of Jesus' actions leading into a long discourse.

[12] For arguments that tie vv. 31-38 to the discourse material see, e.g., Painter, "Farewell Discourse," 526, 529–30; Brown, *Gospel* 2:545–47; Segovia, *Love Relationships,* 136–79.

cry to the Father, and it follows that Jesus' words to the Father, with their theme of glorification, are necessarily linked to Judas' betrayal.

The discussion with Peter in verses 36-38, in which Peter queries Jesus' statement about following him, parallels the discussion in verses 6-11 in which Peter queries Jesus' action of washing his feet. The reference to the "giving" of the commandment in verse 34 recalls the giving of the *hypodeigma* ("example, model") in verse 15. Manns, too, argues for the unity of the entire chapter and points to an *inclusio* formed by the use of *tithēmi* in verses 4 and 38.[13] These structural features situate verses 31-38 within the footwashing narrative as the full pericope's conclusion. Verses 31-38 look back to the footwashing, and 14:1 initiates an *inclusio* with what follows, marked by the repetition of the phrase "Let not your hearts be troubled" (14:1, 27). Even though there is no change in scene, time, or characters, 14:1 marks the beginning of a new stage in the discourse.

a, a'. DIALOGUE WITH PETER

The emphasis in the first unit (13:6-11) is on Peter, and this is reflected in the final unit (vv. 36-38) as well. Formal aspects of the text in verses 6-11 are repeated in verses 36-38: "Simon Peter said to him, 'LORD'" (vv. 6, 36; cf. vv. 8, 37); "Jesus answered" (vv. 7, 36; cf. vv. 8, 38); "betray" (v. 11); "denied" (v. 38). The parallelism is shown not only in the structure of the dialogue between Jesus and Peter, but also in the indications of time—"now" (*arti*, v. 7; *nun*, v. 36) and "later" (*meta tauta hysteron*, vv. 7, 36)—and the failure of two of the disciples, Judas and Peter (vv. 10b-11, 38b).

6. Coming to *Simon Peter, he said to him*: "LORD, you wash my feet?"	36. *Simon Peter said to him*, "LORD, where are you going?"
7. *Jesus answered* and said to him: "What I am doing you do not understand *now*, but you will know *after*."	*Jesus answered*, "Where I am going you cannot follow me *now*; but you shall follow *later*."
8. *Peter said to him:* "You will never wash my feet." *Jesus answered* him: "Unless I wash you, you can have no part with me." 9. Simon Peter said to him: "LORD, not only my feet but also my hands and my head." 10. Jesus said to him: "Whoever has bathed has no need to wash, except for his feet, but is wholly cleansed; and you are cleansed, but not all." 11. For he knew who was *to betray* him: therefore he said, "not all are cleansed."	37. *Peter said to him*, "Why couldn't I follow you now? I will lay down my life for you." 38. *Jesus answered*, "You will lay down your life for me? Amen, amen, I say to you, the cock will not crow till you have *denied* me three times."

[13] Manns, "Lavement," 151.

b, b'. JESUS' TEACHING

The next sections begin with identical expressions, *hote oun* (vv. 12, 31), and introduce the idea of gift-giving. In verses 12-15 Jesus speaks of *giving* (*edōka*) a model, and he teaches, "what I have done, you also do" (v. 15). The parallel unit of verses 31-35 also concludes with Jesus' *giving* (*didōmi*) a new commandment, "love each other as I have loved" (v. 35). The two "gifts," *model* and *commandment,* link both units, as does the rhetoric also: "as I have done (*kathōs*) you also do" (vv. 15, 34); "wash each other's (*allēlōn*) feet" (v. 14); "love each other" (*allēlous,* v. 34).

| 12. *When he had* washed their feet, and taken his garment and reclined again, he said to them: "Do you know what I have done to you?

 13. You call me 'the teacher' and 'the master,' and you say rightly, for so I am.

 14. If I then, the master and teacher, wash your feet, *then you ought to wash each other's feet. 15. I gave you a model, that what I have done to you, you also do.*" | 31. *When he had* gone out, Jesus said, "Now the Son of Man is glorified, and God is glorified in him. 32. If God is glorified in him, God will glorify him in himself, and immediately glorify him. 33. Little children, I am with you a little while; you will seek me, but as I said to the Jews that where I go you are not able to go, now I say to you. 34. *A new commandment I give you,* that you *love each other; as I have loved you, so also you love each other.*
 35. In this everyone will know that you are my disciples, if you have love for each other." |

c, c'. THE BETRAYER

The pivotal units in each major part concentrate on Judas, the betrayer, and have solemn statements of Jesus introduced by "Amen, amen, I say to you" (vv. 16, 21). The *inclusio* formed by the double "amen" and the repetition of "the one who sent" (vv. 16, 20) indicate that verses 16-20 are a unit. Verse 30 has no double "amen," but the terse statement "So after receiving the morsel, he immediately went out; and it was night" (v. 30) brings to closure Jesus' words about betrayal in verse 21. In the center of both units the emphasis is on betrayal in the eating of bread (vv. 18, 26) where verse 26 fulfills the words of Ps 41:10 cited in verse 18.[14]

---

[14] The evangelist has altered the wording of the text of this Psalm. The LXX version (40:10) reads *ho **esthiōn** artous mou emegalunen ep' eme pternismon,* while the gospel reads *ho **trōgēn** mou ton arton epēren ep' eme tēn pternan autou.* The gospel's use of *trōgō* reflects Jesus' earlier teaching in 6:51c-58 and therefore makes the link between the morsel and the Eucharist. On this point see Moloney, *Glory not Dishonor,* 20–22. Maarten Menken analyzes the possible sources for the Johannine version of the psalm

16. *"Amen, amen,* I say to you, the slave is not greater than his master, or the one who is sent greater than the *one who sent* him.	21. After saying these things Jesus was troubled in spirit and testified and said, *"Amen, amen,* I say to you that one of you will betray me." 22. The disciples looked at each other puzzled about whom he spoke. 23. One of the disciples whom Jesus loved was lying close to the breast of Jesus, 24. so Simon Peter beckoned to
17. If you know these things, blessed are you if you do them.	him and said, "Ask him about whom he speaks." 25. So leaning back on the breast of Jesus, he said to him, "Lᴏʀᴅ, who is
18. I speak not about all of you: I know whom I have chosen: but so that the scripture might be fulfilled, *'One who ate my bread has lifted his heel against me.'*	it?" 26. Replying Jesus said, *"It is the one to whom I give this morsel when I have dipped it."* He dipped the morsel and gave it to Judas Iscariot son of Simon.
19. I say this to you before it happens, so that when it happens you may believe that I Aᴍ.	27. After the morsel, Satan entered into him then. Jesus said to him, "Do what you must quickly." 28. But no one reclining at
20. *Amen, amen,* I say to you, whoever receives anyone whom I send receives me, and whoever receives me, receives the *one who sent* me."	the table understood why he said this to him. 29. Since Judas had the common purse, some thought that Jesus had said to him, "Buy what we need to have for the feast," or that he should give something to the poor. 30. After taking the morsel he immediately went out. It was night.

Structurally the entire chapter can be shown thus:

Prologue to the "hour": vv. 1-3.	
Washing of the Feet: welcome to the final meal, vv. 4-5	
a. Dialogue with Peter, vv. 6-11	a'. Dialogue with Peter, vv. 36-38
b. Teaching and "gift," vv. 12-15	b'. Teaching and "gift," vv. 31-35
c. The betrayer, vv. 16-20	c'. The betrayer, vv. 21-30

A Narrative Reading of the Passage

A. *The Prologue to the "Hour"*

"Now before the feast of the Passover, when Jesus knew that his hour had come . . ." (13:1)

---

and concludes that it is the evangelist's own translation of the MT based on Jewish exegetical methods of the time; see Maarten J. J. Menken, "The Translation of Ps 41:10 in John 13:18," *JSNT* 40 (1990) 61–79, at 62–63.

Now the "hour" has come. Throughout the first part of the gospel there have been many mentions of a future time called the "hour" (2:4; 7:30; 8:20; 12:23, 27), which is now situated here within the context of love. As 12:27 noted, this "hour" brings to a climax the purpose of Jesus' life, which has already been described as a gift of divine love (3:16). Now the fullness of that love is to be shown.[15] The Prologue to the gospel said "he came to his own (*eis ta idia*), but his own did not receive him" (1:11); now he gathers the few of "his own" (*tous idious*) who have received him (13:1). These have been promised that they would be given the "power to become children of God" (1:12), and the mention of "his own" recalls this promise, even as the reader waits to see how the narrative will show this being accomplished. The expression "his own," with its evocation of intimacy, trust, and friendship, highlights the enormity of Judas' betrayal (13:2).

Verse 2 contains two serious textual and grammatical difficulties: (1) the time of the footwashing in relation to the meal, and (2) the identity of the one in whose *kardia* the treachery is conceived. The expression *deipnou ginomenou* does not necessarily mean that the meal has begun, and Rudolf Bultmann translates this phrase "on the occasion of a meal."[16] The meal may not yet have started, but the use of the term *palin* (again) in verse 12 indicates that all have taken their places at the table. If one accepts Bultmann's translation on grammatical and contextual grounds one could place the footwashing before the beginning of the meal. This interpretation makes better cultural sense, because it was customary for guests to have their feet washed prior to the meal (cf. Luke 7:44), and I will argue that this timing accords with the Gospel's christology.

R. Alan Culpepper recognizes in this verse a Semitic idiom; he translates "The devil had already made up his mind that Judas should betray him."[17] Culpepper's rendering makes clear that it is the *kardia* of the devil,

---

[15] At this point I am giving the expression *eis telos* its qualitative sense. The temporal sense of the root word is most profoundly revealed in Jesus' dying word, *tetelestai*, "it is finished" (19:30). According to Culpepper ("The Johannine *hypodeigma*," 136), "The *double entendre* serves the vital function of linking the footwashing to Jesus' death and interpreting Jesus' action as the culmination of his love for his own."

[16] Bultmann, *The Gospel of John,* 465 n. 2. In this note Bultmann also discusses a textual variant, *genomenou*, and explains it as a later scribal error or correction. Similarly Édouard Delebecque, *Évangile de Jean: Texte traduit et annoteé* (Paris: Gabalda, 1987) 183.

[17] Culpepper, "Johannine *hypodeigma*," 136; also Moloney, *Glory not Dishonor*, 13 n. 39. For a discussion on this grammatical form and its background in Hellenistic Greek see Delebecque, *Évangile de Jean,* 183, who states emphatically, "le coeur n'est pas celui de Judas, mais du diable" ("the heart is not that of Judas, but of the devil").

not of Judas, that is the object of *ballō eis*. This reading also makes sense of verse 27, which reports that Satan entered into Judas "after the morsel." The lapse in time between Satan's decision (v. 2) and action (v. 27) indicates that Satan's power has been undermined. It is the word of Jesus (vv. 21-26), not the decision of Satan, that instigates Judas' departure (v. 30). Satan may appear to be the "ruler of this world" (12:31; 16:11), but with the arrival of Jesus' "hour" judgment has already been passed.[18] Édouard Delebecque recalls that a compound of this same verb (*ekballō*) was used in 12:31 to announce the ultimate outcome of Jesus' "hour" in the judgment passed on "the ruler of this world."[19] It follows that the use of *ballō* in 13:2 referring to a decision of the devil may be read as high irony. Furthermore, Culpepper's translation sets up the contrast between the mind of Jesus (v. 1) and the mind of the devil (v. 2).

B. *The Footwashing*

In his full awareness of the "hour" (v. 1), Jesus acts with a solemn and deliberative gesture toward the disciples who have spent time with him. Laying aside his clothes (*tithēsin*), and girding himself with a towel, he washes the feet of the disciples, and the description of his "laying aside" and later "taking up" (*elaben*) his garments recalls the image of Jesus the Good Shepherd, who is able to "lay aside" (10:11, 15, 17, 18) and "take up" his life (10:17, 18). Sandra Schneiders comments: "Jesus is presented as acting in full awareness of his origin and destination, i.e., of his identity and mission as agent of God's salvific will and work in the world (13:1, 3). The introduction, therefore, makes it clear that what follows is not simply a good example in humility but a prophetic action."[20]

Footwashing in the NT culture was performed on occasions such as "(1) cultic settings, (2) domestic settings for personal hygiene and comfort, and (3) domestic settings devoted to hospitality."[21] By the first century C.E., while it may have been most unusual for a host to wash personally the feet of his guests, the action could be seen in the light of Abraham's hospitality. According to Frédéric Manns, footwashing had a particular religious significance within Judaism as it recalled the hospitality shown by Abraham

---

[18] Note the use of the perfect *kekritai* (has been judged) in 16:11.

[19] Delebecque, *Évangile de Jean*, 183.

[20] Sandra M. Schneiders, "The Foot Washing (John 13:1-20): An Experiment in Hermeneutics," *CBQ* 43 (1981) 76–92, at 81. The interpretation of this prophetic action will follow below.

[21] Thomas, *Footwashing*, 27; so also Arland Hultgren, "The Johannine Footwashing (13. 1-11) as Symbol of Eschatological Hospitality," *NTS* 28 (1982) 539–46, at 541.

in welcoming his divine guests under the oaks of Mamre (Gen 18:4).[22]
While the original Hebrew text portrayed Abraham merely providing water
for his guests to wash their own feet, the Septuagint suggests that someone
else washes their feet.[23] By the first century this tradition had developed to
present Abraham himself washing the feet of the guests as an act of gracious
hospitality.

Masoretic Text	Septuagint	Testament of Abraham
"Let a little water be brought to wash your feet, and rest yourselves under the tree." (Gen 18:4)[24]	"Let some water be brought and your feet be washed, and make yourselves cool under the tree." (Gen 18:4)	"Then Abraham went forward and washed the feet of the Commander-in chief, Michael. Abraham's heart was moved and he wept over the stranger." (T. Ab. 2:9).

According to Manns, *Targum Neofiti* has the same tradition as the
Testament of Abraham, where Abraham is the one who fetches water and
washes the feet while the strangers are only the active subjects of the following verb "to rest." In Genesis 18:4 the MT reads "Let a little water be
brought, and wash your feet, and rest yourselves under the tree." Manns'
rendering of this verse from *Targum Neofiti* is significantly different; here
Abraham says "I will go and get some water in order to wash your feet."
In this version Abraham, as the host, washes the feet of the travelers. Abraham's role in washing the feet of the divine messenger is brought out also
in the *Testament of Abraham*: "Then Abraham went forward and washed
the feet of the Commander-in chief, Michael. Abraham's heart was moved
and he wept over the stranger" (T. Ab. 2:9).[25] In his act of personally wash-

---

[22] Manns, "Le Lavement des Pieds."

[23] Thomas, *Footwashing*, 35.

[24] While the MT uses second person plural imperative "you (pl.) wash," the con-
sonantal text can also be read as a third person plural; see John William Wevers, *Notes
on the Greek Text of Genesis* (Atlanta: Scholars Press, 1993) 247. The third person would
continue the sense of the first verb, as in the above translation; see Claus Westermann,
Genesis 12–36: A Commentary, trans. John J. Scullion (Minneapolis: Augsburg, 1985)
273. Both Westermann (p. 278) and Gerhard von Rad note that Abraham's speech uses
the third person, avoiding the use of "I" and thus showing profound respect for his visi-
tors; see Gerhard von Rad, *Genesis: A Commentary* (London: SCM, 1972) 206.

[25] Although the Targumic evidence may not be conclusive because of difficulties in
dating, evidence of this tradition is found in the *Testament of Abraham* (dated 75–125
C.E.), thus in a Jewish pseudepigraphon contemporary with the Johannine community.

ing the feet of his guests, Abraham is established in the Jewish tradition as the great model of hospitality.[26]

These texts show that by the first century Abraham and his personal gesture of footwashing are established in the Jewish tradition as the epitome of hospitality.[27] Even though there is no explicit mention of Abraham in the Johannine footwashing, there may be clues to indicate that there are intertextual echoes from Genesis 18.[28] Both Genesis and John describe the host offering a small piece of bread, frequently translated as a "morsel." Abraham says "I will fetch a morsel of bread" (Gen 18:5). Following the footwashing, in the context of Judas' betrayal, Jesus offers him a morsel (13:26). Genesis and John both use the language of master/LORD (*kyrie*) and servant (*paida*, Gen 18:3; *doulos*, John 13:16). Although the Targums have dating difficulties and cannot provide conclusive evidence, *Neofiti* gives this scene a possible Passover context, for Sarah is told to make *unleavened* bread. "Hurry and take three seahs of fine flour, spread it and make unleavened bread" (*Tg. Neof Gen* 18:6).[29] Culturally, and within the Jewish religious traditions about Abraham, there is evidence to suggest that a first-century community would understand the Johannine footwashing primarily as a gesture of hospitality and welcome.

Footwashing also had a cultic purpose, for it was necessary to wash one's feet before entering the precincts of the Temple. The Mishnah records: "[A man] . . . may not enter into the Temple Mount with his staff or his sandal or his wallet, or with the dust upon his feet" (*m. Ber.* 9:5). This cultic purpose predates the compilation of the Mishnah, since the first-century Jewish philosopher Philo offers a number of comments on the practice of

For discussion of this dating see James Charlesworth, ed., *The Old Testament Pseudepigrapha.* 2 vols. (London: Darton, Longman & Todd, 1985) 1:875.

[26] J. T. Fitzgerald, "Hospitality," in Craig A. Evans and Stanley E. Porter, eds., *Dictionary of New Testament Background* (Downers Grove: InterVarsity Press, 2000) 522–25, at 522.

[27] Fitzgerald, "Hospitality," 522.

[28] In examining the possible scriptural echoes in the Pauline literature, Richard Hays proposes seven criteria to test the likelihood that the author is using such a technique: availability, volume, recurrence, thematic coherence, historical plausibility, history of interpretation, satisfaction. See Richard B. Hays, *Echoes of Scripture in the Letters of Paul* (New Haven: Yale University Press) 29–32. Five of these seven criteria are satisfied in trying to assess whether John 13 has possible echoes of Genesis 18: The text was available, there are other points of contact with the Abraham scene, there is coherence and satisfaction in understanding the footwashing as a gesture of hospitality, and it is plausible that first-century readers would understand it in this way.

[29] Martin McNamara, *Targum Neofiti 1: Genesis* (Edinburgh: T&T Clark, 1992) 104.

footwashing prior to entering the presence of God. In commenting on Exodus 12:3, 6, Philo explains that the keeping of the sacrificial lamb for four days was to ensure the proper piety of the one offering the sacrifice: "He who was about to offer sacrifice should first prepare his soul and body . . . for, according to the saying, one should not enter with unwashed feet on the pavement of the Temple of God" (*QE Sup* 2.1:2). In a treatise on special laws, commenting on the washing of the sacrificial victim, he transfers the significance of the washing to the person offering the sacrifice. "By the washing of the feet is meant that his steps should be no longer on earth but tread the upper air. For the soul (*psychē*) of the lover of God does in truth leap from earth to heaven and wing its way on high, eager to take its place in the ranks and share the ordered march of sun and moon and the all-holy, all-harmonious host of the other stars" (*Spec. Laws* 1.207). These comments indicate that footwashing was a customary gesture prior to entering the Temple in the first century, which the Mishnah will later encode.[30] The precedent for washing one's feet prior to entering the Temple was established in Moses' instructions that Aaron and his sons should wash their hands and feet prior to entering the Tent of Meeting or approaching the altar (Exod 30:17-21; cf. 2 Chr 4:6; Ps 25:6).

In discussing footwashing as a gesture of welcome into a house and also as the prelude to entering the Temple, the artistry of the Fourth Evangelist is apparent, for these two aspects of "house" and "Temple" come together in the Johannine theology. Following the footwashing in chapter 13, Jesus acts as the one sent and authorized by the Father to welcome his disciples into "my Father's house/hold" (14:2).[31] Since the term "my Father's house" carries the earlier sense of "Temple" from chapter 2:16, it is doubly appropriate that the disciples' feet are washed prior to entry.

a, a'. DIALOGUE WITH PETER

The meaning of this action is not clear to the disciples, and Peter's words could well voice the discomfort of the entire group: "LORD, *you* wash my feet?" Peter's difficulty is not with having his feet washed *per se*, but having them washed by Jesus. Peter perceives this as a degrading act for Jesus to perform, for it was customary in Peter's society that a slave would

---

[30] This same conclusion is reached by Herold Weiss with regard both to Hellenistic synagogue practice and also the Jerusalem Temple: ". . . the notion that in order to walk on the pavement of the temple disciples were supposed to have washed their feet was a well established and recognized one in the Judaism of the second temple"; see Weiss, "Foot Washing in the Johannine Community," *NovT* 21 (1979) 298–325.

[31] In the previous chapter I summarized the significance of the phrase "in my Father's house/hold" (14:2), showing its dual meaning as Temple and household.

bring a bowl of water and a person would wash his/her own feet.[32] This, however, is Peter's perception, not necessarily the perception of Jesus. The Fourth Evangelist frequently uses misunderstanding as a literary device, so Peter's view of the footwashing may be an instance of such misunderstanding. Jesus even states that this action will not be understood until a "later" time (v. 7).

The terminology of "now" and "later" requires an understanding of John's use of time as a tool in the development of his hermeneutical perspective. "Now" and "later" in this gospel are not simply references to time in a neutral sense; these terms have a rich theological purpose. On several occasions in the narrative thus far there have been indicators that the full understanding of their experience is not accessible to the participants in the story, but will be known only after Jesus' death and resurrection. "When therefore he was raised from the dead, the disciples remembered that he had said this and they believed the scripture and the word which Jesus had spoken" (2:22). The disciples did not understand at first, but after Jesus was glorified they remembered what had been written in the Scriptures and what had been done to Jesus (12:16; cf. 20:9). In both cases understanding occurs as a recollection, a remembering; both cases also involve the Scriptures. This retrospective understanding is seen as a particular function of the Paraclete, who will "teach you all things, and bring to your remembrance all that I have said to you" (14:26). It is only in the "later" post-Easter time, when the community has the gift of the Paraclete, that the fullness of understanding will be possible. This is a unique Johannine understanding of revelation, and it means that the post-Easter disciples (i.e., the Johannine community) continue to experience, in the Spirit, a revelation that the first disciples experienced in the person of Jesus. In fact, the post-Easter disciples can have access to even greater understanding than those first disciples. Jean Zumstein comments: "The Paraclete is the memory of Jesus grasped at the point of its fruition, the post-Easter retrospect upon the incarnate Christ."[33] In this pericope it is said that the disciples will grasp the meaning of Jesus' act of footwashing only after his death.

---

[32] In the scriptural instances a person usually washes his/her own feet, whereas in the Greco-Roman world this act of washing would be done by a slave. See Thomas, *Footwashing*, 35–42, 46–56.

[33] "Der Paraklet ist die im Vollzug begriffene Anamnese Jesu, die österliche Retrospektion des inkarnierten Christus." See Jean Zumstein, "Der Prozess der Relecture in der Johanneischen Literatur," *NTS* 42 (1996) 394–411, at 410. Zumstein also notes that the small prologue (13:1–3) establishes that the footwashing needs to be understood retrospectively in the light of "the hour." See also Zumstein, *Kreative Erinnerung*, 166.

In response to Peter's objection, Jesus begins to unfold the meaning *he* gives to this action. "Unless I wash you, you can have no part with me" (v. 8). The term used here, *meros*, implies the sense of "share in my inheritance," "participate with," or "be drawn into my destiny."[34] Footwashing is an invitation to the disciples to become participants with Jesus in his "hour." As he, with deliberate foreknowledge, moves from this world to the Father, they too are to be involved. That the term *meros* involves Jesus' future death, which in this chapter is presented as his departure to the Father (v. 1), is borne out in the parallel section. Jesus says to Peter: "Where I am going you cannot follow me now; but you shall follow after" (v. 36). The "now" is the "hour" of Jesus, but by having a "part/*meros*" with him, disciples will follow him "later," even a disciple who denies him (v. 38).

b, b'. TEACHING AND "GIFT"

The next unit (13:12-15) adds to the deeper understanding of the meaning of Jesus' action. Jesus instructs the disciples that they too should wash each other's feet, that what he has done is a "model" (*hypodeigma*)—though what he means by this is not yet clear. The term *hypodeigma*, in the New Testament, is only found here (John 13:15), in Hebrews (4:11; 8:6; 9:23), 2 Peter (2:6), and James (5:10). In these texts it is usually translated "example," which is commonly understood in ethical terms as a good example of humility.

In his discussion of the term *hypodeigma*, R. Alan Culpepper cites a number of passages in Jewish literature where the word is used "to exhort the faithful to mark an exemplary death."[35] Although an exemplary death is not the only sense of the term, there are indicators in the Johannine text suggesting that this meaning must be considered in the context of the footwashing. The opening verse of the chapter sets the scene at the "hour" of Jesus' departure to the Father. Jesus' action in laying aside (v. 4) and taking up (v. 12) his garments symbolically dramatizes his identity as the Good Shepherd who can lay down (10:11, 15, 17, 18) and take up (10:17, 18) his life. Jesus' appearance, girded with a towel, indicating a role reversal from master to slave, suggests that the model is only that of humble service; but the solemnity of the occasion, together with his words to Peter about having a "part with him," and the term *hypodeigma*, suggest a deeper meaning related to the cross. Here again it is important to take seriously Jesus' words to Peter: "What I do you do not understand now, but you will know later" (v. 7). It is still too soon to grasp the meaning of Jesus' actions.

---

[34] Brown, *Gospel* 2:565.

[35] 2 Maccabees 6:28, 31; 4 Macc 17:23; Sir 44:16. See Culpepper, "The Johannine *hypodeigma*," 142–43; also Heinrich Schlier, ὑπόδειγμα, *TDNT* 2 (1964) 32–33.

The term *hypodeigma*, as well as referring to an exemplary death, has another usage that I consider to be even more significant for understanding why the gospel uses this word to describe Jesus' action. What is meant by saying "I have given you a *hypodeigma*" (13:15)? In the OT background it appears that *paradeigma* and *hypodeigma* are interchangeable.[36] In the LXX we find *para/hypodeigma* used in two senses. It can be used to describe human behavior, and so Enoch is presented as an example of repentance (Sir 44:16) and similarly the Maccabean martyrs are held up as examples in their fidelity unto death (2 Macc 6:28, 31; 3 Macc 2:5; 4 Macc 6:19; 17:23).[37] This is the meaning discussed by Culpepper.

Apart from these usages, which refer to human behavior, there is a further use in which the term acquires the sense of a physical "model" or prototype from which something is to be copied. Moses is shown the pattern (*paradeigma*) of the heavenly tabernacle and its furniture, which he is to make (Exod 25:9). David gives Solomon the model (*paradeigma*) of the Temple he is to build (1 Chr 28:11, 12, 18, 19). Similarly, Ezekiel is shown a vision of the Temple as the model (*hypodeigma*) of the new house of God (42:15).[38] It is this meaning of *hypodeigma* as a prototype of the tabernacle and Temple that I believe lies behind the Johannine use.

Chapter 13 symbolically anticipates the crucifixion, as Zumstein notes: "the footwashing scene is a metaphor for the cross."[39] In welcoming disciples into his Father's household, Jesus proleptically draws them into his own divine sonship within his Father's household. What is acted out here in symbol will be realized at the cross. In his life and death Jesus is the Temple of his Father's presence. In the post-resurrection time the disciples, as children of the Father, will continue to be the dwelling place of God in history. Jesus is now the *hypodeigma* or prototype of the future house/hold of God, which his disciples will become through their having a part (*meros*) in his hour.

Through his death Jesus raises up the new house/hold of God, and his life provides the model on which future disciples will become this house/hold. The parallel unit (vv. 31-35) takes up this aspect of *hypodeigma*. Jesus calls his disciples "little children" (v. 33), which recalls both the promise that those who receive the incarnate Word would become children of God

---

[36] Schlier, ὑπόδειγμα.

[37] A similar sense relating to human behavior is found in Jer 8:2 and Nah 3:6, where the term is used in the sense of public shame or exposure.

[38] "When he had finished measuring the interior of the house, he led me out through the East gate and measured the model (*hypodeigma*) of the house around the outside (Ezek 42:15, author's own translation).

[39] Zumstein, *Kreative Erinnerung*, 174.

(1:12) and the characterization of Jesus' task as gathering God's "scattered children" (11:52). In this unit Jesus gives a new commandment to these little children to love one another as he has loved. The two instructions, featuring the verb *didōmi*, 13:15, 34, reciprocally interpret each other through their parallelism.[40] The action of Jesus in washing the feet of the disciples can now be seen as a model of loving "as I have loved." In both segments of these parallel statements Jesus is the model or standard he proposes to his disciples: wash each other's feet *as* I have done, love each other *as* I have loved. Read this way, the footwashing is an expression of love rather than just a good example of humble service. To the observer it may appear to be service, as it did to Peter, but in the experience of the one doing the deed it is love.[41] Furthermore, the placement of these two gifts highlights the extraordinary depths of Jesus' love. In the structure I propose, the two units (vv. 12-15 and 31-35), in which Jesus speaks of his actions in terms of a gift, are framed by a description of two of "his own" who receive these gifts: Peter, who will deny him (vv. 6-11, 36-38), and Judas, who will betray him (vv. 16-20, 21-30). Truly, here is love displayed *eis telos*, where love is given in the knowledge that those who receive it will fail. Such love is utterly gratuitous, given unreservedly—which shows that the dynamism of this love lies solely with the lover.[42] "It is precisely in his unconditional gift of himself to people who do not love him that Jesus reveals who he is and what he is doing. . . . Revealed here is God's love which transcends and challenges all human criteria and human experience."[43]

c, c'. THE BETRAYER

The pivotal units express the enormity of Judas' deed. Middle Eastern hospitality would require that even your enemy, if he has broken bread with

---

[40] Although he presents a different structure, Yves Simoens also emphasizes the parallelism of these two gifts and the importance of relating them to each other in the process of their interpretation. See Simoens, *La gloire d'aimer: Structures stylistiques et interprétives dans le Discours de la Cène (Jn 13–17)* (Rome: Biblical Institute Press, 1981) 92.

[41] Schneiders' work ("Foot Washing," 81–86) on "a phenomenology of service" has been particularly helpful in sharpening my interpretation of this text. She describes three models: (1) service between unequals, where one party has some rights over the other, (2) service given to another to meet some need within the one serving (even if this is an unconscious need), and (3) service between friends.

[42] Francis J. Moloney develops the three models of service proposed by Schneiders and suggests a fourth model: "a love unto death of friends who have betrayed and denied the one who loves still." See Moloney, "A Sacramental Reading of John 13:1-38," *CBQ* 53 (1991) 237–56, at 249 n. 4.

[43] Moloney, "A Sacramental Reading," 249.

you, should be safe within your home.[44] To turn against one who has welcomed you and given you bread to eat is the height of betrayal. The words of the psalm are fulfilled when Judas receives from Jesus the morsel of bread.[45] Judas is now aligned with Satan, and the powers of darkness close in. He leaves the presence of Jesus, the light of the world (8:12; 9:5), and goes out into the night (13:30). In terms of Middle Eastern hospitality, Judas leaves the meal as enemy.[46]

Interpreting the Footwashing as Welcome into God's Household

At this point I move from the *now* of the narrative time to the *later* of the post-Easter community and the time when Jesus promised that the disciples would understand the meaning of his action. Between *now* and *later*, the events of the "hour" intervene. Jesus completes his Passover to the Father, and in this moment draws his disciples into his own filiation, fulfilling the promise of the Prologue that believers would become children of God (1:12). From the cross the Nazarene Temple-builder raises up a new house(hold) of God in the new relationships formed between the mother of Jesus and the Beloved Disciple (19:25-28).[47] The reader, who has followed the narrative hints, realizes that this scene brings to completion the promises made across the gospel text.

From the first eighteen verses the evangelist begins to develop a metaphorical framework based on the Middle Eastern social structure of the "household." The relationship between Jesus and God is described as "father-son" (1:18), and believers are told that they will become "children" who will be "born of God" (1:13). This familial imagery continues throughout the gospel.[48] In his work on metaphor in John, Jan Van der Watt uses

---

[44] Bruce J. Malina, "The Received View and What It Cannot Do: III John and Hospitality," *Semeia* 35 (1986) 171–89, at 185. Malina comments (p. 183): "Frequently the ritual of footwashing marks the movement from stranger to guest (see Gen 18:4; 19:2; 24:32)."

[45] See n. 14 above on the eucharistic implications of the morsel. The term *psōmion* need not necessarily mean bread; it could also be a morsel of meat. However, given the link with Ps 41:10 and the use of *trōgō* with cross-reference to the discourse on the "Bread of Life" in 6:51c-58, *psōmion* is best understood as a morsel of bread.

[46] "The stranger-guest will leave the host either as friend or enemy" (Malina, "Received View," 186).

[47] The role of Jesus as the builder of the new Temple is developed in my earlier work, *God Dwells with Us*; on the Nazarene and the scene in 19:25-28 see pp. 171–74, 186–90.

[48] Klaus Scholtissek (*In Ihm sein und bleiben: Die Sprache der Immanenz in den johanneischen Schriften.* Herder's Biblical Studies 21 [Freiburg: Herder, 2000] 249, 267)

the expression "*Family* of the King";[49] I propose that the term *household* more accurately expresses the Johannine theology within its cultural context. Carolyn Osiek rightly points out that our experience of a nuclear family was not the experience in the biblical world; indeed, the Bible does not even have a word for family.[50] The closest expression in the MT to what we understand as family is the *beth ʾabh* ("father's house"), or, in the LXX, *oikos tou patrou*. This terminology is culturally more accurate and is also found twice within the Fourth Gospel (2:16; 14:2); I would therefore substitute "household" for "family" in Van der Watt's proposal. The meaning of the narrative of the footwashing for the community emerges from this vantage point of the community's self-perception as "the household of God" and of the new insight into Jesus' mission to reveal and make possible this household. For the disciples, footwashing is a proleptic experience of the welcome into the Father's household that will be accomplished at the cross.[51]

The parallelism between the two units (vv. 12-15 and vv. 31-35) brings together the footwashing, interpreted as a model, and the command that disciples love one another as Jesus has loved [them]. Jesus' love is demonstrated by the laying down of his life (15:13), which, I have argued, the footwashing symbolically enacts. Those who have a part (*meros*) in Jesus and are drawn into the household of his Father (14:2) will pattern their lives on Jesus' love, since loving after this pattern (*hypodeigma*) is what constitutes relationships within the household (15:9, 10). The footwashing in its entirety (vv. 3-38) may be described as a Johannine *sēmeion*, which the rest of the farewell discourse will interpret.

These final chapters 13–17, leading into Jesus' Passion, have the rhythm of a dinner with invited guests. Rather than present a detailed literary analysis of the structure here, I propose a simpler format in five phases:[52]

---

calls this "family-metaphor" the semantic axis of the gospel, presented first in 1:11-13 and returning in this image of the Father's *Hausgemeinschaft*.

[49] Jan Gabriël Van der Watt, *Family of the King: Dynamics of Metaphor in the Gospel According to John* (Leiden: Brill, 2000).

[50] Carolyn Osiek, "The Family in Early Christianity: 'Family Values' revisited," *CBQ* 58 (1996) 1–24, at 10–11. Similarly Halvor Moxnes, "What is Family? Problems in Constructing Early Christian families," in idem, ed., *Constructing Early Christian Families: Family as Social Reality and Metaphor* (London: Routledge, 1997) 13–41.

[51] Anticipating the formation of the Father's household, the disciples are called "children" during this meal (13:33).

[52] A formal literary structure can be found in a number of commentaries; see, e.g., Simoens, *La gloire d'aimer*, 52–76, with a summary on p. 77.

Phase 1. 13:1-3. Jesus gathers "his own" for a final meal.

Phase 2. 13:4-11. He washes their feet to welcome them into the household that his departure will form, namely "my Father's house" (see 14:2).[53]

Phase 3. 13:12-38. The disciples, including Judas, share food and Jesus gives these "little children" a paradigm of the Father's household through the requirement to love.

Phase 4. Chapters 14–16. As the meal progresses, Jesus offers final teaching and explains the meaning his death will have for the disciples.

Phase 5. Chapter 17. At the end of the meal Jesus prays that the disciples may share in the union between Father and Son (17:21-23).

According to Dennis E. Smith and Shemuel Safrai there are various features of this Johannine meal that are typical of the tradition of the Greco-Roman banquet or symposium.[54] Guests would come to the home; their feet would be washed; they would partake in a meal; there would be discussion; and finally, the host would conclude the meal with a hymn or prayer. In the OT, too, the most frequent occasion for footwashing, apart from cultic cleansings, is to welcome guests. "A common greeting in ancient Israel is to offer water to a guest and to invite him to wash his feet (Gen 18:4; 19:2;

---

[53] Christoph Niemand, *Die Fusswaschungserzählung des Johannesevangeliums: Untersuchungen zu ihrer Entstehung und Überlieferung im Urchristentum.* Studia Anselmiana 114 (Rome: Pontificio Ateneo S. Anselmo, 1993) 404–11, takes a similar approach, suggesting that the historical situation that gave rise to the need for a footwashing ritual within the Johannine community was the need to initiate and welcome the disciples of John the Baptizer, who had already undergone baptism.

[54] Shemuel Safrai, "Religion in Everyday Life," in Shemuel Safrai and M. S. Stern, eds., *The Jewish People in the First Century: Historical Geography, Political History, Social, Cultural and Religious Life and Institutions* (Amsterdam: Van Gorcum, 1976) 793–833, describes the following stages for the usual evening meal: ablutions, a blessing, the breaking of bread ("bread" standing for the whole meal), and a grace or blessing following the meal. He notes that some groups would meet for a communal meal with a discussion or lecture from their teacher. Among the elements noted by Dennis E. Smith (*From Symposium to Eucharist: The Banquet in the Early Christian World* [Minneapolis: Fortress Press, 2003] 222), the following apply to John 13: reclining at table (v. 23), washing the feet prior to reclining (v. 5), ranking at table (v. 23), discourse on an appropriate theme (chs. 14–16), and ending the meal with a hymn (ch. 17). Elsewhere (p. 153) Smith refers to a prayer at the conclusion of the meals at Qumran. See also Blake Leyerle, "Meal Customs in the Greco-Roman World," in Paul F. Bradshaw and Lawrence A. Hoffmann, eds., *Passover and Easter: Origin and History to Modern Times* (Notre Dame: University of Notre Dame Press, 1999) 29–61.

24:32; 43:24; Judg 19:21; 1 Sam 25:41; cf. 2 Sam 11:8) and to rest (Gen 18:4), spend the night (Gen 19:2), or accept food (Gen 24:32-33; Judg 19:21)."[55] Although Phase 3, the actual meal, is given only brief attention in John's narrative, it nevertheless remains a significant backdrop to the discussions: it is designated as the overarching context of what follows (v. 2), mention is made of dipping a morsel, probably bread (v. 26), and the beloved disciple is described as "reclining" close to the breast of Jesus (v. 23), which indicates the posture of one dining at a table. The evangelist's major interest is in Jesus' teaching, Phase 4 (chapters 14–16) and his prayer at the conclusion of the meal (chapter 17).[56]

The five phases listed above, which are typical components of the first-century meal, allow the footwashing to be seen for what it is—a gesture of welcome into "my Father's house/hold" (14:2).[57] Jesus, as the Son who intimately knows the Father's heart, is able to make this gesture of welcome on his Father's behalf. For commentators who come from a Western background, as I do, footwashing is not a common experience, but it is still such in many Middle-Eastern societies,[58] where it is understood primarily as an act of welcome. Although it is unusual for the host to perform this deed, the biblical tradition of Abraham's welcome to his guests emphasizes hospitality rather than humility. The primary perception of this act as a gesture of welcome would be taken for granted, even though, within narrative time, questions would still remain.[59] Welcome to what? Why is Jesus performing this action? What do his words mean?

---

[55] Hultgren, "Johannine Footwashing," 541. Hultgren also notes that the verb *niptein* (John 13:5, 7, 8, 10) is the same verb used to translate these examples of footwashing in the LXX.

[56] Recent commentators have appealed to the genre of a "farewell speech" or "testament" as the likely model that has been used in shaping these chapters. For a summary of this approach see Moloney, *John*, 376–78.

[57] Hultgren ("Johannine Footwashing," 542–43) comes to the same conclusion based on the normal use of footwashing in the OT. My work on the meaning of "my Father's house" (John 14:2) develops this insight further by showing how the narrative bears this out; see Coloe, *God Dwells with Us*, 160–64, 171–74, 185–90.

[58] Hultgren ("Johannine Footwashing," 546 n. 28) points out that footwashing as an act of hospitality has continued up to modern times in some cultures.

[59] Using a very different methodology, Niemand (*Fusswaschungserzählung*) comes to the same conclusion about the meaning of the footwashing. He proposes that the *Sitz im Leben* for this passage lies in the problem surrounding the disciples of John the Baptizer and how these disciples were to be received into the Johannine community. They had already received John's baptism of purification and so did not need a second baptism, but they did need a ritual of initiation to draw them into the Christian community (383). For these former disciples of the Baptizer, "die Fusswaschung . . . ihren Konnotationen

Conclusion

In laying aside his garments and donning the garb of a household servant, Jesus demonstrates the essential relationships within God's "household." There may be differences in roles and tasks, but there is an equality made possible by love. The example Jesus gives is not that of servitude, but of the depths of his love (13:1) and of God's love for us (3:16). The Fourth Gospel does not present Jesus as the "Servant of God" as do the Synoptics; Jesus is rather the Shepherd-King who freely lays down his life for love of his friends (15:13). To the outside observer love may appear to be service, as it can also seem to be duty; but the experience of love transcends and transforms service and duty.[60] This is why the attitude of love among disciples is so critical, for love is the essential dynamism of any household. At one level Jesus' relationship with his disciples remains that of teacher and master, but as the "hour" approaches there is a deeper level of loving intimacy that he now reveals, knowing that it will not be understood until *later.*

As the Prologue announced, Johannine christology is incarnational (1:14), making possible the transformation of humanity into "children of God" (1:12). As Jesus gathers his own, the process of his "hour" begins, and Jesus enacts a loving welcome into the Father's household with the simple, homely implements of a towel, a basin, and water.

---

gemäss, für Wertschätzung und *Aufnahme* in Haus und Gemeinschaft der Gemeinde steht und zudem den Aspekt des *Freuden- und Hochzeitsmahles* evoziert" ("Footwashing . . . in its connotations, represents esteem and *acceptance* into the house and society of the community, and also evokes the aspect of *the meal of rejoicing and nuptials*") (p. 384; emphasis in original). Footwashing was thus a welcoming ceremony.

[60] "By the foot washing Jesus has transcended and transformed the only ontologically based inequality among human beings, that between him and us." See, Schneiders, "Foot Washing," 87.

Dwelling in the Household of God

JOHN 14:1–15:17

What is enacted in the footwashing is explained and developed in the discourse that follows across chapters 14–16 and is the theme of Jesus' final prayer in chapter 17. In the footwashing, disciples participate in a ritual act of welcome into the household of Jesus and his Father. In chapter 2 the dwelling place of God was named "my Father's house" (2:16), and in chapter 14 this terminology returns with a deeper, personalized image that more properly is named "my Father's household." The incorporation into the divine household will occur at the cross, but disciples, by their participation in the ritual of footwashing, anticipate the gift that will be fully accomplished in the post-Easter time. John 14 presents an elaborate exposition of the Johannine theology of the cross as the foundation of the household of God. In John 19:26-27 a few verses narrate the moment when the Beloved Disciple is drawn into Jesus' own sonship through the change of relationship with Jesus' mother. "Woman, behold your Son . . . behold your mother." This verse names a change in the relationship between Jesus and disciples, who now shift from being "friends" (15:14), to being sisters and brothers of Jesus (cf. 20:17), and therefore children of God (cf. 1:12).[1] All the promises of the gospel reach their fulfilment in this scene, disciples are born anew (3:3), born of the Spirit (3:5). As the blood and water testify to Jesus' death (19:34), they also bear witness to a moment of birth;[2] as one

[1] Mary Coloe, *God Dwells with Us*, 186–90.
[2] On the "birth" symbolism of the blood and water see Dorothy Lee, *Flesh and Glory*, 82, 152–59.

Temple is destroyed, a new Temple is raised up. The discourse of John 14:1–15:17 anticipates this narrative.

The Household Metaphor

"In my Father's house/hold are many dwellings" (14:2). This statement begins the rich and evocative theme of Johannine mutual immanence between Father and Son, and Jesus and believers, through the indwelling gift of the Paraclete. I have developed the structure and theology of John 14 in my earlier work,[3] and so this chapter will not repeat the earlier study but will briefly revise some of its major findings and offer further development in the light of recent European scholarship.

The verb *menō* was used in the introductory gathering of the disciples who asked Jesus, "Where do you dwell (*pou meneis*)?" (1:38). In response to his invitation to come and see, the disciples dwelt (*emeinan*) with him that day (1:39). Dwelling with Jesus is the first and primary activity of disciples. Later, the Samaritan villagers ask Jesus to dwell (*menai*) with them and he remains (*emeinen*) there for two days (4:40). In these episodes the verb *menō* begins to reveal its particular meaning to express the Johannine theology of immanence. The faith of disciples is expressed by their being drawn into the place where Jesus dwells (1:39), and Jesus responds to the faith of the Samaritans by dwelling with them (4:40).

In John 14 the verb *menō* occurs in four verses to describe the activity of God.

- v. 10: the Father dwells in (*menōn en*) Jesus.[4]

- v. 17: the Paraclete now dwells (*menei*) with believers and in the future will be in (*estai en*) them.

- v. 23: the Father and Jesus will make their dwelling with (*monēn para*) the believer.

- v. 25: Jesus dwells with (*menōn para*) the disciples.

These verses speak of a future dwelling of the Father, Jesus, and the Paraclete with believers. The Temple, which was once conceived as the divine dwelling place, i.e., "my Father's house" (2:16), is now reimaged, for in the future the dwelling of God will be the Christian community. In the terminology "my Father's house," Temple and household themes are intertwined, for consistently across the Old Testament the term "my father's

---

[3] Coloe, *God Dwells with Us*, ch. 8.

[4] This verse is followed by a statement of reciprocal immanence of Father and Son using the verb "to be" (*eimi*): "I am in the Father and the Father is in me" (v. 11).

house" refers to people considered part of the household. This includes the *paterfamilias* with his wife (wives), married sons, unmarried daughters, relatives, clients, dependent slaves, as well as future descendants.[5] "My Father's house" is simultaneously the Temple of the divine dwelling and the household of God. John 14 introduces the concept of God's dwelling with the verbal noun *monē* (dwelling) and the idiom "my Father's house/hold." Together these two expressions constitute a rich metaphorical field that will be developed in chapters 14 and 15.

Klaus Scholtissek's work on the Johannine theology of immanence came out around the same time as my own.[6] His fine study offers a number of insights that enrich and support my earlier presentation. He argues that there is a close correlation between John 14 and the earlier confrontation between Jesus and "the Jews" in chapter 8, where Jesus challenges their claim to be Abraham's children (8:39).[7] In this context Jesus says to them: "the slave does not dwell in the household for eternity (*ho doulos ou menei en tē oikia eis ton aiōna*); the son dwells for eternity (*ho huios menei eis ton aiōna*)" (8:35). This confrontation takes place in the Temple, "my Father's house," but Jesus is warning those who will not accept his words that they, like the slave, will not have a permanent place within the household. Only those who are free, who keep Jesus' words as his disciples, can form a lasting household with the Son and the Father. Scholtissek argues that John 14 is a revised and developed form (*réécriture*) of John 8:12-59.[8] The farewell discourse in John 14 develops the household image of 8:35 in an extended metaphor describing the dwelling of the Father, Son, and Paraclete with the believers in the post-Easter time.[9] The one point on which I disagree with Scholtissek is when and where this household is to be actualized. For Scholtissek the metaphor speaks to a future-eschatological heavenly dwelling, "the post-mortal completion of the paschal Christian life."[10]

---

[5] Frank-Lothar Hossfeld, "Die alttestamentliche Familie vor Gott," in Josef Schreiner, ed., *Freude am Gottesdienst: Aspekte ursprünglicher Liturgie.* (Stuttgart: Katholisches Bibelwerk, 1983) 218.

[6] Scholtissek, *In Ihm sein und bleiben.*

[7] On this conflict based on "paternity" see Coloe, "Like Father, Like Son," 1–11; also *God Dwells with Us*, 138–42.

[8] Scholtissek, *In Ihm sein und bleiben*, 241–44. He presents points of contact between the two passages to show their intertextual relationship. For his description of the two literary processes of *réécriture* and *relecture*, see ibid. 131–39. Briefly, *réécriture* is a synchronic development of previously introduced material. The author returns to an earlier theme and develops it further. *Relecture* is both a synchronic and a diachronic elaboration of an earlier theme, rewritten to meet the needs of a later community situation.

[9] Ibid. 244.

[10] Ibid. 271.

I have argued that the metaphor describes the present participation in Jesus' divine filiation and present communion of life with God, initiated at the cross in the raising of the new Temple/household of God.[11] By understanding the Johannine crucifixion as the place where Temple and household symbolism come together, one has no need to project the metaphor of dwelling in the Father's household to a future eschatological heavenly reality. The whole point of the farewell discourse is to assure the disciples that the departure of Jesus will not leave them orphans (14:18), but will simultaneously bestow the Paraclete upon them, enabling believers of all times to experience the indwelling of God.

The household metaphor is developed further in John 15:1-17 with the introduction of a new image: the vine. Together these two images offer the distinctly Johannine perspective on salvation as a communion of life formed by the mutual indwelling of God and the believer. "On that day you will know that I am in my father, and you in me, and I in you" (14:20). Where chapter 14, using the image of the household/Temple of God, describes a series of divine indwellings, chapter 15 focuses on the indwelling of the believer in Jesus. Before I offer an analysis of John 15 it is necessary to give my understanding of the relationship between 13:1–14:31 and what follows. While my primary methodology is narrative criticism, the apparent disjunction created by Jesus' words, "Rise, let us be on our way" (14:21), begs some explanation.

John 15:1-17 Within the Farewell Discourse

The complexity of the farewell discourse means that there is great variety of opinions among scholars about the limits of individual sections, the history of the tradition behind these sections, and therefore the purpose of individual sections within the discourse and the gospel as a whole. The following views provide a sample of scholarly opinions on the position of John 15:1-17 in the discourse.[12]

- Rudolf Bultmann suggests the following as the original sequence, which has been dislocated to give the current arrangement: 13:1-30; 17; 13:31-35; 15; 16; 13:36–14:31. Thus Bultmann proposes that 15:1-17 follows directly after the love command in chapter 13.[13]

---

[11] Coloe, *God Dwells with Us*, ch. 9; eadem, "Raising the Johannine Temple," 47–58.

[12] For a detailed discussion of scholarly views see Segovia, *Love Relationships*, 82–101.

[13] Bultmann, *Gospel of John*, 523.

- In 1967 Rainer Borig presented a study in which he argued that John 15–17 is an alternative version of John 13:31–14:31, and within that alternative 15:1-10 is a distinct unit.[14]

- Raymond E. Brown's study of John 12–21 appeared in 1970, and Brown's conclusion was similar to Borig's in that John 15–17 constitutes a second addition to an original discourse. Brown differs from Borig in delineating three distinct subdivisions within these additional chapters and continuing the section on the vine imagery to verse 17, giving the following divisions: 15:1-17; 15:18–16:4a; 16:4b-33.[15]

- Rudolf Schnackenburg also identifies 15:1-17 as a subsection, but places it within a larger literary unit, 15:1–16:4a.[16]

In considering the relationship between chapters 15–17 and 13–14, recent European scholarship has been using the expressions *réécriture* and *relecture*. Jean Zumstein,[17] Andreas Dettwiler,[18] and Klaus Scholtissek[19] have applied these literary and hermeneutical understandings in their analysis of the gospel.[20] What these new approaches add to earlier suggestions of different versions (Borig) and additions (Brown) is a more developed hermeneutical theory of a community guided by the Paraclete reinterpreting the Scriptures and their own tradition.[21] Moloney's summary of the process

---

[14] Rainer Borig, *Der Wahre Weinstock, Untersuchungen zu Jo 15: 1-10*. SANT 16 (Munich: Kösel, 1967) 19.

[15] Brown, *Gospel* 2:658.

[16] This is the position of John Painter, "Farewell Discourses," 526. Yves Simoens and Francis J. Moloney have the larger unit conclude at 16:3 rather than 16:4a; see Simoens, *La gloire d'aimer*, 42–43, and Moloney, *Glory not Dishonor: Reading John 13–21*, 56–59.

[17] Zumstein, *Kreative Erinnerung*, 15–30.

[18] Dettwiler, *Die Gegenwart des Erhöhten: Eine exegetische Studie zu den johanneischen Abschiedsreden (Joh 13,31–16,33) unter besonderer Berücksichtigung ihres Relecture-Charakters* (Göttingen: Vandenhoeck & Ruprecht, 1995) 46–52.

[19] Scholtissek, *In Ihm sein und bleiben*, 131–39. Where Scholtissek relates 15:1-17 to John 8 and the saying about the son and slave in the household, Dettwiler argues that this passage is a *relecture* of the footwashing in 13:1-17.

[20] A helpful summary of these two processes can be found in Brown, *Introduction to the Gospel of John*, 291–92.

[21] The role of the Paraclete as the guide in the process of reflection and rearticulation of both the Scriptures and earlier aspects of the gospel tradition is described by Zumstein: "The Paraclete brings no new revelation, but reduplicates the eschatological event. He is the concrete remembrance of Jesus, the paschal retrospective of the incarnate Christ. He guides the *relecture* of the Jesus tradition." See Zumstein, *Kreative Erinnerung*, 29.

of *relecture* as articulated by Zumstein, Dettwiler, and Scholtissek is as follows:[22]

    i. *Relecture* is an intertextual phenomenon that must be analyzed both synchronically and diachronically.

    ii. The reread text (*der Rezeptionstext*) looks back on the original text (*der Bezugstext*) for its original meaning, which it has further developed.

    iii. *Relecture* happens in the twofold action of further developing the original text and applying it to a different context.

    iv. The final text is always to be understood as a rereading of the original text.

    v. The reasons for *Relecture* may, on the one hand, be a need for the further theological development of an original theological position within the narrative itself (synchrony), or on the other hand may be called for because of a new historical or social situation of the community (diachrony).

    vi. The question of authorship plays little or no part in understanding the process of *Relecture*.

The process of reinterpreting and revising earlier forms of the narrative does not necessarily require different authors. There is no need to postulate an original evangelist and a later editor when considering John 1–20. Even allowing for the process of *relecture*, the entire narrative could have been formulated by the creative theological reflection of one mind. The unity of theme, style, and theological perspective across these chapters, in my opinion, argues for one author,[23] even though this author may have returned to his original narrative to offer further development in responding to the needs of his community. In the following discussion I read chapters 13–17 as a coherent narrative. As Segovia writes, "The present text of the farewell speech undoubtedly did represent to someone, somewhere, at some time, not only a unified and coherent literary whole but also a proper and meaningful form of communication."[24] Although some sections may be a later reformulation of an earlier discourse, I make no attempt to reconstruct a hypothetical historical situation that might have been the stimulus for these later reflections.[25] Instead, I postulate sections of the text based on their internal themes.

---

[22] Brown, *Introduction to the Gospel of John*, 291.

[23] "All the units of discourse could well have come from one individual who responded to a variety of different rhetorical situations with different strategies." See Segovia, *Farewell of the Word*, 320.

[24] Ibid. 48.

[25] One such reconstruction can be found in John Painter, "Farewell Discourses," 525–43. Painter bases his historical hypotheses on the three Paraclete sections found

There are two primary reasons why the majority of scholars takes 15:1–17 as a distinct unit: first, the language associated with the vine, its branches, and fruit in verses 1-8 recurs in verse 16 as a way of expressing Jesus' teaching in verses 9–15. This language drawn from viticulture then disappears from the rest of the discourse; second, verses 1–17 focus on the internal relationships between Jesus and the disciples while, beginning with verse 18, the remaining part of the discourse involves the relationship of disciples with the outside world.[26]

Structure of 15:1-17

If we accept 15:1-17 as a distinct unit, the next point of discussion is the unit's internal arrangement. Along with a number of scholars, I detect a parallelism across these verses, forming two major units: verses 1-8 and verses 9-17.[27] Verses 1 and 9 take their starting point in the relationship

---

across the discourse. He suggests the original discourse, 13:31–14:31, followed by a first revision, 15:1–16:4a, followed by a second revision, 16:4b-33. Chapter 17 is new material and not a revision of earlier material. Segovia also postulates a development in three stages, but with 15:1-17 as a final stage. His suggestion is: Stage 1, 13:31–14:31; Stage 2, 15:18–16:33 (with two small subdivisions); Stage 3, 15:1-17. Stage 2 emerges in a situation of tension and conflict with the outside world, particularly with post-70 Judaism, while Stage 3 reflects intramural tension and the possibility of community rupture; see Segovia, *Farewell of the Word*, 319–28. Along similar lines, Dettwiler also makes the cautious suggestion that the pericope 15:1-17 arose out of a need to reaffirm the community's self-identity in the time after the destruction of the Temple; Dettwiler, *Die Gegenwart des Erhöhten*, 100–107. In a situation of mounting tension with the synagogue the text functions to remind believers that their identity rests solely on their relationship to Jesus, and also that this relationship is conditional on their remaining faithful (102). Dettwiler discusses the work of Klaus Wengst, *Bedrängte Gemeinde und verherrlichter Christus. Ein Versuch über das Johannesevangelium* (Munich: Kaiser, 1990) and his critics and, while not fully accepting the details of Wengst's position, he agrees with his general proposal and states his own position: Historically we presuppose only the hypothesis of an extremely strained relationship between the Jewish synagogue and the Johannine community (106). This represents my own position regarding the historical situation of the gospel generally.

[26] As well as Brown, some other scholars who read vv. 1-17 as a distinct unit are Barnabas Lindars, *The Gospel of John*. NCB (London: Oliphants, 1972) 486; C. K. Barrett, *Gospel According to St John,* 470; Jürgen Heise, *Bleiben. Menein in den johanneischen Schriften*, HUT 8 (Tübingen: J. C. B. Mohr [Paul Siebeck], 1967) 81; Segovia, *Farewell of the Word*, 125–127; Sharon H. Ringe, *Wisdom's Friends: Community and Christology in the Fourth Gospel* (Louisville: Westminster John Knox, 1999) 65–66; Dorothy Lee, *Flesh and Glory*, 92; and Scholtissek, *In Ihm sein und bleiben*, 276–77.

[27] See, for example, Bultmann, *Gospel of John*, 529; Segovia, *Farewell of the Word*, 126; Scholtissek, *In Ihm sein und bleiben*, 276–77.

between Jesus and the Father "I am the vine and my father is the vine-dresser"; "As the Father has loved me. . . ." Verse 8 brings to a conclusion the development of the vine imagery established in verse 1, while verse 9 introduces the motif of "love," which extends through verses 9-17 (vv. 9, 10, 12, 13, 17).[28] In verses 14-15 the word "love" disappears and is replaced by "friend," which, according to Brown, is a term very close to "beloved" and so may be considered synonymous.[29] As well as the vine image in verses 1-8, these verses are also united by the constancy of the term *menein* (dwell/remain) (vv. 4[3x], 5, 6, 7[2x]).[30] Within the two major sections verses 1-8 and verses 9-17, the initial verses (vv. 1-3b; 9-11) establish a "model" that the rest of the section develops and applies to the disciples. Both these small units conclude with the expression "I have spoken to you," and in the second section verses 12-17 are established as a unit, with the love command stated in verse 12 and then repeated in verse 17.

Part A	Part B
vv. 1-3b: Image: the vine	vv. 9-11: Model: the Father and Jesus
vv. 4-8: application to disciples	vv. 12-17: application to disciples

Closer examination of the text reveals further balancing of ideas and language across both sections. In verse 4 and verse 12 there is a strong imperative tone coupled with a statement of a reciprocal relationship between Jesus and disciples. In verse 4 the imperative mood is used, "remain in me as I in you"; in verse 12 the imperative continues in the commandment to "love one another as I have loved you." Verses 5 and 14 describe the relationship between Jesus and the disciples in terms of a new identity, "you are the branches," "you are my friends." Verses 7 and 16 express the consequence that will follow if the disciples act on Jesus' words; this consequence is that whatever is asked will be given: "you may ask whatever you desire and it will be done," "whatever you ask the Father in my name he will give you." The parallelism across these verses is shown in the following table:

---

[28] The vine imagery appears again in v. 16, but it is not developed any further.

[29] Brown, *Gospel* 2:664 n. 13; also Ringe, *Wisdom's Friends*, 65, and Lee, *Flesh and Glory*, 99.

[30] Moloney (*Glory not Dishonor*, 56–57) sees the term "dwell" (*menein*) as the controlling theme of the passage rather than the imagery of the vine. While agreeing with him that the "metaphor is not an end in itself but serves as a vehicle to articulate the importance of abiding" (ibid. 58), I believe the parallelism across the section requires the first major break after v. 8 rather than after v. 11.

A. vv. 1-8	**B. vv. 9-17**
Image 1. I am the true vine and my Father is the vinedresser 2. Every branch in me not bearing fruit he cuts away and every branch bearing fruit he prunes so it bears more fruit.	*Image* 9. Just as the Father has loved me, so have I loved you. Dwell (*meinate*) in my love. 10. If you keep my commandments you will dwell in my love, just as I have kept my Father's commandments and dwell in his love.
Aside[31] 3. You are pruned now by the word I have spoken to you.	*Aside* 11. This I have spoken to you so that my joy may be in you and your joy may be fulfilled.
Teaching imperative: remain in me 4. Dwell (*meinate*) in me and I in you. Just as the branch is unable to bear fruit by itself unless it remains (dwells, *menē*) in the vine, neither can you unless you dwell (*menēte*) in me.	*Teaching imperative: love one another* 12. This is my commandment; love one another just as I have loved you. 13. Greater love than this has no one than to lay down his life for his beloved/friends.
Disciples: you are the branches 5. I am the vine, **you are the branches.** The ones dwelling in me and I in them bear much fruit, for apart from me you can do nothing. 6. If anyone does not dwell in me s/he is cast out as a branch and withers, and is gathered up and thrown into the fire and burned. 7. If you dwell (*meinēte*) in me and my words dwell (*meinē*) in you,	*Disciples: you are my friends/beloved* 14. **You are my friends** if you do what I have commanded. 15. No longer do I call you servants, for the servant does not know what his master does. I have called you friends because everything I heard from my Father I made known to you. 16. You did not choose me, but I chose you and appointed you that you go and bear fruit, fruit which remains (*menē*),
Consequences[32] you may **ask whatever you wish and it will happen.**	*Consequences* so that whatever you **ask** the Father in my name **he will give you.**
Climax 8. In this my Father is glorified: that you bear much fruit and thus be my disciples.	*Climax* 17. This I command you: love one another.

[31] In his earlier work (*Love Relationships*, 101, 110) Segovia used the term "aside" to describe the function of vv. 3 and 11; his later work (*Farewell of the Word*, 138, 150) ties v. 3 to his next subsection, vv. 3-7, and v. 11 is linked to a smaller subsection, vv. 9c-11. I believe his earlier assessment was correct for the following reasons. With the repetition of the expression "I have spoken to you" a parallelism is established between v. 3 and v. 11. In v. 3 Jesus turns from the vine imagery to address the disciples for the first time, but his words about being "pruned now" are not developed any further; then in v. 4 dwell (*menein*) is used and this term is developed through to v. 7. Similarly, v. 11 makes a statement about joy, but this also is not developed in the following verses, while the words "love" and "commandment" are. Thus vv. 3 and 11 stand apart as expressions of

Literary Genre

The imagery of the vine and branches is difficult to categorize. In his review of previous scholarship Fernando Segovia notes that the image has been variously classified as *Bildrede, mashal*, extended metaphor, parable, and allegory.[33] Segovia favors the expression "sustained metaphor," while the complexity of the imagery in 15:1-8 leads Jan van der Watt to speak of a "metaphorical network."[34] Van der Watt provides the following functional description of a metaphor: "two lexical items of disparate meanings are linked on the basis of some form of comparison, with specific semantic implications."[35] A metaphor draws together in one statement two different realities while inviting the reader to see "an intuitive perception of the similarity . . . in dissimilars."[36] When Jesus says "I am the true vine," a metaphor is formed and the reader is expected to puzzle over what aspects of a vine could relate to a human person and what aspects of a human person could relate to a vine. The incongruity of comparing a person with a vine sets up a tension that opens up the possibility for the reader to transcend the literal meaning and enter into a new, creative perception of reality.

Perhaps the only way to classify this example of Johannine imagery is to use the term the gospel itself uses, "I have said this to you in figures (*paroimiais*)" (16:25; see also 10:6; 16:29).[37] According to Van der Watt the term *paroimia* implies a "double vision" or "two realities," which is very close to the way he describes metaphor.[38] The gospel has certainly demanded that readers have a "double vision" when it uses expressions such as "born again" (3:3, 5) or "living water" (4:10). In these expressions, Jesus speaks from the perspective of his mission as the incarnate Son sent from the Father

---

a single idea that is mentioned and then left. The term "aside" correctly describes this type of expression.

[32] The terms "consequences" and "climax" are also taken from Segovia (*Love Relationships*, 107).

[33] Segovia, *Farewell of the Word*, 133–34. See also the summary table in Van der Watt, *Family of the King*, 29.

[34] Ibid. 125.

[35] In his analysis of metaphor in John, Van der Watt provides an extended discussion of the meaning and types of metaphor; see *Family of the King*, 6–24; the quotation is from p. 6.

[36] Paul Ricoeur, *The Rule of Metaphor: Multidisciplinary Studies of the Creation of Meaning in Language* (London: Routledge & Kegan Paul, 1977) 23.

[37] Klaus Scholtissek describes these verses as a unique Johannine form that is *sui generis,* and suggests it can only be compared to other Johannine "figurative language" such as the shepherd and sheepfold material in ch. 10. See Scholtissek, *In Ihm sein und bleiben*, 278. He reads 15:1-8 as a *relecture* of 10:1-18.

[38] Van der Watt, *Family of the King*, 158–60.

"that the world might be saved" (3:17), while the characters in the narrative can only understand his words in their literal sense.

John 15:1-17 as *Relecture* of 14:1-31

As we examine the relationship between 15:1-17 and the preceding chapters, the process of *relecture* offers a helpful way of explaining both the disjunction at 14:31—"Arise, let us go"—and the repetitions of themes and words particularly across chapters 14 and 15:1-17. I offer the following hypothesis.

Within chapter 14 there are three occasions where disciples interrupt Jesus' discourse, revealing their lack of comprehension. Thomas says: "Lord, we do not know where you are going. How can we know the way?" (v. 5), Philip says: "Lord, show us the Father, and we will be satisfied" (v. 8), and Judas (not Iscariot) wonders: "Lord, how is it that you will reveal yourself to us, and not to the world?" (v. 22). In narrative time these are issues raised by disciples prior to Easter, but their questions may also voice issues faced by the post-Easter believers who, puzzled by the delay of the *parousia* and troubled by tension with their Jewish heritage, are forced to clarify their own religious identity and to make a clear choice for Jesus. In chapter 14 an initial response is made to each of these interjections. In response to Thomas, Jesus affirms: "I am the way, and the truth, and the life. No one comes to the Father except through me" (14:6). To Philip's request that he reveal the Father, Jesus says, perhaps with a degree of exasperation, "Have I been with you all this time, Philip, and you still do not know me? Whoever has seen me has seen the Father. How can you say, 'Show us the Father'? Do you not believe that I am in the Father and the Father is in me? The words that I say to you I do not speak on my own; but the Father who dwells (*menōn*) in me does his works. Believe me that I am in the Father and the Father is in me" (vv. 10-11). And to Judas, Jesus replies: "Those who love me will keep my word, and my Father will love them, and we will come to them and make our dwelling (*monēn*) with them" (14:23).

In chapter 15 a number of the themes in Jesus' responses to these interjections are repeated and developed further, particularly in verses 9-17.

[to Philip] 14:10 Do you not believe that **I am in the Father and the Father is in me** (*egō en tō patri kai ho patēr en emoi estin*)? The words that I say to you I do not speak on my own; but **the Father who dwells in me** (*ho patēr en emoi menōn*) does his works. 14:11 Believe me that **I am in the Father and the Father is in me;** (*egō en tō patri kai ho patēr en emoi estin*).	15:10 just as I have kept my Father's commandments and **dwell in his love** (*menōn aotou en tē agapē*). 15:15 everything I heard from my Father I made known to you

14:13 I will do **whatever you ask in my name** (*ho ti an aitēsēte en tō onomati mou*) so that **the Father may be glorified** in the Son. 14:14 **If in my name you ask me for anything** (*ean ti aitēsēte me en tō onomati mou*), **I will do it.**	15:7 If you dwell (*meinēte*) in me and my words dwell (*meinē*) in you, **you may ask whatever you wish and it will happen.** 8. In this **my Father is glorified,** that you bear much fruit and thus be my disciples.
	15:16 The Father will give you **whatever you ask him in my name** (*ho ti an aitēsēte ton patera en tō onomati mou*).
14:21 They who have my **commandments** and **keep** them are those who **love** me; (*entolas mou kai tērōn autas ekeinos estin ho agapōn me*), and those who love me will be loved by my Father, and I will love them and reveal myself to them."	15:10 If you **keep** my **commandments,** you will abide in my **love,** just as I have **kept** my Father's **commandments** and abide in his **love** (*ean tas entolas mou tērēsēte, meneite en tē agapē mou, kathōs egō tas entolas tou patros mou tetērēka kai menō autou en tē agapē*).
14:23 Jesus answered him, "Those who **love** me (*agapa me*) will **keep** my word, and my Father will **love** them (*ho patēr mou agapēsei auton*), and we will come to them and make our dwelling (*monēn*) with them.	15:9 Just as the Father has **loved** me (*ēgapēsen me*), so I have **loved** you (*egō humas ēgapēsa*); **dwell** in my love (*meinate en tē agapē tē emē*).
14:25 "I have said these things to you while I **dwell** with you (*par' humin menōn*).	15:4 **Dwell** in me and I in you (*meinate en emoi, k'agō en humin*).

I note the following themes:

> the indwelling love of the Father and Jesus (14:10, 23, 25; 15:4, 9, 10)
> the glorification of the Father (14:13; 15:8)
> asking in Jesus' name (14:13, 14; 15:16 [7])
> keeping the commandments linked to love (14:21; 15:10)

Within these themes there is the repetition of key words: commands (*entolas*), love (*agapē, ktl.*), dwell (*menō, ktl.*), asking in Jesus' name. These repetitions in such close proximity lead me to suggest that 15:9-17, and its introductory image of the vine and the branches (15:1-8), is a *relecture* of 14:1-31. In chapter 15 the major focus is on the reciprocal indwelling of Jesus and the Father, and its implications for the disciples (15:9-17). The intimate relationship between Jesus and the Father is not a new theme, since it has been present across the gospel (e.g., 1:1, 18; 5:20; 10:30, 38). What is new is the teaching that disciples can also participate in this divine indwelling by their mutual indwelling in Jesus. Throughout chapter 14 Jesus had taught that he, the Father, and the Paraclete would dwell in the disciples (14:17, 23, 25), but as the interjections make clear, Jesus' words were not fully grasped. Chapter 15:9-17 repeats and elaborates on this teaching. As an introduction, and as a further explication of Jesus' response to Thomas, Jesus provides the disciples with an image. The image of the vine and the branches is a teaching tool, a device to illustrate the close and necessary mutual indwelling of Jesus and disciples. This is the one and only means that makes possible the mutual indwelling with the Father. Jesus says to Thomas, "I am the way," and he repeats this in the image: "Just as the branch cannot bear fruit by itself unless it remains (*menē*) in the vine, neither can you unless you dwell (*menēte*) in me. I am the vine, you are the branches" (15:4-5). Only through Jesus can disciples be drawn into the Father's love. By dwelling in Jesus, disciples will be enabled to dwell in the Father. "In that day you will know that I am in my Father, and you in me, and I in you" (14:20). Through keeping Jesus' command to love, disciples will dwell in Jesus' love and will in turn be loved by the Father, and the Father will dwell with them.

Recalling the earlier description of *relecture* provided by Moloney, we see that the six aspects of this process are satisfied in the comparison between 15:1-17 and 14:1-31. The themes and terminology of chapter 15 draw on the text of John 14, establishing that it is an intertextual development (i). These themes are found within chapter 14, which is considered by most scholars to have been the original form of the discourse (ii). The teaching of divine indwelling, presented in chapter 14, is further developed in chapter 15 with an emphasis on the role of Jesus as the sole mediator of this indwelling. To this end, the image of the vine and the branches is used to illustrate and emphasize the necessity of relationship with Jesus (iii). Within the narrative the confusion shown by the disciples would provide sufficient cause for a teacher's further elaboration. If, as I believe, the discourse material has probably developed over a period of time, it is also possible that 15:1-17 was developed in response to later community needs for further clarification, particularly of the role of Jesus as the sole mediator (v). One of the reasons why scholars approach 15:1-17 as a distinct unit is that the image and terminology used are found only here in such a concentrated way, closely linked to the use of the verb "dwell" in chapter 14 (iv). Nothing in my reading of the text suggests, let alone requires, another author. On the contrary, the sensitivity to language and style and the unity in theological thinking are indicators to me of a single author (vi).

The teaching in 15:1-17 recapitulates and develops Jesus' response to the disciples' perplexity in chapter 14. Thomas' question is critical: "How can we know the way?" (14:5). Jesus' mission has been to reveal the way by making known his Father. This is not simply intellectual knowing, but an experience of a quality of God's own life, named in the gospel as "eternity life" (e.g., 3:15, 16; 6:47, 54). Those believing in Jesus are invited into this quality of life by being "born anew" (3:3). Now, on the eve of Jesus' departure, Thomas is still confused. If, while Jesus is present, his revelation is still shrouded in mystery, what hope will these disciples have in his absence?

Jesus' response to Thomas in chapter 14 is to assure him: "I am the way" (v. 6). In chapter 15, using the image of the vine to illustrate his point, Jesus restates his singular role in mediating the relationship with the Father, and thus the life of God. The branches live only in their relationship to the vine.

Philip's request—"Show us the Father" (14:8)—is met with Jesus' affirmation that to see him is to see the Father, "I am in the Father, and the Father is in me" (14:10). In chapter 15 the union of Father and Son is re-affirmed and explained even further as a communion of will and love (15:10). When Judas wonders how Jesus will be manifest (*emphanizein*) to the disciples and not to the world (14:22), Jesus responds by speaking of an indwelling presence of himself and the Father: "Those who love me will keep my word, and my Father will love them, and we will come to them and make our dwelling with them" (14:23). In chapter 15 Jesus explains further what keeping his word means in practice: "If you keep my commandments, you will dwell in my love . . . this is my commandment, that you love one another as I have loved you" (15:10, 12). As a *relecture* of Jesus' response to the disciples' lack of comprehension, 15:1-17 offers further clarification and development of his teaching in the initial discourse of chapter 14.

The Vine and Branches: vv. 1-8

The first part of this section (vv. 1-8) develops the imagery of the vineyard so familiar to people of that time.[39] Verse 1 begins by establishing the relationship between the vine and vinedresser and identifying the roles of Father and Son in this metaphor.[40] The vinedresser's role is not mentioned after verse 2, as the metaphor concentrates on describing the relationship between the vine and the branches. By establishing the vine/vinedresser connection first, the metaphor grounds all further developments in this primary relationship. Verses 2 and 3 exploit the double meaning of the word *kathairō*: to make clean and to prune.[41] Stepping outside the imagery and

---

[39] For a description of vine farming in antiquity see Van der Watt, *Family of the King*, 26–29. On the Jewish background for the image see Schnackenburg, *Gospel* 3:104–107; Scholtissek, *In Ihm sein und bleiben*, 279–81.

[40] Elsewhere I have discussed the emphatic statement "I am the true vine (literally "I am the vine, the true") and suggested that this comparison may have arisen in a context where there was some confusion yet again about the respective roles of John the Baptizer and Jesus; see Mary L. Coloe, "Was there another vine? Questions on John 15:1a," *Australian E-Journal of Theology* 4 (2005), accessed March 30th, 2006, available from http://dlibrary.acu.edu.au/research/theology/ejournal/aejt_4/coloe.htm. Such historical issues are not the focus of this study and so will not be part of the following analysis.

[41] "In Jn 15.2 the meaning of *kathairō* may also be understood as 'to prune branches,' thus playing on two distinct meanings of *kathairō*." See Louw and Nida, eds., *Greek-English Lexicon* 1:699 § 79.49.

speaking directly to his disciples, Jesus tells them that they are pruned/ cleansed now through his word. In his discussion of verse 3, Scholtissek relates it to what was said by Jesus in chapter 8. "If you remain (*meinēte*) in my word, you are truly my disciples, and you will know the truth, and the truth will make you free" (8:31-32), and also his words to Peter in the footwashing scene: "He who has bathed does not need to wash, except for his feet, but he is clean (*katharos*) all over" (13:10).[42] While chapter 8, with its use of the future "will know," looks ahead to the time after the Passion, 15:2 is spoken with the post-Easter perspective of disciples who have remained in Jesus' word and have therefore been cleansed/made free by their participation in his Passion as symbolized in the act of footwashing.[43]

The image resumes in verse 4 with the command, "abide/dwell in me as I in you (*meinate en moi kagō en humin*). For the first time in this chapter the verb *menō* is used, and this term will dominate the rest of the passage as a means of describing a number of relationships: between vine and branch (v. 4), disciples and Jesus (vv. 5, 6, 7), the word of Jesus and the disciples (v. 7), the disciple and Jesus' love (vv. 9, 10), Jesus and the Father's love (v. 10), and also the enduring quality of the fruit (v. 15). In verse 4 there is a uniquely Johannine shift in the vine imagery that was not foreshadowed in any previous Jewish literature. The image is now used to carry the meaning of reciprocal immanence and a profound divine/human intimacy. The term "dwell, abide" (*menō ktl.*) was used in chapter 14 to describe the dwelling of the Father, Jesus, and the Paraclete with and in the disciples;[44] here in chapter 15 the subject changes to the disciples and the verb is used to describe a reciprocal abiding between disciples and Jesus. The reciprocity or intersubjectivity of the verb "dwell" is developed through this natural image of vine and branch: "dwell in me and I in you" (v. 4).

The image is given a direct application to Jesus and his disciples in verse 5. Here the disciples are identified as the branches and Jesus as the vine. The consequences of dwelling or not dwelling in the vine are explained; the disciples who dwell in Jesus will bear fruit (v. 5) and their requests will be heard (v. 7), while the disciples who do not dwell in Jesus are cast away (v. 6). The final verse in this section returns to the image of the vine, only now the relationship is directly between the disciples and the Father. Just as a vinedresser receives great renown and honor (*doxa*) by the

---

[42] Scholtissek, *In Ihm sein und bleiben*, 288–90.

[43] With Scholtissek, I also read the footwashing as a symbolic action drawing the disciples into the salvific meaning of Jesus' Passion. For more on this see the earlier discussion in ch. 7.

[44] The verb dwell (*menō*) is used in 14:10, 17, 25; the noun form "dwelling" (*monē*) is used in 14:2, 23.

amount and quality of the fruit of his vineyard, so will the Father be glorified (*edoxasthē*) by the fruit-bearing of the disciples. While this section (vv. 1-8) speaks often of bearing fruit (vv. 2, 4, 5) there is no explanation of its meaning when applied to the disciples. This explanation requires a different image, drawing no longer on nature but on the quality of the relationship between a father and son. In a sense the vine image begins to break down from verse 4, where it begins to be used to express the mutual intimacy between Jesus and disciples. This intimacy, unlike the natural flow of life within a vine and its branches, is based on the divine choice to love (3:16), and will be expressed by Jesus in a love unto death (17:13). For disciples it is conditional on their choice to remain faithful.

Father and Son (vv. 9-17)

The vine imagery in verses 1-8 gives way to a new image of the dynamic love-relationship between the Father and Son. "Just as the Father has loved me, so have I loved you. Remain in my love" (v. 9). The imagery of this verse is so taken for granted that its metaphoric use can be missed. The gospel began with the relationship of God and the Word outside time (1:1). When the Word enters the human story this relationship is described in human terms as being *like* the relationship of a father and his only son (1:14, 18). The gospel then continues to use this image as a means of expressing the loving union between God and the incarnate Word, as well as differentiating them and not allowing the relationship to collapse into a singularity. It is on the basis of Jesus' loving union with his Father that he claims the Sabbath prerogative of God to give life and make judgments (cf. 5:19-20). As one who constantly rests in the heart of his Father (1:18), he can say "the Father and I are one" (10:30). It is only when the image of the vine and branches is read in the light of the more personal image of Father and Son that its full emotive force is realized.

Image	Image
1. I am the true vine and my Father is the vinedresser.	9. Just as the Father has loved me, so have I loved you. Dwell (*meinate*) in my love. 10. If
2. Every branch in me not bearing fruit he cuts away, and every branch bearing fruit he prunes so it bears more fruit.	you keep my commandments you will dwell in my love, just as I have kept my Father's commandments and dwell in his love.
Aside	**Aside**
3. You are pruned now by the word I have spoken to you.	11. This I have spoken to you so that my joy may be in you and your joy may be fulfilled.

The imperative "remain in my love" (v. 9) is revealed as the same love existing between Father and Son. Disciples are drawn into the very heart of the divine intimacy. The parallelism across the images now makes clear that the expression "bear fruit" means "keeping my commandments," which is to love as I have loved in laying down my life (v. 10). To speak of verses 9-17 as the ethical dimension of verses 1-8 misses the point of the image in verse 9 and its relationship to the vine image in verses 1-8.[45] It is not possible to differentiate between the Father/Son relationship and their mutual love. A definition of God that underpins the theology of the Fourth Gospel is *Being-in-Love*. God's "being" is God "loving"; the loving is not an ethical activity that can be distinguished from God's being, as the First Letter of John states: "God is love" (1 John 4:8, 16). This same mode of being is applied to the disciples, since remaining in the vine is loving one another "as I have loved" (v. 12). Love is to *be* the essence of Christian discipleship, not simply an ethical response.

The rich theology of divine/human intimacy that is the basis for the logic across these verses (14:1–15:17) is sustained by the word dwell/remain (*menein*). In looking at the many places where this word is employed across the gospel, it is difficult to determine when it has a theological use and when it can be understood in the neutral sense of "stay."[46] There have been a number of studies of the use of this expression in the Fourth Gospel,[47] and to my knowledge only Klaus Scholtissek has brought out the ecclesial and soteriological meaning the Fourth Evangelist gives to this word.

Scholtissek perceives that in 15:1-17 the evangelist describes the ultimate revelation of Jesus' mission, which is to draw believers into the communion of life and love he shares with the Father. The same dynamism of love between Father and Son now exists between Jesus and his disciples. But whereas the relationship between Father and Son is constant and so can be described with the verb "to be" (*eimi*), a verb expressing the reciprocal "being" of the Father in the Son, the relationship with believers is contingent on their loving, and this could fail, so the verb "dwell" (*menō*) is

---

[45] Segovia (*Love Relationships*, 119–21) makes this distinction of "faith" and "ethic."

[46] Scholtissek, *In Ihm sein und bleiben*, 155–56, identifies only six places where *menō* is used in a local sense meaning "stay" (2:12; 4:40; 7:9; 10:40; 11:6; 19:31); and thirty-two times in a theological sense: 1:32, 33, 38, 39(2x); 3:36; 5:38; 6:27, 56; 8:31, 35(2x); 9:41; 12:24, 34, 46; 14:10, 17, 25; 15:4(3x), 5, 6, 7(2x), 9, 10(2x), 16; 21:22, 23; I would also add the use of *monai* (14:2) and *monēn* (14:23).

[47] See, for example, Heise, *Bleiben: Menein in den johanneischen Schriften*; Dorothy A. Lee, "Abiding in the Fourth Gospel: A Case-study in Feminist Biblical Theology," *Pacifica* 10 (1997) 123–36; Ignace de la Pottérie, "Le Verbe 'demeurer' dans la Mystique Johannique," *NRTh* 117 (1995) 843–59. De La Potterie counts sixty-seven studies within the Johannine literature (ibid. 843).

more appropriate.[48] The disciples' love for each other is the condition that determines their being caught up in the love, also described as friendship, of Jesus, who in turn exists in the love of the Father. Jesus is the mediator of this divine intimacy, for the believer does not dwell "immediately" in the Father; Jesus is "the Way," as he says to Philip (14:6). Through friendship with Jesus the disciple is drawn into the filial love existing between Father and Son. Where Scholtissek uses the expression *vita communis*, I use the term "household," for this retains the image of "the Father's house" used in 14:2.[49]

Johannine Ecclesiology: The Household of God

Since the image used to describe the loving being of God is the love between a father and son, it is appropriate to describe this as an image of the divine "household." The image of the Father's household (14:2) thus unites the text of the gospel across 13:1–15:17; chapter 13 is included here because the ritual of footwashing welcomes disciples into the household. Chapter 14 speaks of God's dwelling *with* believers and a future dwelling of the Spirit *in* believers. Chapter 15:1-8 employs an image from the natural world in order to describe the reciprocal indwelling of disciple and Jesus. Then verses 9-17 return to the image of the household of God by applying the love between the Father and Son to the love between Jesus and his disciples, with the command that they live this love in the relationships within the community by loving "one another as I have loved you" (v. 12). What Jesus meant by "bearing fruit" is clarified in these verses as the reality of disciples loving one another, and so in their communion-in-love they are a living symbol of the divine *communio*, the household of God.

Both the image of the vine and the model of father-son intimacy directly engage the pre-Easter disciples present in the narrative, and more especially the post-Easter believers. In Jesus' teaching the sign of love is the readiness to gives one's own life for the beloved. This sign is only realized at the cross, and so verse 13 presupposes that this event has already happened. Similarly, Jesus has made known (*egnōrisa*) all he has heard from his father; this

---

[48] Scholtissek, *In Ihm sein und bleiben*, 365.

[49] At times Scholtissek also uses "familial" terms recognizing that "household" is part of the metaphorical language of this gospel. "Diese nachösterliche Glaubenserfahrung lotet Joh 14 *haus- und familienmetaphorisch* aus" ("John 14 plumbs the depths of this post-Easter faith experience through *metaphors of household and family*"). Ibid. 374; also 265, 267.

statement also presupposes the completion of his revelation on the cross.[50] While the narrative setting is Jesus with his disciples prior to his arrest and crucifixion, the Johannine perspective is that of Jesus, the already risen and glorified Lord, encouraging post-paschal believers to remain faithful.[51] In Jesus' words the relationship of love for his own can also be named as friendship.[52] "Greater love (*agapēn*) than this has no one than to lay down his life for his friends (*philōn*). You are my friends (*philoi*)" (vv. 13-14a). In the ancient world friendship and household relationships overlap. "A man's friends are part of his *oikos*. They determine the social position of the *oikos* and are determined by it."[53] Through friendship, someone beyond the household could be incorporated into the household. Sjef van Tilborg describes Jesus' early activity in the gospel as creating "an *oikos* of mutual friends who have found each other on the basis of freedom and kinship relationships."[54] Following the wedding at Cana, Jesus went with his mother, his siblings, and his disciples and dwelt (*emeinan*) with them (2:12). Immediately after this, Jesus and his disciples go to his Father's house (2:16). Read against a first-century *oikos* ideology, disciples have been brought by the beloved son into the household of the Father.[55] As members of the *oikos*, and because of their friendship with the son, they can make requests to the Father in his son's name and be assured that they will be granted (15:7, 16).[56] The proof of friendship Jesus proposes is the same as that discussed in Hellenistic philosophy.[57]

---

[50] There is a mixture of present, perfect, and aorist forms of the verbs across vv. 1-17, indicating a retrospective telling of the story of Jesus' final meal. See ibid. 277, 300.

[51] Segovia, *Farewell of the Word*, 327, suggests that the danger of falling away expressed in this section indicates the beginnings of an internal rupture that will lead to the situation of the Johannine letters.

[52] A helpful summary of the meaning of friendship within Greco-Roman and Jewish philosophy can be found in Sharon Ringe, *Wisdom's Friends*, 64–83, and J. Massyngberde Ford, *Redeemer-Friend and Mother: Salvation in Antiquity and in the Gospel of John* (Minneapolis: Fortress Press, 1997) 76–92.

[53] Sjef van Tilborg, *Imaginative Love in John*. Biblical Interpretation Series 2 (Leiden: Brill, 1993) 149. On this point Tilborg cites a number of classical authors of *amicitia* literature.

[54] Ibid. 116.

[55] The *oikos* ideology described by van Tilborg is further enriched by the narrative progression across these opening chapters using nuptial imagery, as I have proposed in ch. 2.

[56] Van Tilborg, *Imaginative Love*, 150.

[57] I follow the translation offered by van Tilborg (ibid. 150–53).

> To die for one another is only possible for people who love. (Plato, *Symposium* 179b)

> Truly, the honorable person does many things because of his friends and his country; if necessary, he will even die for them. (Aristotle, *Eth. Nic.* IX 8.9)

> Epicurus on the wise man: And he will on occasion die for a friend. (Diogn. Laër. X 120).

> Why do I seek someone's friendship? So as to have someone for whom I would be willing to die. (Seneca, *Ep.* 1.9.10)

In the philosophical writings, to die for one's friend is presented as the ideal, and it is also a hypothetical ideal. On the lips of Jesus this statement of love moves from hypothesis to fact, from idea to reality. The depth of his love for his friends is shown by the extent to which he is prepared to go so that they too can become members of his *oikos* and "children of God" (1:12), and thus can participate in the love shared between Father and Son. Where kinship is a matter of blood ties, friendship is a matter of free choice, and the love of friendship can have an affective quality deeper than some family ties.

Friendship speaks also of a bond of the spirit rather than ties of blood or patronage. Although Jesus speaks frequently of his relationship with God using the metaphor of Father-Son, as the gospel reminds us, "God is spirit" (4:24). The inner dynamism within God's being can never be adequately expressed. Words such as "love," "father," "household," "son" can only be used analogically. The gospel likewise struggles to convey the rich revelatory experience of God's love revealed in Jesus, and the bonds between believers that this love creates, sustains, and obliges. Whether using the image of household and/or friendship, the creative dynamic at the heart of the Christian community is divine love, made possible by believers being drawn into God's own "Being-in-love." The community is given a model of the relationships that exist in the divine household (my Father's house), and this model of life is to exist in their own relationships. When proposing that the image of the household describes the Johannine ecclesiology I am not therefore advocating a model of the patriarchal household of the first century. The gospel provides its own point of reference for this image, the divine household governed by the singular dynamic of self-giving love, even unto death. "The immanence relationship between the disciples and Jesus is neither static nor individualistic; it is neither magical nor private; it is a personal and community-promoting 'Living'—a reality modeled on the fullness of life in the Father-Son immanence."[58]

---

[58] Scholtissek, *In Ihm sein und bleiben*, 301.

Conclusion

Across the entire gospel, the reader has been introduced to various expressions that come to their clearest and richest exposition in these seventeen verses. *Menein* has been used to speak of the indwelling Spirit and Jesus (1:32) as well as the gathering of disciples/believers around Jesus (1:38-39; 2:12; 4:40; 6:56; 8:31). Believers have been told that they will receive a particular quality of life, "eternity" life (3:15, 36; 6:27; 10:28). Situated on the eve of his return to his Father, Jesus gathers his own, those who have received his word (15:3) and have abided with him. Now he discloses that if they dwell in him, his return to the Father will draw them into his own indwelling reciprocal love. Abiding in Jesus, disciples of all times will be able to participate in the loving and dynamic life of God in eternity. Participation in this communion of life and love is not relegated to the eschaton, but with the gift of the indwelling Spirit this *communio dei* is a post-paschal reality. Participation in the divine "household" is the Johannine equivalent of salvation; this is the gift given in its fullness (1:16), enabling believers to become children of God (1:12). As Scholtissek states, "The reciprocal immanence between the Son and Christians articulates a living and relationship-rich salvation reality: the post-Easter union of the Christian with Christ. This reciprocal immanence is not only a praxis (namely the presence of love), but the reality of salvation."[59] In the narrative at this point, this revelation still has the character of a promise, but for the post-Easter community it is the living experience that grounds their faith and praxis.

The image of the vine and the branches (15:1-8), situated within passages that describe abiding within the divine household (14:1-31; 15:9-17), invites disciples into a union with Jesus that will draw them into his own abiding as Son in the household of the Father for eternity (8:35). The initiative for this divine filiation comes from God, who comes to dwell with us in Jesus. Those who believe in Jesus and become his friends can, in and through Jesus, experience his dwelling close to the heart of the Father (1:18). This profound insight into the meaning of Jesus' mission must have been the post-Easter experience of the Johannine community, for only one who has experienced such union would be bold enough to propose such divine-human intimacy. I conclude with the words of Dorothy Lee, who succinctly expresses the arguments of this chapter:

> Abiding is a quality of the divine realm, an aspect of eternal life that in John's Gospel is offered to human beings. As a divine quality, abiding expresses the intimacy and reciprocity which, for John, lie at the heart of the universe. The

---

[59] Ibid. 314.

relationship between God and Jesus, father and son, is the symbol and arche-type of abiding. . . . To be a disciple means to be in union with Jesus, and through Jesus with God—a union that is reciprocal and oriented towards community.[60]

[60] Lee, "Abiding in the Fourth Gospel," 131.

Resurrecting the Household of God

JOHN 20:19-29

Following his discourse and final prayer to his Father, Jesus leaves Jerusalem and crosses the Kedron to enter a new space: the garden. Jesus is betrayed and buried in a garden (18:1; 19:41) and this *inclusio*, unique to John, along with the emphasis on Jesus' cross in the middle (19:18), echoes the first garden of creation with its tree of life in the middle (Gen 2:9). The Johannine crucifixion is not an act of abandonment or abasement. It is the culmination of Jesus' work and his hour of triumph. Jesus reigns from the cross as he deliberately displays a depth of love unto death for his friends. The cross is a new tree of life, as Jesus, the Nazarene Temple-builder, creates the Father's house/hold as a community of beloved disciples.[1] In this garden Jesus is the divine creator breathing the lifegiving Spirit (19:30), and the new Adam from whose side flow the blood and waters of birth (19:34). As the Spirit is breathed onto this new creation, Jesus proclaims the divine judgment on this work: "it is finished (*tetelestai*)" (19:30), recalling God's assessment of creation: "Thus the heavens and earth were finished (*synetelesthēsan*)" (Gen 2:1). In the theology of the Fourth Gospel

---

[1] Ruben Zimmermann offers a rich interpretation of the garden theme across John 18–20 and links this theme with that of the Temple, especially Jewish traditions of the eschatological Temple. "Since the expectation of the eschatological temple was linked in early Jewish time expressly with garden symbolism, it may be concluded that, in John 20, the evangelist is consciously linking the garden and Temple symbolism. From John 2:21 it becomes clear in the first encounter with the Risen One in a garden that Christ is the new, eschatological temple." See Zimmermann, *Christologie der Bilder*, 160.

creation has only now been brought to completion in this holy Passover.[2] The Sabbath can now begin (19:31).

With the cross as Jesus' hour of exaltation, the reader may wonder what more can follow. Unlike the Synoptics, where the resurrection is the vindication of Jesus after his apparent defeat, John 20 is not needed to witness to Jesus' triumph. Jesus has already been lifted up and glorified on the cross. In the Fourth Gospel there are no "Passion predictions" in which Jesus speaks of his death and rising. The Passion/resurrection predictions fit within the theology of the Synoptic Gospels,[3] but when we turn to the Fourth Gospel we find no equivalent.[4] There is a statement about death, described as a lifting up (3:14), but this is not followed by a statement about "being raised." The only time the "three day" language associated with the Synoptic resurrection predictions is used is when Jesus speaks of raising the Temple "in three days" (2:19).[5] Although, two verses later, this Temple is identified as "the Temple of his body" (2:21), the statement about destroying and raising the Temple takes on a far richer meaning than simply the death and resurrection of the body of Jesus. Resurrection in the Fourth Gospel will have a different focus.

John 20:19-29

The household scene in John 20 is a fitting and necessary narrative conclusion to the theology of the gospel. While this chapter is not needed to testify to Jesus' resurrection understood as his vindication, it is needed to witness to the resurrection of faith for the disciples, and to the reality of the new house/hold of God promised by the narrative plot as I have presented it in this work. The first scene at the tomb (vv. 1-18) testifies to the faith of two of the disciples who, having been present at the foot of the cross, represent all newborn children of God. In the appearance to Mary Magdalene, the Risen One states the Johannine *kerygma*: "Go to *my brothers and sisters* and say to them, 'I am ascending to my Father and *your Father*, to my God and your God'" (20:17). With the cross now a past event, dis-

---

[2] Throughout the gospel Jesus had insisted that God was still working (5:17) and that he had been sent to complete God's creative work (4:34; 5:36; 17:4).

[3] In the Gospel of Mark we find three passages in which Jesus speaks of his future death and resurrection in Jerusalem (Mark 8:31; 9:31; 10:33-34 *par.*).

[4] Maarten J. J. Menken, "Interpretation of the Old Testament and the Resurrection of Jesus in John's Gospel," 197.

[5] The pericope of the wedding at Cana is also introduced by "On the third day," but in this passage there is no association with death and resurrection, as there is in ch. 2. For the meaning of this phrase in the Cana pericope see Francis J. Moloney, *Belief in the Word*, 91.

ciples have become "brothers and sisters"; the household of God has begun to gather God's children (cf. 1:12). Disciples can now approach God as brothers and sisters of Jesus and say "Father." The next scene (vv. 19-23) depicts the reversal within the household of believers as they move from fear to joy in the presence of the Risen One. Although, with the exception of a few women, these disciples were not present at Jesus' death, they also receive the creative breath of the Spirit (v. 22) and are then commissioned to forgive sin (v. 23).

The gospel could have finished at this point, with the disciples gathered around the Risen Jesus and commissioned to continue the ministry the Father gave him. This is where Matthew concludes his gospel (Matt 28:16-20). Authors of an article in *Biblica* express the puzzlement of many about the need for this final pericope:

> In a sense, we might well ask what is the point of the Thomas episode. Mary has seen Christ as he is about to ascend to the Father. The disciples have seen Christ risen and glorified. We have already reached the summit: the balance is perfect, the identity of the historical Christ with the eternal Word is fully manifest. What more is there to add?[6]

What more indeed! This gospel has self-consciously testified to Jesus for the readers/hearers of the text.[7] The final scene continues this narrative device in its portrayal of Thomas. Through Thomas the readers are not simply presented with a narrative of things past. Through Thomas, time is stretched and the past is brought into God's eternal present.

Thomas in the Fourth Gospel

Thomas is not new to the reader of this gospel. He was first introduced in the Lazarus episode as one expecting to find death: "Let us also go that we may die with him" (11:16), but who instead witnesses a resurrection (11:44). The naming of Thomas in John 20 recalls the Lazarus scene and Thomas's lack of understanding. Jesus has invited the disciples to accompany him to Jerusalem so that "they might come to have faith" (v. 15).[8] However, Thomas sees only an invitation to death,[9] and it appears that even

---

[6] Liliane Dupont, Christopher Lash, and Georges Levesque, "Recherche sur la structure de Jean 20," *Bib* 54 (1973) 482–98, at 493.

[7] Note the use of first-person pronouns in the Prologue (1:14, 15, 16) and the testimony of the witness at the cross (19:35).

[8] Brown, *Gospel* 1:424.

[9] Many scholars see in Thomas's words a parallel to Mark 8:34 as a model for Christian discipleship to the point of martyrdom. Sproston North's comments are typical of this interpretation: "Here from one faithful disciple to the others, the call to martyrdom

the events he witnesses at Bethany are unable to shift his misunderstanding that there is no return from the grave. This earlier experience of a household where there was the transition from death to life provides a narrative link to the household of John 20, which also experiences a movement from death to life. Thomas has accompanied Jesus to Bethany and so has been a witness to this dramatic overturning of death, but it seems that even this has not been sufficient for him to have faith in Jesus' words, "I am the resurrection and the life" (11:25).

The second appearance of Thomas is in John 14, where Thomas is the first to speak after Jesus' description of his death as a means of preparing the Father's household:

> "In my Father's Household there are many dwellings. . . . I go to prepare a place for you. And you know the way to the place where I am going." Thomas said to him, "Lord, we do not know where you are going. How can we know the way?" (14:2, 4–5).

I am presuming that Thomas, as one of Jesus' disciples, was present at the Festival of Tabernacles when Jesus said, "I will be with you a little while longer, and then I am going to him who sent me" (7:33), so Thomas, even if he does not know the "way," should at least know where Jesus is going: "to him who sent me." As a character in both John 11 and here in chapter 14, Thomas comes across as particularly obtuse. More important, he is a character associated with the household of a resurrection and Jesus' teaching about the Father's household. Both of these themes will be developed in the Thomas scene in John 20, to which I now turn.

Structuring the Narrative

20:19 On the evening of that day, **the first day of the week,** the **doors having been shut** where the disciples were, for fear of the Jews, **Jesus came and stood in their midst** and said to them, **"Peace be with you."**

20:20 **When he had said this, he showed them both his hands and his side. Then the disciples rejoiced when they saw the Lord.**

---

is used by the evangelist to his readers in the plainest possible terms." See Sproston North, *The Lazarus Story within the Johannine Tradition*, 56–57. Such interpretations misunderstand the context of this statement within the Johannine narrative. As Dorothy Lee writes, "the structure of these verses points to life rather than death. Through the metaphor of light in v. 9, Jesus reveals that in going to Judaea he is walking not into darkness but in the light." See Lee, *Symbolic Narratives*, 200. For more on the misunderstanding of Thomas at this point see Francis J. Moloney, "Can Everyone be Wrong?" 512–13.

20:21 **Jesus said** to them again, **"Peace be with you.** As the Father has sent me, I also send you." 22 And saying this, he breathed on them, and said to them, "Receive the Holy Spirit. 23 If you forgive the sins of any, they are forgiven; if you hold them, they are held."

20:24 But Thomas, one of the twelve, called the Twin, was not with them when Jesus came. 25 So the other disciples told him, "We have seen the Lord." But he said to them, "Unless I see in his hands the print of the nails, [and place my finger in the mark of the nails], and place my hand in his side, I will not believe."

20:26 **Eight days later,** his disciples were again in the house, and Thomas was with them. **The doors were shut, but Jesus came and stood in their midst,** and said, **"Peace be with you."**

20:27 Then he said to Thomas, "Put your finger here, and see **my hands;** and put out your hand, and place [it] in **my side;** do not be faithless, but believing."

20:28 Thomas answered him, "My Lord and my God!"

20:29 Jesus said to him, "Have you believed because you have seen me? Blessed are those who have not seen and yet believe."

As this structure shows, verses 26-29 are almost a mirror image of verses 19-23 in the repetition of words and actions occurring across the scene. Both sections begin with naming the day, the Sunday, which can be called both the first day (v. 19) and the eighth day (v. 26). The disciples are inside with the doors shut (vv. 19, 26). The expression "Jesus came and stood among them and said, 'Peace be with you'" occurs on both occasions (vv. 19, 26). In verses 20 and 27 Jesus reveals his hands and his side, leading in both cases to a response of faith: "The disciples were glad when they saw the Lord" (v. 20); "Thomas answered him, 'My Lord and my God'" (v. 28). Both units conclude with the words of Jesus (vv. 21-23; v. 28). Both sections of this diptych therefore frame verses 24-25, making it the narrative hinge.[10]

A Possible Eucharistic Setting

There are a number of features in this section (vv. 19-29) that suggest the worship experience of the early church. The very points named above are repeated across the units and are features that will be present in the

[10] Raymond F. Collins, "'Blessed are those who have not seen': John 20:29," in Rekha M. Chennattu and Mary L. Coloe, eds., *Transcending Boundaries: Contemporary Readings of the New Testament.* Biblioteca di Scienze Religiose 187 (Rome: Libreria Ateneo Salesiano, 2005) 184.

eucharistic gatherings of later households of believers.[11] The repetition serves to emphasize the following seven points:

1. The day of both gatherings is the Sunday.
2. The disciples gather inside a house.
3. The doors are shut.
4. Jesus comes to them.
5. Jesus shows the disciples and Thomas signs of the crucifixion.
6. Jesus greets them with "Peace."
7. There is a response of faith.

In drawing parallels between the Johannine text and later liturgical practice I am not arguing either that the gospel led directly to liturgical forms or that liturgical forms led directly to the gospel. Such claims of development in either direction seem impossible to prove conclusively. The difficulty of obtaining any historical knowledge of the eucharist in the first century, due to the scarcity of sources, must also be acknowledged. My aim is simply to observe the parallels between gospel and liturgy and make the more modest claim that there is a relationship, if not of dependence, then at least of development out of a common tradition and spiritual experience. In this I support the thesis of Helge Nielsen that the appearance report in verses 19-29 has been shaped by the worship experience of the Johannine community.[12] Commenting on the lack of textual information, Hartmut Gese makes a most important observation: "those for whom the New Testament texts were written knew how this worship service was observed, and thus there was no need to be exhaustive."[13]

I realize that in drawing comparisons with later texts I am venturing onto hermeneutical "thin ice." However, while this may be venturous to the point of danger, I still believe I am working within the hermeneutical paradigm that emerged throughout the last century and continues to be used in most Johannine criticism. This paradigm understands the text as the product of a particular community; it therefore addresses the needs of that com-

---

[11] The eucharistic background of some of these repetitions was first noted by John Suggit, "The Eucharistic Significance of John 20:19-29," *Journal of Theology for Southern Africa* 16 (1976) 52–59.

[12] Helge K. Nielsen, "Der erste Gottesdienst. Eine Analyse von Joh 20, 19-23," SNTSU 28 (2003) 67, 81.

[13] Hartmut Gese, *Essays on Biblical Theology*, trans. Keith Crim (Minneapolis: Augsburg, 1981) 117–18.

munity and to some extent reflects the community's life and concerns.[14] Working with this paradigm leads to various hypothetical reconstructions of the community life and history behind this gospel, based on evidence from written and archaeological sources in the Jewish and Greco-Roman worlds of the first century.[15] This paradigm presumes that the gospel uses the language, images, conventions, perceptions, and theological understanding of its historical situation in order to communicate to people living within that situation. From the letters of Paul, the testimony of Pliny (*Ep.* 10.96.7), and the descriptions of the early church recorded in Acts, we can conclude that liturgical worship in general, and some form of Eucharist, was part of the life of early communities. What we do not have are texts providing details of how this worship occurred, what structure(s) was/were followed, and what words were used. There is a gap of centuries before we have such details. However, once this gap is breached and we begin to have written sources, the seven elements listed above are already present. So, although looking to later liturgical writing to understand a first-century text must be approached with great caution,[16] these texts are all we have to shed any light on a critical aspect of early Christian life. We cannot discount the close relationship between the text and liturgy, particularly when it seems that our Christian texts were used in the worshiping assembly (Col 4:16; 1 Thess 5:27; Rev 1:3),[17] and it is possible that the worship of the community helped

---

[14] Among numerous articles and monographs that adopt this understanding, that the gospel addresses issues within the community, see, for example, Sandra M. Schneiders, "Death in the Community of Eternal Life," 44–56; Jörg Frey, *Die johanneische Eschatologie* 3, ch. 2; Martin Asiedu-Peprah, *Johannine Sabbath Conflicts as Juridical Controversy*, especially 237–45.

[15] For a recent overview of proposals about the historical circumstances and composition of the Johannine community see Raymond E. Brown, *Introduction to the Gospel of John*, 69–78.

[16] I thus work in parallel with scholars of Judaism and Christianity who use material from the Mishnah (ca. 200) to try to reconstruct the religious life of the first century. These scholars use the Mishnah cautiously, but do so presuming that what has been codified in the Mishnah reflects much earlier traditions, even though there is no longer written evidence from the first century of these traditions; e.g., "There is no question that some of its [the Mishnah's] legislation reflects a much earlier period when the Temple was still in operation," Gale A. Yee, *Jewish Feasts in John's Gospel* (Wilmington, DE: Michael Glazier, 1989) 74. On the prehistory of the Mishnah see Günter Stemberger, *Introduction to the Talmud and Midrash*, trans. Markus Bockmuehl (2nd ed. Edinburgh: T&T Clark, 1996) 124–39.

[17] The use of some texts within Christian worship is one of the factors that led to their inclusion in the NT canon. "Gradually, some Christian writings came to be read in Christian worship alongside Jewish Scripture and thus acquired a similar scriptural

in the formation of the text.[18] With these cautionary remarks, I now turn to each of the seven features common to both parts of the diptych, showing their possible link with the eucharistic experience of the early church.

1. The first day of the week is associated with "the breaking of bread," which was an early name for the Eucharist:[19] "On the first day of the week, when we were gathered together to break bread" (Acts 20:7; cf. *Did.* 14:1).[20] The second gathering of disciples, including Thomas, occurs "eight days later," again making this the Sunday evening, since the beginning and end day of a period of time are both counted.[21] This deliberate time frame, "eight days later," indicates that this scene is to be understood against the liturgical background of the community.[22] The first day of the week was also called "the Lord's day" (1 Cor 16:2; Rev 1:10) and later came to be called Sunday.[23]

---

status. Indeed, the Christian movement was actively interpreting Scriptures, both Jewish and Christian, well before it possessed a canon of either. This precanonical interpretation of Scripture was not only propaedeutic but prerequisite to the creation of the canon of the New Testament, and decisively influenced its content and shape." See Harry Y. Gamble, "The Formation of the New Testament Canon and its Significance for the History of Biblical Interpretation," in Alan J. Hauser and Duane F. Watson, eds., *A History of Biblical Interpretation: Volume One, The Ancient Period* (Grand Rapids: Eerdmans, 2003) 410.

[18] Etienne Trocmé situates the development of the Passion in its narrative form within a liturgical context: "A number of features of the original Passion narrative thus point towards a liturgical setting for this tradition unit." See Trocmé, *The Passion as Liturgy: A Study in the Origin of the Passion Narratives in the Four Gospels* (London: SCM, 1983) 80. Brown also raises the liturgical context as a possibility: see Raymond E. Brown, *The Death of the Messiah: From Gethsemane to the Grave*, 2 vols. (New York: Doubleday, 1994) 1:51.

[19] This expression, "the breaking of the bread," is considered one of the earliest names given to the Eucharist. See Eugene LaVerdiere, *The Eucharist in the New Testament and the Early Church* (Collegeville: Liturgical Press, 1996) 20–22; Xavier Léon-Dufour, *Sharing the Eucharistic Bread: The Witness of the New Testament* (Mahwah, NJ: Paulist, 1987) 21–28; Josef A. Jungmann, *The Early Liturgy: To the Time of Gregory the Great*, trans. Francis A. Brunner (London: Darton, Longman & Todd, 1959) 29.

[20] In Luke's Gospel, the Emmaus story also has the "breaking of the bread" on the first day of the week, the resurrection day (Luke 24:13-35).

[21] Schnackenburg, *Gospel* 3:331.

[22] Ibid.

[23] Oscar Cullmann, *Early Christian Worship*. SBT 10 (London: SCM, 1953) 10; the name Sun-day developed from the pagan sun cult when Christians transferred the symbolism of the rising sun to the rising of Jesus. The term Sunday is first attested in Justin's *Apology* 1, 67, 3 (ibid. 12).

Harald Riesenfeld suggests that originally the day after the Sabbath was chosen as the day for Christian worship to reflect the early community's understanding that their worship was a continuation and fulfilment of their Sabbath worship. Following their Sabbath worship in the Temple (and possibly synagogue), the early Christians returned to their own homes (Acts 2:46; 5:42) to listen to apostolic teaching, for prayer, and for the breaking of the bread.[24] The Sabbath was not only a day to celebrate God's initial creative activity, in post-exilic times it was also characterized by a strong eschatological hope in God's future act of re-creation/salvation of Israel (*Gen Rab.* XVIII, *m.Tam.* VII, 4). In time the terminology of the "first day" shifted to the "eighth day" to reflect Christian belief that they were living in the new eschatological age. The "eighth day" terminology first appears in Christian literature in the *Epistle of Barnabas* (ca. 95–135 C.E.).

> He further says to them, *Your new moons and Sabbaths I disdain.* Consider what he means: Not the Sabbaths of the present era are acceptable to me, but that which I have appointed to mark the end of the world and to usher in the eighth day, that is, the dawn of another world. This, by the way, is the reason why we joyfully celebrate the eighth day—the same day on which Jesus rose from the dead; after which He manifested himself and went up to heaven. (*Ep.Barn.* 15:8-9)[25]

In the gospel the disciples gather "on the first day," and then again "eight days later." The eschatological new creation theme is suggested by these two details of time, particularly given the placement of the crucifixion, burial, and resurrection in a garden (18:1; 19:41). The naming of these days therefore accords with what we know of early Christian worship practice and its eschatological character, which can be seen already in the Synoptic institution narratives: "Truly I tell you, I will never again drink of the fruit of the vine until that day when I drink it new in the kingdom of God" (Mark 14:25 *par.*).

---

[24] Harald Riesenfeld, "Sabbat et Jour du Seigneur," in Angus J. B. Higgins, ed., *New Testament Essays: Studies in Memory of Thomas Walter Manson* (Manchester: Manchester University Press, 1959) 212.

[25] The eschatological "eighth day" also appears in the Jewish apocalyptic source *2 Enoch* (1st century B.C.E.). "And I appointed the eighth day also, that the eighth day should be the first-created after my work, and that the first seven revolve in the form of the seventh thousand, and that at the beginning of the eighth thousand there should be a time of not-counting, endless, with neither years nor months nor weeks nor days nor hours" (33:1).

2. Although the word "house" is not used explicitly, it can be inferred by the mention of the "closed doors." The witness of the early church is that Eucharist was celebrated in ordinary houses rather than places reserved for cultic activity: "And day by day, attending the Temple together and breaking bread in their homes, they partook of food with glad and generous hearts" (Acts 2:46).[26] The Pauline Epistles cite numerous examples of the Christian assembly gathering in houses of community members (1 Cor 16:19; Rom 16:3-5, 23; Phlm 1-2, Col 4:15).

3. The disciples are gathered behind closed doors, and in the narrative this is explained as being "for fear of the Jews" (v. 19). In the narrative context of the crucifixion this comment needs little further elaboration. "The Jews" in the gospel, who have consistently opposed Jesus to the point of orchestrating his death, also planned to kill Lazarus (12:10), and so the disciples' fear and the closed doors are readily understood from a narrative perspective. In John 9, the reason given for the hesitancy of the parents of the blind man is their fear of "the Jews" (9:22). This expression is understood to reflect the post-Easter experience of the Johannine community in its situation of tension and possible conflict with a local synagogue.[27] However, the gathering of disciples behind closed doors may be more that just a narrative description of frightened post-Easter disciples. In addition to this indicator that the text reflects the post-Easter time, the closing of the doors to unbelievers is an action in early liturgies to mark the ending of the "Mass of the Catechumens" and the beginning of the "Mass of the Faithful." In the liturgy of the Apostolic Constitutions, known as the Clementine Liturgy and dated in the fourth century, we read:[28]

> Let the deacon ascend upon some high seat, and proclaim, "Let none of the hearers, let none of the unbelievers stay."[29]

---

[26] On the reliability of Acts for its description of the Jerusalem church see Roger W. Gehring, *House Church and Mission*, 62–63.

[27] Nielsen uses the terms "der erzählten Welt" and "der Erzältwelt" to describe the reported time of the narrative, told through the experience of the time of the narrator; Nielsen, "Der erste Gottesdienst," 65–66.

[28] On the dating of this document see R.C.D. Jasper and G. C. Cuming, eds., *Prayers of the Eucharist: Early and Reformed* (2nd ed. New York: Oxford University Press, 1980) 70.

[29] ἀναστάντων ἀπάντων ὁ διάκονος ἐφ᾽ ὑψηλοῦ τινό ἀνελθῶν κηρυττέτω Μή τι τῶν ἀκροωμένων, μή τι τῶν ἀπίστων. Frank Edward Brightman, *Liturgies Eastern and Western* (Oxford: Clarendon Press, 1896) 3.

Similarly, The Liturgy of St. James, dated about 400 states:[30]

> Let none of the catechumens; none of the uninitiated; none of those who cannot pray with us. Recognize one another. The doors![31]

In later Eastern liturgies the deacon cries out "The Doors" to mark the conclusion of the catechumenal instruction and the start of Eucharist for the fully initiated believers.[32] While these descriptions are later, the structure of Justin's liturgy, dated around 155, seems to indicate that this division between the Mass of the Catechumens and the Mass of the Faithful was already happening in the second century.[33]

4. The coming of Jesus, and his remaining present with the community, is one of the features of early Christian worship as it was in Israel's Temple liturgy.[34] "In Israelite worship, the theophany, or cultic 'coming' of Yahweh occupied the central moment of the cultic act."[35] According to Oscar Cullmann, the Aramaic prayer *Maranatha* is a very early cultic prayer found in Paul's letter to the Corinthians and the *Didache*, and is given its Greek translation at the end of Revelation (1 Cor 16:22; *Did.* 10:6; Rev 22:20).[36] This prayer connects Christian worship with the day of the resurrection. "On this day Christ appeared at a meal with the disciples. So now he ought to appear again, in the Christian celebration of the Meal, since, 'where two or three are gathered together in my name, there am I in the midst of them' (Matt 18:20)."[37] The *Maranatha* prayer therefore looks back to his coming to the disciples in his resurrection; at the same time it looks to his present coming in the eucharistic meal of the community and looks forward to his coming at the end. David Aune situates the uniquely realized eschatology found in the Fourth Gospel in the worship experience of the community. Inspired and illuminated by the Spirit, the worshiping community experienced

---

[30] For the dating see Jasper and Cuming, *Prayers of the Eucharist*, 60.

[31] Μή τι τῶν κατηξουμένων. Μη τι τῶν ἀμυήτων. Μή τι τῶν μὴ δυναμένων ἡμῖν συνδεηθῆναι. Ἀλληλού ἐπίγνωτε. Τὰ θύρὰ. Brightman, *Liturgies*, 41.

[32] Suggit, "Eucharistic Significance," 54.

[33] Geoffrey G. Willis, *A History of Early Roman Liturgy: To the Death of Pope Gregory the Great*. Subsidia 1 (London: Henry Bradshaw Society, 1994) 4–6.

[34] Nielsen names the presence of the Risen One and the presence of the Spirit as two prerequisites for Christian worship; see Nielsen, "Der erste Gottesdienst," 69.

[35] Aune, *Cultic Setting*, 89.

[36] Oscar Cullmann and Franz J. Leenhardt, *Essays on the Lord's Supper.* Ecumenical Studies in Worship (Richmond: John Knox, 1958) 13–14.

[37] Cullman, *Early Christian Worship*, 13–14.

proleptically the parousial "coming" of Christ. He cites the visionary imagery of John 1:51 and 12:39-41 as evidence of a particular Johannine understanding that the heavens have been opened, and in worship the community can anticipate the *parousia* still to come.[38]

> This recurring [cultic] "coming" of the exalted Jesus was conceptualized in terms of traditional Christian Parousia imagery, and was directly experienced by the worshiping congregation "in the Spirit," or alternately as a presence mediated through the office of prophetic personalities.[39]

5. Disciples who were not present at the crucifixion are shown signs of this event when Jesus reveals his hands and his side. Thomas's words in verse 25 and the following scene emphasize the tangible nature of these signs. Thomas is singled out and told to *ballō* ("put" or "throw") into the side of Jesus (v. 27). This is strange wording. There is no direct object to the verb "throw," although most translations supply one "put [it, your hand] in my side."[40] But it is not just Thomas' hand that is to be placed in Jesus' side; this expression invites Thomas himself to participate in the meaning of the pierced side. In an earlier work I argued that the most probable Old Testament passage alluded to by the flow of blood and water from the pierced side is the description of the Temple waters in Ezekiel 47.[41] The blood and water flowing from the side of Jesus at the conclusion of this Passover day mirror the flow of blood and water from the Jerusalem Temple as the priests wash away the signs of the bloody sacrifices of thousands of Passover lambs. Beneath the Temple were large cisterns of water, and the blood of the sacrifices would mingle with the water and flow out into the Kedron (*m. Mid.* 3:2). In the Fourth Gospel Jesus dies on the Day of Preparation (19:14, 31, 42) and Pilate hands Jesus over to death at the time when the Jews were sacrificing the lambs for the Passover meal (19:14). At the end of the day the Temple would be washed to be ready for the following day's prayers. The pierced side therefore not only testifies to the death of Jesus, but once again, in this unique Johannine symbolism, presents Jesus as the Temple. The pierced side of Jesus is the definitive sign of his death, the destruction of one Temple and the bringing to birth of the new Temple/household of God. Thomas, who was not present at the

---

[38] Aune, *Cultic Setting*, 89–101.

[39] Ibid. 101–102.

[40] The first use of *ballō* in v. 27 has a direct object, "your finger"; the second *ballō* is not followed by an object.

[41] Coloe, *God Dwells with Us*, 206–209.

cross, is invited to "stretch out your hand" and throw (himself) into the sign of the pierced side, to become a participant in Jesus' death and thereby in the new Temple raised up in his death. Later disciples will also be able to participate in the meaning of Jesus' Passion when they, too, can "stretch out their hands" to receive the eucharistic bread, which for them is the sign of Jesus' flesh and blood given in death "for the life of the world" (6:51c).[42]

The verb used here to describe Thomas's action, *ballō*, may have been deliberately chosen because of its etymological links with the Jewish term "praise" or "confess," *todah*.[43] While *todah* is usually translated as praise or thanksgiving, Jerome Kodell notes that "the verb root of *todah* is an intensive form of the word *yadah* ("throw")."[44] A number of scholars of early eucharistic origins look to the *Todah* meal rather than the Passover meal as the basis for the eucharistic meals in the New Testament.[45] The *todah*, as a literary genre, recounts the reason for praising and thanking God and so can begin with a communal lament that becomes a confession of faith and praise. Psalm 22 is typical of this form. The *todah* is

> a thank offering by an individual or group which has experienced deliverance from some sickness or other threat. The worshiper offers an animal in sacrifice in the midst of friends and celebrates a new beginning with a meal offering (the *todah*) recounting the past troubles and the Lord's deliverance.[46]

The *todah* meal has strong elements of remembering and of thanksgiving, elements central to Eucharist, as testified in the earliest text we have from Paul's teaching at Corinth:

---

[42] The connection between the invitation to Thomas to "stretch out your hand" and the action of later believers at Eucharist was brought to my attention in Schneiders, "Resurrection Narrative," 604–606.

[43] G. Mayer, יָדָה תְּהָדִי תִּדְשֹׁה תַּדְרֵ *TDOT* V (1986) 427–43.

[44] Jerome Kodell, *The Eucharist in the New Testament* (Wilmington, DE: Michael Glazier, 1988) 49. The etymological link with *ballō* may explain why the Hebrew verb יָדָה found in 2 Chr 26:15; Isa 37:33; Job 38:6 is translated with *ballō* in the LXX.

[45] Léon-Dufour, *Sharing the Eucharistic Bread*, 42–44; Kodell, *Eucharist in the New Testament*, 48–52; Gese, *Essays on Biblical Theology*, 117–40.

[46] Kodell, *Eucharist in the New Testament*, 48. See also Léon-Dufour, *Sharing the Eucharistic Bread*, 42; John Reumann, *The Supper of the Lord: The New Testament, Ecumenical Dialogues, and Faith and Order on Eucharist* (Philadelphia: Fortress Press, 195) 22–23.

For I received from the Lord what I also delivered to you, that the Lord Jesus on the night when he was betrayed took bread, and when he had given thanks, he broke it, and said, "This is my body which is for you. Do this in remembrance of me." In the same way also the cup, after supper, saying, "This cup is the new covenant in my blood. Do this, as often as you drink it, in remembrance of me." For as often as you eat this bread and drink the cup, you proclaim the Lord's death until he comes. (1 Cor 11:23-26)

If the early Eucharist drew upon the *todah* form, then the rather strange use of *ballō* may further link this text with the community's worship.

6. The greeting of "Peace" (vv. 19, 26) is attested to in the early communities in the manner of a formal greeting at the start of a letter (e.g., Rom 1:7; 1 Cor 1:3; 2 Cor 1:2; Gal 1:3; Eph 1:2; Phil 1:2). The greeting of peace is also incorporated into the liturgies of Justin, the Clementine Liturgy, and the Liturgy of St. James. In Justin's *Apology* 1.65 we read: "At the end of the prayers we salute one another with a kiss." The Liturgy of St. James makes explicit that this kiss is associated with a greeting of peace.

> The priest says: "Peace to everyone." The people respond "And with your spirit." The archdeacon then says: "Let us greet one another with a holy kiss."[47]

Paul's letters frequently conclude by encouraging members of the community to greet each other with "a holy kiss" (Rom 16:16; 1 Cor 16:20; 2 Cor 13:12; 1 Thess 5:26). The Pauline letters are thus framed by a greeting of peace at the beginning, and a "holy kiss" at the end. John Suggit argues that since liturgies are generally conservative, "the existence of this common feature in so many early liturgies is strong indication of its early date."[48]

7. The disciples respond with joy and Thomas with a profession of faith, "My Lord and my God" (20:28). This statement of faith has no parallel in the gospel narrative, but forms an *inclusio* with the high christology found in the opening verse of the Prologue (1:1). The confession of Jesus as Lord was part of the confession of faith within the Pauline

---

[47] Εἰρήνη πᾶσιν. Καὶ τῷ πνεύματι σοῦ. Ἀγαπήσωμεν ἀλλήλου ἐν φιλήματι ἁγίῳ. Brightman, *Liturgies*, 43–44. For the kiss of peace in the Clementine Liturgy see ibid. 13.

[48] Suggit, "Eucharistic Significance," 55.

community,[49] and Cullmann writes: "We may assume with certainty that Confession formulae were recited in the early Christian service of worship."[50] Raymond E. Brown also places this confession of Jesus as "God" within a cultic or liturgical context,[51] and C. K. Barrett believes the entire passage from verse 19 "may be liturgical in origin."[52] The letter of Pliny to the emperor Trajan (111–112 C.E.) describes Christian worship as a gathering of Christians before sunrise at which they sing a song "to Christ as to a god."[53] In the Greek-speaking Jewish world, *Lord* was a reverential way of speaking to God. Larry Hurtado argues that in the earlier Aramaic-speaking communities believers were invoking Jesus as Lord in the prayer *Marana tha* (1 Cor 16:22).[54] The words of Thomas, "My Lord and my God" (*ho kyrios mou kai ho theos mou*) find their closest parallel in Ps 34:23 LXX, "my God and my Lord" (*ho theos mou kai ho kyrios mou*), which has characteristics of the *todah*, where there is a recitation of suffering moving to thanksgiving and praise. Dorothy Lee draws attention to the significance of Thomas's confession taking place outside the foundational events of Easter Sunday, even though related to these events.[55] She sees in this an implicit link to the liturgical life of the community. Thomas's words, "My Lord and my God," express "the faith of the ongoing community of faith Sunday by Sunday, where the Easter events are celebrated."[56]

Symbol or Fact?

The repetition of these seven features of the two resurrection appearances in verses 19-29 suggests that they have been given a deliberate emphasis and are not to be read simply as "just facts." In chapter 2, I noted an early study on Johannine symbolism by Juan Leal in which he named four criteria indicating that aspects of the narrative may have a symbolic as well as a literal meaning. These criteria bear repeating in support of my reading

---

[49] According to Larry Hurtado there are about 180 occurrences of *Kyrios* applied to Jesus in the seven undisputed letters of Paul; see Larry W. Hurtado, *Lord Jesus Christ: Devotion to Jesus in Earliest Christianity* (Grand Rapids: Eerdmans, 2003) 111.

[50] Cullmann, *Early Christian Worship*, 22.

[51] Brown, *Gospel* 2:1047.

[52] Barrett, *Gospel According to St John*, 573.

[53] Pliny, *Ep.* 10.96.7.

[54] Hurtado, *Lord Jesus Christ*, 110.

[55] Dorothy A. Lee, "Partnership in Easter Faith: The Role of Mary Magdalene and Thomas in John 20," *JSNT* 58 (1995) 37–49, at 48.

[56] Ibid.

a symbolic interpretation into this appearance narrative. Leal notes the following:

  i. inconsequential details that seem to play no part in the narrative,

 ii. a discourse set within the narrative of an event such that discourse and narrative are mutually illuminating,

iii. accentuating the importance of a person who has no significant role in context,

 iv. use of later liturgical and Christian expressions.[57]

The attention given to the first and the eighth day and the closed doors seem to be inconsequential details. The repetition of these seven features accentuates their importance. The greeting "Peace be with you" and Thomas's confession of faith are found in later liturgical usage. In a recent study of Johannine imagery Ruben Zimmermann proposes two criteria to determine if an element in the text should be understood symbolically.[58] He suggests that if a motif such as "light," "water," or "shepherd" holds a great deal of religious meaning within a community due to prior tradition, then it is most probable that this element has a symbolic significance due to its conventional usage. He names this "conventional plausibility." Other elements may be identified as having symbolic significance based on clues given in the text. This criterion he names "textual plausibility." In John 20 it is difficult to apply Zimmermann's criteria of conventional plausibility, because we are dealing with the earliest beginnings of a new religious community. We have only the earlier Synoptic Gospels and Pauline letters to establish whether some aspects of a text have become part of the Christian tradition and so meet the criteria of conventional plausibility. The gospel itself is participating in a symbolizing dynamic that later believers will draw upon in their writings and liturgical forms. With respect to the second criterion he proposes, that of textual plausibility, I have tried to identify, with the assistance of Juan Leal's criteria, the textual clues suggesting that a symbolic interpretation is appropriate. Apart from these seven common features, there are two further elements found only in the first household scene in which Thomas is absent; these also have parallels with eucharistic practice: namely, the gift of the Spirit and the forgiveness of sins (20:22-23).

The Easter gift of the Spirit in John 20 is associated with Jesus breathing on the gathered community, recalling the breath of God giving life to

---

[57] Leal, "El simbolismo," 344–46.
[58] Zimmermann, *Christologie der Bilder*, 140–41.

Adam in Genesis 2.[59] The Spirit is given to the community, and this gift is situated between Jesus' greeting of "Peace" (v. 21) and the command to forgive sin (v. 23).[60] The context of the gift of the Spirit places an emphasis on the Spirit's role in maintaining harmony within the community. Where the later liturgies invoke the Spirit on the bread and wine in order to change them into the body and blood of Christ, the earliest extant liturgy, that of the Apostolic Tradition of Hippolytus, dated around 217,[61] invokes the Spirit upon the community.

> And we ask that you would send your Holy Spirit upon the offerings of your Holy Church; that gathering them into one, you would grant to all who partake of the holy things (to partake) for the fullness of the Holy Spirit for the confirmation of faith in truth.[62]

This petition comes after the words of consecration, "hence it is an epiclesis which does not ask for the transformation of the gift, but for a fruitful communion."[63] There is some doubt whether this was part of the

---

[59] Martin Hengel sees in this *hapax legomenon, enephysēsen,* a direct reference back to Gen 2:7 LXX, describing God breathing the lifegiving Spirit into the nostrils of Adam. See Hengel, "The Old Testament in the Fourth Gospel," in Craig A. Evans and W. Richard Stegner, eds., *The Gospels and the Scriptures of Israel.* JSNTSup 104 (Sheffield: Sheffield Academic Press, 1994) 391; also Raymond E. Brown, "The Resurrection in John 20—A Series of Diverse Reactions," *Worship* 64 (1990) 203–204; Ignace de la Pottérie, "Genèse de la Foi Pascale D'Après Jn. 20," *NTS* 30 (1984) 37.

[60] D. A. Carson reads v. 22 as a symbolic promise of the Spirit: *The Gospel According to John* (Grand Rapids: Eerdmans, 1991) 652–54. For contrary arguments see Thomas R. Hatina, "John 20,22 in Its Eschatological Context: Promise or Fulfillment?" *Bib* 74 (1993) 196–219. With Hatina, I read v. 22 as the bestowal of the Spirit, fulfilling the promise in 7:37-39. With the gift of the Spirit, the transfer of the Temple symbolism from the person of Jesus to the future community of believers so that they can be sources of living water is brought to completion. What was a promise in the Feast of Tabernacles occurs in the hour, as the disciples become children in the *oikia tou patrou* and *adelphoi* of Jesus (20:17). As children of God (20:17), they are now God's dwelling place in history, making them the raised-up Temple (2:19) and thus able to be sources of living water. There is no need to impose on the Fourth Gospel the Lukan time schedule for Pentecost.

[61] On the authenticity of the Apostolic Tradition and its reliance on an early Greek text reflecting characteristics of Hippolytus' thought see Arthur H. Couratin and David H. Tripp, eds., *Liturgical Studies [of] E. C. Ratcliff* (London: SPCK, 1976) 20.

[62] Jasper and Cuming, *Prayers of the Eucharist,* 23.

[63] Jungmann, *The Early Liturgy,* 70. On the dating of the Eucharistic Prayer of Hippolytus see ibid. 52–58.

original Greek prayer or was a later interpolation,[64] but in support of an earlier dating it must be noted that the later trend in this part of the Eucharistic Prayer is to invoke the Spirit on the elements to pray that through the Spirit they may be changed into the body and blood of Jesus. In these later prayers the Spirit becomes the agent of change. The above Prayer of Hippolytus does not ask the Spirit to effect a change in the eucharistic elements, but to effect a communion and strengthening of faith in the community.

Even closer to the Johannine structure is a prayer found in the Maronite Church, possibly dating to the third century.

> Let your living and Holy Spirit, Lord, come and descend upon this offering of your servants, and may it avail to those who partake for propitiation of offenses and forgiveness of sins, for the blessed resurrection from the dead, and for new life in the kingdom of heaven forever.[65]

As with the Liturgy of Hippolytus, the invocation of the Spirit comes after the words of consecration, suggesting an early dating, and this prayer follows the Johannine pattern in linking the coming of the Spirit to the forgiveness of sin.

The earliest indication of a confession of sin within the Eucharist is found in the *Didache*:

> Come together on the dominical day of the Lord, break bread and give thanks, having first confessed your sins so that your sacrifice may be pure. Anyone who has a quarrel with his fellow should not gather with you until he has been reconciled, lest your sacrifice be profaned. (*Did.* 14:1)[66]

The Last Supper narrative of Matthew's Gospel provides further first-century evidence of a similar theological perspective that links Eucharist and the forgiveness of sin: "And he took a cup, and when he had given thanks he gave it to them, saying, 'Drink of it, all of you; for this is my blood of the covenant, which is poured out for many for the forgiveness of sins'" (Matt 26:27-28). The letter of Clement, dated 95–96, contains a long prayer that may be a type of eucharistic prayer in a time when there was no

---

[64] See the discussion of the dating in Couratin and Tripp, eds., *Liturgical Studies*, 22–27.

[65] Jasper and Cuming, *Prayers of the Eucharist*, 33.

[66] Similarly, "in the assembly you will confess your sins and you will not go to prayer with a bad conscience" (*Did.* 4:14); "If anyone is holy, let him come; if anyone is not, let him repent" (*Did.* 10:6).

set pattern.[67] In this prayer the leader prays: "Forgive our sins and injustices, our failures and faults. Do not take account of every sin of your servants and handmaids, but purify us with your purifying truth" (*1 Clem.* 60:1-2).[68] If the household scene in John 20 reflects the eucharistic experience of the Johannine community, it may explain why the exhortation to forgive sins occurs here in this final chapter, although the Fourth Gospel has paid little direct attention to this theme. So strange are these words about forgiveness that Terence Forestell even considers 20:23 a foreign addition to the narrative, introduced later to deal with pastoral issues.[69] There is no need to call on another hand if the Thomas pericope reflects early eucharistic experience such as we see in the texts cited above, where a link is made between the gift of the Spirit and the forgiveness of sin.[70] These two features, combined with those common to both sections of the diptych, add further weight to understanding this scene as emerging from the experience of the community's worship.

There is one element of eucharistic worship that is glaringly absent from John 20, namely bread. In Luke 24, very clearly the link is made between the post-resurrection community and Eucharist in the Emmaus story, where there is a description of Jesus breaking bread with two disciples, with clear echoes of the Last Supper (Luke 24:30; cf. 22:19).[71] Some may wish to see a similar reference to bread to confirm the association between the Thomas scene and Eucharist that I have been presenting, but this is to misunderstand Johannine symbolism. Eucharist is the celebration of the presence of the Absent One. While the community has the presence of the historical Jesus there is no need to have Eucharist also; but when Jesus has returned to the Father, then his presence with the community is experienced and celebrated in and through Eucharist. Eucharist is the real presence of Jesus in symbol. The eucharistic bread is the body of the Risen One in the only form accessible to human experience. This is the nature of symbol, as

[67] Georges Blond, "Clement of Rome," in Willy Rordorf et al., eds., *The Eucharist of the Early Christians* (New York: Pueblo, 1978) 40.

[68] Blond, "Clement of Rome," 34.

[69] J. Terence Forestell, *The Word of the Cross: Salvation as Revelation in the Fourth Gospel.* AnBib 57 (Rome: Biblical Institute Press, 1974) 157.

[70] It is beyond the scope of this book to discuss the very divided interpretive history of 20:23. Brown (*Gospel* 2:1039–45) discusses the issue of forgiveness in the life of the community. What I am pointing out is a possible explanation for the reference to forgiveness, linked to the gift of the Spirit, in this post-Resurrection narrative.

[71] On a possible eucharistic background for the Emmaus narrative see Raymond Orlett, "An Influence of the Early Liturgy upon the Emmaus Account," *CBQ* 21 (1959) 212–19.

Sandra Schneiders says: "The task of the symbol is to make that which by nature is spiritual or transcendent, and therefore sensibly unavailable in itself, intersubjectively available by giving it a 'body,' a sensible form."[72] To have both the symbol (bread) and what is symbolized (the Risen Jesus) within the same scene would be to undermine the sacramental principle that lies at the heart of Johannine theology as expressed in the Prologue: "the Word became flesh" (1:14).[73]

In commenting on criteria for finding Old Testament allusions within the New Testament, Richard B. Hays proposes seven criteria to test the likelihood that the author is using such a technique: availability, volume, recurrence, thematic coherence, historical plausibility, history of interpretation, and satisfaction.[74] I believe his criteria can be used with equal validity for the movement from the New Testament into the later liturgy of the community. Six of these seven criteria are satisfied in trying to assess whether John 20 has possible allusions to the early Christian Eucharist. We know from Paul's first letter to the Corinthians that Christians gathered to celebrate the Lord's Supper (1 Cor 11), so this practice was available for the evangelist to draw upon in the shaping of his resurrection narrative. I have noted many points of contact with early forms of Christian worship. There is coherence in seeing a link between resurrection and Eucharist when one considers the similar link in John 6. There is theological and aesthetic satisfaction in interpreting this pericope in the light of Christian worship, and it is plausible that-first century readers would understand the Johannine text in this way. Some may require more explicit references than the allusions I have outlined, but the comments of David Aune express my own convictions in this regard.

> It would therefore be incorrect to claim, with Ernst Käsemann, that basic elements of congregational life, worship, sacraments and the ministry play only insignificant roles in the Fourth Gospel.[75] *Such elements do not receive explicit treatment precisely because they are the presuppositions of the ecclesial context out of which the Gospel arose.* Since the Fourth Gospel was not

---

[72] Schneiders, *Written That You May Believe*, 70. See also the comments by Francis J. Moloney on the Bread of Life discourse: Moloney, *John*, 223.

[73] The term "sacramental principle" is a found in the writing of Sandra Schneiders to describe the relationship between history and symbolism in Johannine theology. See Schneiders, "Symbolism and the Sacramental Principle in the Fourth Gospel," 233.

[74] Richard B. Hays, *Echoes of Scripture in the Letters of Paul* (New Haven: Yale University Press, 1989) 29–32.

[75] Ernst Käsemann, *The Testament of Jesus,* 27.

written for the consumption of modern scholars, it is necessary for us to break the code in which the Gospel is written, and which it presupposes.[76]

Raymond Orlett makes a similar comment when proposing a possible liturgical background for the Emmaus narrative.

As we read the account in Lk it seems that the author intends his reader to see the parallels, *which would have been much more evident perhaps to his first readers than to us today.* The early community would see a typical sense to be found in the experience of the two disciples on the way to Emmaus. The antitype would be their liturgical experience.[77]

In my analysis of the Thomas scene I have attempted to "break the code" and reveal its relationship to the Eucharistic gatherings of the Johannine community. With such an understanding, I now turn to the narrative function of this scene and its major role in bringing the gospel to its conclusion.

The Narrative Function of the Scene

The Fourth Gospel began with a Prologue that invited the reader to move from the timelessness of God's eternity, "in the beginning," into the narrative time of the gospel, "the Word became flesh and dwelt among us." In this way the Prologue is a bridge from eternity into history. The household scene in John 20 has a similar bridging function, for it moves the reader from the narrative time of the first Easter household gathered around the Risen One into the reader's own experience of gathering in the household of God around Eucharist. Where the original disciples could see and touch Jesus in the flesh, later disciples can see, touch, and be nourished by the eucharistic body of Jesus. The risen body of Jesus in the midst of his disciples is foundational for Christian faith in the ongoing presence of the risen and glorified Jesus within the believing community, now mediated through the Spirit.

The structure of John 20 moves the reader from a place of death, the tomb, to a place of life, the household of disciples gathered around Jesus.[78]

---

[76] Aune, *Cultic Setting*, 73 (italics supplied). Although cited earlier, Aune's comments are particularly appropriate in this context and so are repeated here.

[77] Orlett, "Emmaus Account," 218, emphasis supplied.

[78] With a number of other scholars I structure John 20 into two major scenes (vv. 1-18; vv. 19-29) determined by the two locations, namely, the tomb (v. 1) and a house (v. 19); see Moloney, *John*, 517; Brown, *Gospel* 2:965; Schneiders, *Written that you May Believe*, 190.

The gospel narrative therefore depicts the theological meaning of the crucifixion as the raising of the new Temple/household of God. Before this gospel closes, the readers are invited to see the reality of this new household in the post-Easter time. However, this picture of the new household of God is not to be a glimpse back into the distant past, which could simply remain as nostalgic longing; the gospel invites readers to become participants in this new household by seeing in the reality of their own eucharistic gatherings the continuation of the disciples' experience. In this way the household scene of John 20 opens out to the household gatherings of all future believers, asking them to see the signs and believe.

That this is its intention is made clear by Jesus' final words in which he speaks of those beyond the narrative: "Blessed are those who have not seen and yet believe" (v. 29). Brown draws the comparison with a stage play and writes evocatively:

> Throughout the Gospel, and more particularly in the last discourse, in what the evangelist has been describing on the stage of early 1st-century Palestine, he has had in mind an audience seated in the darkened theatre of the future, silently viewing what Jesus was saying and doing. True to the limitations and logic of the stage drama imposed by the Gospel form, the Johannine Jesus could address that audience only indirectly through the disciples who shared the stage and gave voice to sentiments and reactions that were shared by the audience as well. But now, as the curtain is about to fall on the stage drama, the lights in the theatre are suddenly turned on. Jesus shifts his attention from the disciples on the stage to the audience that has become visible and makes clear that his ultimate concern is for them—those who have come to believe in him through the word of his disciples (17:20).[79]

Conclusion

Thomas was absent from the first gathering of the household, and in this situation, even having heard the Easter proclamation, "We have seen the Lord" (v. 25), Thomas voices the strongest rejection of faith in this gospel: "I will not believe" (v. 25). Before Thomas will believe the disciples' testimony, he demands that certain criteria be met. He places conditions on his believing: "Unless I see . . . and place . . ." (v. 25).[80] Being outside the household of disciples has placed Thomas outside the experience of Jesus' presence and outside their Easter faith.

---

[79] Brown, *Gospel* 2:1049.
[80] Ignace de la Potérie, "Genèse de la Foi Pascale D'Après Jn. 20," 42.

Thomas's state as an outsider is corrected in verse 26. Now Thomas is gathered within the household on the first day of the week, the day of later eucharistic gatherings, and Jesus reveals his presence in the midst of the household. In very strange wording, Jesus offers to meet the criteria for faith that Thomas had earlier expressed. Jesus does not say, "Open your eyes and see," but "put your finger here and see." Thomas is given an opportunity to "see" with his sense of touch. He is challenged to come to faith by stretching out his hand and "throwing" into the side of Jesus. Faith for Thomas is to be first a physical placing and touching. Thomas is to experience the presence of Jesus, where before he knew only absence, but only when he gathers within the eucharistic household. Thomas thus functions as a representative character who brings into the text the experience of future believers. They, too, are absent from the experience of the historical Jesus and his resurrection appearances. They, too, know the apparent absence of Jesus. By narrating this scene, drawing on features of early Christian Eucharist, the evangelist makes available to later believers the Easter experience of the disciples.

If my arguments are correct, this scene has been shaped by the Johannine community's experience of Eucharist in which future believers can, like Thomas, stretch out their hand in a physical act of faith. Thomas's words, the words of one not present for the initial Easter experience, now express the perfect act of faith: "My Lord and my God" (v. 28). Thomas has let go his previous criteria for faith. There is no suggestion in the text that he did place his finger in the mark of the nails and his hand in Jesus' side. The sight of the Risen One bearing the marks of the cross is sufficient. In this experience he recognizes the true identity of Jesus and makes a personal commitment to him: "my Lord," "my God."[81] Although Thomas has been privy to a visionary experience, this need not detract from his faith confession.

Thomas voices an understanding not only of Jesus' identity, but also of the significance of that identity for himself. In naming Jesus "my God," Thomas has moved away from strict Jewish monotheism, in which YHWH alone is God, into a new faith community of the brothers and sisters of Jesus (20:17). In an article published in 1984, Timothy Radcliffe discusses the significance of the community context for understanding this confession of Jesus as God.[82] He compares the christological claims of Paul and of John

---

[81] According to Brown there are only three NT passages that indisputably call Jesus "God" (John 1:1; 20:28; Heb 1:8). See Raymond E. Brown, *Jesus God and Man. Modern Biblical Reflections* (New York: Macmillan, 1967) 23–29.

[82] Radcliffe, "The Locus of Confession," 52–62.

and concludes that the Fourth Gospel is able to call Jesus "God" because it has begun the process of moving apart from Judaism.

> But John writes on the other side of the break with Judaism . . . with clearer boundaries between insiders and outsiders, and between the language of those who belong and those who do not. It was this ecclesial transformation that made possible, though it did not demand, Thomas' confession before Jesus, "My Lord and my God."[83]

He further notes the frequent claim that christological development occurred first in hymns and prayers and adds that this is so, not necessarily because hymns and prayers used in worship are more poetic and therefore open to greater freedom of expression, but because the language of worship lies at the very heart of community. "It is there that the language of the community is at its greatest distance from the language of outsiders."[84] Taking these insights further, if the language of worship expresses the "heart of the community gathered together," then this language will reflect not only the community's understanding of God, but also, and perhaps most importantly, its own self-identity in relation to God.

Before Easter, disciples were outsiders to Jesus' experience of God. Through his death, resurrection, and gift of the Spirit, outsiders have become insiders (12:32), participating in Jesus' own filiation, able to call God "my Father" (20:17) and knowing themselves to be dwelling in the *oikia tou patrou* (14:2). In coming to know their own new identity as children of God, disciples come to know the identity of the one who made this possible, the Son who has made them truly free (8:36). As Paul Bradshaw comments, "It is only after the Resurrection that Jesus calls the disciples his brothers, and it is only when they are called his brothers that they can call him God."[85]

---

[83] Ibid. 52.

[84] Ibid. 53.

[85] Ibid. 61. In this article Radcliffe discusses the different historical and religious contexts exhibited by the Pauline letters and the Fourth Gospel. He argues that in the early years believers saw themselves continuing within the faith of Judaism. Only when there had been a social transformation separating Jews and Christians, such as we find in the Gospel of John (9:42; 12:42; 16:2), could the early believers move away from strict Jewish monotheism. He speaks of an "ecclesial transformation" that made possible Thomas' confession. On the complex issue of Jewish-Christian relations in the first two centuries I draw attention to Judith M. Lieu, *Image and Reality: The Jews in the World of the Christians in the Second Century* (Edinburgh: T&T Clark, 1996); eadem, *Neither Jew nor Greek? Constructing Early Christianity.* Studies of the New Testament and its World (Edinburgh: T&T Clark, 2002); and Kåre Sigvald Fuglseth, *Johannine Sectarianism in Perspective: A Sociological, Historical and Comparative Analysis of Temple and*

Thomas's confession is the high point of Johannine faith, giving voice to the community's faith in Jesus' identity and its own self-identity as the household of God.[86]

Then, from within this Easter household, symbolic of all eucharistic households, Jesus speaks from the narrative to the future believers. These are the final words of Jesus, now the Risen Lord, and they are a beatitude spoken into history to all communities of faith: "Blessed are those who have not seen and yet believe." With this blessing on the future households of faith, the gospel narrative ends.[87]

Social Relationships in the Gospel of John, Philo and Qumran. NovTSup 119 (Leiden: Brill, 2005).

[86] With Brown, (*Gospel* 2:1047), Moloney (*John*, 537) I see Thomas's confession as the high point of Johannine faith, forming an *inclusio* with the pronouncement at the start of the Prologue (1:1c) and appropriately bringing the narrative to its conclusion. As a character in the narrative, Thomas of course has had the privilege of faith through seeing Jesus, but his faith is not therefore inferior to that of those who do not see Jesus but come to faith through hearing the Gospel word and experiencing the community. The beatitude expresses that this privilege of seeing Jesus is not the only way of "possessing the joy and blessings of the risen Jesus" (Brown, *Gospel* 2:1049).

[87] Raymond F. Collins ("Blessed are Those Who Have Not Seen," 189) points to the gnomic character of beatitudes phrased in the third person, which therefore have a general sense not limited to the immediate hearers of this gospel.

The Household of God

In *God Dwells with Us*, I proposed that the Temple was the major christological image in the Fourth Gospel.[1] The Temple spoke of Jesus' identity as one in whom God dwelt, and of his mission, to build a new Temple wherein God would continue to dwell in the world. In the gospel Jesus speaks of the Temple as "my Father's house" (2:16), echoing the most frequent name of the Temple in Israel's Scriptures as "the LORD's house." Across the gospel there are indicators that the image of the Temple will be transferred to the Christian community, so that they will become a new house of God. This is particularly clear in chapter 14 when Jesus speaks again of "my Father's house" (14:2) and then reveals the future dwellings of the Father, the Spirit, and himself within the believer. Since the terminology "my Father's house" is given a personal sense, in keeping with its Old Testament usage, where it means "my Father's household," this current work has given attention to household imagery across the gospel.

The Prologue offers the first clues that the Fourth Gospel is going to draw on household imagery. The object of Jesus' coming into the world is stated in terms of believers becoming "children of God" (1:12). The relationship between the enfleshed Word and God is described analogically as a father-son relationship (1:14, 18) and this analogy will dominate the gospel. God is named "Father" in the Fourth Gospel more than in all the Synoptic Gospels combined.[2] Correlative with the title "Father" to speak of God is the title "Son" to speak of Jesus. The metaphorical dimension of

---

[1] As well as my own work see also Franz Mussner, "Jesus und 'das Haus des Vaters' —Jesus als 'Tempel,'" in Josef Schreiner, ed., *Freude am Gottesdienst: Aspekte ursprünglicher Liturgie* (Stuttgart: Katholisches Bibelwerk, 1983) 267–75.

[2] Mark, 4x; Luke, 17x; Matthew, 43x; John, 124x.

these terms must not be lost because of their familiarity in the Christian tradition. Read in its first-century context, the father-son relationship presupposes a concept of a divine household, which was already part of the pre-Johannine Christian tradition (Gal 6:10; Eph 2:19; Heb 3:6). It is the genius of the Fourth Evangelist to take this foundational terminology and develop it into a metaphorical network, not only describing Jesus but extended also to include believers.[3]

Review

I began with the premise that the community behind the Fourth Gospel perceived itself as a gathering of children within the household of God. This self-identity is also their underlying spirituality, giving rise to theological reflection on the meaning of Jesus' life, death, and resurrection. Experiencing themselves as beloved children of God through their participation in Jesus' relationship with God, this community reshaped and retold the Jesus traditions from this post-Easter faith perspective. The gospel text is the product of their experience and theological interpretation of the Jesus event.[4]

To test the validity of this premise I re-read the gospel, giving particular attention to the household scenes. The initial gathering of disciples occurred in the context of John's witnessing to Jesus (John 1–3). In examining the different emphasis the Fourth Gospel gives to John's testimony, I drew on Middle Eastern customs surrounding a marriage. These customs explained the Johannine characterization of John as the witness (1:6), the voice (1:23), and the friend of the bridegroom (3:29). The movement of the narrative across the first three chapters follows the normal progression in the development of a household: the initial seeking of a bride, the betrothal, wedding, incorporation into the groom's family, coming to the father's house, all culminating in the birth of a child.

Chapters 5 and 6 examined the household of Bethany, with the raising of Lazarus (John 11) and the scene of the anointing (John 12:1-8). The earlier Nicodemus scene introduced the Johannine understanding of life, i.e., eternity life, begun now through belief in Jesus' word. The Lazarus episode raised the painful issue of Jesus' apparent absence in the face of

---

[3] In his concluding summary Klaus Scholtissek sees in John 1:11-13 the semantic axis of the gospel. He proposes that across the Johannine corpus the family and house metaphor is the basic one, "eine ekklesiologische Leitmetapher"; see Scholtissek, *In Ihm sein und bleiben*, 371.

[4] Sandra Schneiders, *Written That You May Believe*, 48.

death. What is the meaning of death in a community promised eternity life? The raising of Lazarus confirms Jesus' teaching that in him eternity life has become a present reality. Those believing the word of Jesus, who is Wisdom incarnate, only "seem to die" (Wis 3:2). A household of death is transformed into a household of life through the word of Jesus. Post-Easter believers may no longer have the physical presence of Jesus, but belief in his word assures them of seeing "the glory of God" (11:40), as the first disciples saw that glory in the flesh of Jesus (1:14). In the anointing that followed this episode the gospel is clearly moving from Jesus' ministry into his "hour." Caiaphas has already determined that "one man should die for the people" (11:50). The flesh of Jesus, introduced as the tabernacling presence of the divine Word (1:14), is anointed as Moses once anointed Israel's tabernacle (Exod 40:9-13). Mary repeats the actions of generous-hearted Israelites in the wilderness in offering fine ointment to mark the sanctity of Jesus' body (Exod 35:5-8). The fragrance of her anointing oils fills the entire household, echoing the description of God's glory filling the Tabernacle and Temple (Exod 40:34-35; 1 Kgs 8:10-11). The "hour" of Jesus has implications for his disciples, and so the entire household is touched by her action.

From chapter 11 onward, characters in the gospel address Jesus as "Lord" (*Kyrie*). This title dominates the chapters in which Jesus is within a household setting, e.g., the household of Bethany (11:3, 12, 21, 27, 32, 34, 39), the household of "his own" (13:6, 9, 25, 36, 37; 14:5, 8, 22), and the Easter household (20:20, 25, 28). In my examination of chapter 11, I discussed the theological meaning of *kyrios*, given its usage in the Septuagint to translate the name YHWH; but *kyrios* also has a social meaning as "the master of a household." The Bethany household of chapter 11 marks a transition from the public ministry of Jesus to a more private setting. In the privacy of his own friends and disciples Jesus is called *kyrios* (13:13), reflecting a self-perception of this inner group as members of his household. It is significant that this title is used of Jesus primarily within household settings,[5] for "Lord" (*kyrios*) is a distinctly relational title that Jesus reinterprets in terms of friendship to the point of death (15:13-14).[6] Interpreted through the lens of Easter, the title *kyrios* offers insight into the christology of the Johannine community and its own self-perception, i.e., its ecclesiology. In its theological sense *kyrios* acknowledges the divinity of Jesus. In its social sense it names the community as members of his household.

---

[5] It is used only twice before the Bethany household episode, and in both these cases it is a profession of faith (6:68; 9:38).

[6] Ruben Zimmermann, *Christologie der Bilder*, 175–76.

Chapters 7 and 8 explore the inner dynamism of the household as articulated in the final discourse (13:1–15:17). In the footwashing Jesus symbolically draws disciples into the meaning of his death, which is then explained in the following discourse. In the Fourth Gospel, Jesus' death is his return to the Father in order to enable a new, more inclusive mode of presence for believers of all times. Jesus' return will make possible the mutual indwelling of Father, Son, and Spirit with all disciples. The post-Easter dwelling of God in the world is named in terms of Israel's Temple traditions as "my Father's house" (14:2)—or more accurately, "my Father's household." Temple and household symbolism come together in this phrase, and the footwashing, in this perspective, is a ritual of welcome to the Temple/household of God. In this context Jesus interprets his death as a self-giving act of love, the model of love within the divine household (15:9). This model of self-giving love he proposes is the one essential requirement for the disciples. "As I have loved you, so also you should love one another" (13:34). Love is the blueprint, the paradigm (*hypodeigma*) of the new Temple/household of God.[7]

The discourse following the footwashing (ch. 14) teaches the disciples the meaning of Jesus' death, but the questions posed by Thomas (14:5), Philip (14:8), and Judas (14:22) show that they have not understood his meaning. In chapter 15, which is probably a slightly later elaboration on chapter 14 (*relecture*), Jesus teaches again that the love between Father and Son is to be the model of the relationships between the disciples (15:9, 12). Such love is only possible in Jesus. He is the only mediator, the only Son who permanently dwells in the household (8:35), and as such he is the one who is able to invite others into the household. The image of the vine and branches speaks of the mutual intimacy between Jesus and disciples, which makes possible the mutual indwelling of Father and Spirit. By dwelling in Jesus, who is in the Father's heart (1:18), believers can also dwell in God. The teaching about the reciprocal relationships between Father and Son, and Jesus and believers, is in my opinion the greatest insight of this gospel. The same loving communion of life experienced within the divine Godhead is opened up as a possibility for all.[8]

Since the Johannine theology of the cross was explored in my earlier work, this study moved from the discourse immediately into chapter 20 and proposed that the resurrection narratives in this gospel are primarily focused

---

[7] I noted earlier that the terms *paradeigma* and *hypodeigma* are used to describe the models of the Tabernacle and Temple given to Moses (Exod 25:9), Solomon (1 Chr 28:11, 12, 18, 19), and Ezekiel (Ezek 42:15).

[8] One of the richest explorations of this theme of mutual immanence is the work of Klaus Scholtissek frequently cited in this work.

on its meaning for the community. The cross is Jesus' hour of glorification and the completion of his work. Jesus needs no further testimony to his triumph. Chapter 20 is needed to witness to the meaning of the resurrection for the disciples, and in this gospel it also reaches beyond the narrative into the world of the reader.

The household scene (20:19-29) not only describes the coming to faith of post-Easter disciples, but also addresses the faith experience of later communities. The final scene takes place in a household gathered in the evening on the first day of the week (20:19). This household experiences the presence of Jesus (20:19) and the lifegiving Spirit (20:22). Words of peace are spoken (20:19, 21, 26), hands are invited to reach out in faith (20:27), and within the household there is a confession of faith in Jesus as Lord and God (20:29). I propose that this Easter narrative carries the memory and shape of the eucharistic experience of the Johannine community. Readers of this text are therefore given an opportunity to see in their own eucharistic gatherings the same faith experience as that of the early disciples. The gap between text and reader at this point is bridged. The reader is invited into the narrative, to become part of the household, and with Thomas to proclaim "my *kyrios* and my God."

The above brief review shows that the imagery of the household pervades the gospel in the naming of Jesus, "Son" and "*kyrios*," in the movement of the narrative across the first three chapters, in the household of Bethany (chs. 11–12), and especially in the "hour" (chs. 13–20). Jan Van der Watt and Ruben Zimmermann rightly identify the household/family as one of the major metaphorical concepts of the gospel.[9]

Household Ecclesiology and Spirituality

This book has not been an exercise in academic research divorced from the current issues facing Christian churches and all members of the earth community. In particular, I ask the question: does a household ecclesiology offer an alternative model of church for our time with implications for worship and spirituality? An adequate answer to this question would require further volumes, but here I will note four possible trajectories for further exploration.

1. The household model as imaged in the language of the Fourth Gospel essentially deconstructs the patriarchal household model of antiquity, since it takes as its point of reference the divine communion. The Fourth Gospel, while using "father-son" terminology, reconstitutes the relationship as

---

[9] Zimmermann, *Christologie der Bilder*, 172–83; Van der Watt, *Family of the King*, ch. 4.

a dynamism of mutual self-giving love.[10] In turn, although Jesus can rightly be called *kyrios*, he acts in loving service in washing the feet of disciples, he calls members of the household "friends," and he gives the ultimate sign of love unto death. We do not have within this household a hierarchy of leadership other than the leadership of faith and love, seen particularly in the female characters of the Samaritan woman, Mary of Bethany, and Mary Magdalene, and also the Beloved Disciple, who remains anonymous and in his anonymity includes all beloved disciples, women and men.

2. Cultic ecclesial models, when based on ancient practices, restrict and even exclude the participation of women due to concepts of cultic purity and impurity. While worship in the Temple was primarily the responsibility of adult males, piety and its expressions within the household were shared. Women were managers within the household, and within its domain they took leadership roles in rituals of worship. "In the ancient world religious matters within the household were the woman's classic sphere of influence."[11] Within the Roman world, wealthy women could own property and be managers of households in their own right.[12] In the New Testament house-churches women clearly had such leadership.[13] Over the first six hundred years the church gradually shifted in its self-perception from a household gathered at the Lord's table to a larger congregation gathered to offer sacrifice on the altar. During these centuries we see a gradual decline in women's liturgical leadership.[14]

---

[10] Dorothy A. Lee, "Beyond Suspicion? The Fatherhood of God in the Fourth Gospel," *Pacifica* 8 (1995) 140–54. "The symbol of divine fatherhood is not presented in a dictatorial or subjugating way; on the contrary, authority is seen within the context of intimacy and love, and divine sovereignty is presented, within a relational setting, as life-giving, liberating and inclusive." See Lee, *Flesh and Glory*, 128.

[11] Roger W. Gehring, *House Church and Mission*, 211.

[12] "The Roman woman had few restrictions in engaging with the world beyond the *domus*; she could own all manner of property, including real estate, slaves and commercial businesses, which she could generally control without spousal approval . . . she could attend the public baths, enjoy entertainments such as the theatre and public games, and even participate in significant forms of civic involvement such as holding priesthoods in the imperial cult." See Michele George, "Domestic Architecture and Household Relations: Pompeii and Roman Ephesus," *JSNT* 27 (2004) 12–13.

[13] E.g., Prisca/Priscilla (Acts 18:18, 26; Rom 16:3; 2 Tim 4:19), Lydia (Acts 14:15-16), Phoebe (Rom 16:1-2), Mary (Rom 16:6), Junia (Rom 16:7), Nympha (Col 4:15). "Approximately one-fourth of the co-workers mentioned in the undisputed Pauline Epistles are women," Gehring, *House Church and Mission*, 211.

[14] "[T]he highest level of church office for women was on the decline already by the end of the sixth century. Various reasons are suggested by historians. Certainly the rise

Reclaiming the earlier household model may offer a more liberating way of perceiving the church assembly and its worship, particularly the participation of women.

3. The Johannine story of salvation is in essence a love story. God loved the world, and in love sent Jesus to gather children into the divine communion. This is a salvation story that gives little power to sin as the motive for the incarnation and situates salvation in God's initiative to love and to be known. The Fourth Gospel therefore offers a model of salvation in terms of God's ongoing revelation rather than reparation. From John's perspective creation has been continually in process of unfolding, for God has been continually working (John 5:17).[15] Jesus continues God's creative work, revealing a new depth to the meaning of "life" as a participation in God's own eternity life (3:16). The Fourth Gospel starts "in the beginning" and relates an ongoing story of creation that has its origin in and through the eternal *logos*[16] and is brought to completion only with Jesus' word from the cross, "It is finished" (19:30). The cross ushers in the new creation where, through the indwelling presence of Jesus and the Spirit, men and women can know themselves to be children in God's household (20:17). In a world that is becoming more alert to the fragile ecology of our planet, and our small place in a vast cosmological process, a spirituality of dwelling in God's *oikos* offers a rich biblical and thoroughly Christian dimension to the human desire to live in harmony with all creation.[17]

4. The Johannine vision of mutual indwelling of God and the believer opens to all Christians the possibility of experiencing the divine presence. What is particularly Johannine is the emphasis on reciprocal indwelling. God dwells in us, and we dwell in God. In his use of the verb "dwell"

---

of cultic sacramentalism that highlighted cultic purity as requisite for approaching the increasingly sacred sacramental celebration was a key factor"; see, Kevin Madigan and Caroline Osiek, *Ordained Women in the Early Church: A Documentary History* (Baltimore: John Hopkins University Press, 2005) 205.

[15] See also my discussion of the Prologue: "The six strophe structure of the Prologue, like the six days of creation in Genesis 1, requires one final act to bring it to completion. This act begins in verse 19 as the Gospel narrative of God's final work, to be accomplished in the life and death of Jesus, now begins" (*God Dwells with Us*, 18–23).

[16] Scholtissek and Lee touch on the impact of the incarnation on the whole of created reality. See Scholtissek, *In Ihm sein und bleiben*, 364; Lee, *Flesh and Glory*, 61–62.

[17] The word "ecology" has its root in the Greek term for a house (*oikos*). A proper understanding of the whole of creation as God's *oikos* has much to offer current ecological concerns. Ecclesiology, through the lens of the Fourth Gospel, becomes *oik(os)ology.*

(*menein*) the Fourth Evangelist expresses the mystery of divine interiority known through experience, which is usually termed mysticism.[18] In trying to clarify what it is that is meant by the word "mysticism" or "mystical," Ignace del la Potterie writes:

> This is why, with several recent authors, it seems necessary to us to insert into the definition of the word "mystical," the element of experience; it would be then, according to J. Huby, the "experiential awakening of the life of grace in the heart." In short, one could say with J. Maréchal, that it is about "the intuition of God's presence" in love, or, "of the certainty of the presence of [God]"; in yet other words, it speaks of the awakening of the presence of God in us and us in God.[19]

The evangelist writes of the inner dynamism of love existing between Father and Son, and states that this same dynamism is to be in the life of the believer. He makes this claim with the assertion of experiential knowledge, "he knows that he tells the truth" (19:35). The boldness of the evangelist's claim to know the inner dynamism of God, and to know that this same loving relationship has been made accessible to all, can only have its basis in the living, Spirit-mediated experience of the community. In Scholtissek's words:

> The language and theology of Immanence in the Johannine corpus (likewise the Pauline corpus) is inconceivable without a reference to the faith experiences of the beloved disciples, the Evangelists, the Presbyters and the Christians, to which they give witness. The Immanence statements are the reflective result of early-Christian faith experiences that demand articulation.[20]

Conclusion

This book began where my last book ended, with an insight into the crucifixion as the raising of a new Temple/household of God. The hermeneutical process of this work is best described as a rereading of the gospel with an informed, but nevertheless intuitive guess that the symbolism of the household may provide insight into the spirituality and identity of the

---

[18] Scholtissek uses the term *mystagogisch*, which carries the sense of the experience as an ongoing dynamic process of coming to and following Jesus. See Scholtissek, *In Ihm sein und bleiben*, 379, and especially Scholtissek, "Mystagogische Christologie," 412–26.

[19] Ignace de la Potterie, "Demeurer," 857.

[20] Scholtissek, *In Ihm sein und bleiben*, 378.

Johannine community. Reading the gospel in this symbolic manner, I am aware that, with a few exceptions, the household imagery is not overt. It is the nature of symbol to resist immediate understanding and to engage the reader with puzzling questions. Symbols are subtle, and their meaning will only be unraveled through repeated reading of the text, with each reading deepening the insights and awakening new perceptions to be brought to future readings.[21] In addition, symbolism depends for its meaning on the conventions and culture of the community. Ruben Zimmermann writes that for symbols to communicate effectively the author and reader must share the same symbolic codes.[22] Read from a distance of two thousand years and from a different cultural experience, much of the Johannine symbolism may remain vague and undeciphered for modern readers. Zimmermann's criteria of conventional and textual plausibility offer some measure of testing whether my reading is justified. Besides asking whether this is a plausible interpretation, I ask: is it coherent with the entire gospel narrative, and does it help to make sense of the text? My answer obviously is "yes."

The first Epistle of John is the earliest commentary on the Fourth Gospel, and these ancient words fittingly conclude this study of God's household:[23]

> "Beloved, we are now God's children,
> and what we shall become has not yet been revealed,
> but we know that when it is revealed we shall be like God,
> for we shall see God as s/he is." (1 John 3:2)

---

[21] On this point I agree with Zimmermann's statement that understanding the symbolic network across the entire gospel is only possible through repeated readings. See Zimmermann, *Christologie der Bilder*, 419.

[22] Ibid. 140.

[23] On the relationship between the Fourth Gospel and the Johannine Epistles see John Painter, *1, 2, and 3 John*, SP 18 (Collegeville: Liturgical Press, 2002) 58–74.

Bibliography

Reference Works

Aland, Barbara, Kurt Aland, Johannes Karavidopoulos, Carlo Martini, and Bruce Metzger, eds. *The Greek New Testament*. 4th ed. Stuttgart: United Bible Societies, 1998.

Botterweck, G. Johannes, and Helmer Ringgren, eds. *Theological Dictionary of the Old Testament*. 14 vols. Grand Rapids: Eerdmans, 1974.

Brenton, Lancelot. *The Septuagint with Apocrypha: Greek and English*. Peabody, MA: Hendrickson, 1980.

Buttrick, George A., et. al., eds. *The Interpreter's Dictionary of the Bible*. 5 vols. Nashville: Abingdon Press, 1962.

Charlesworth, James H., ed. *The Old Testament Pseudepigrapha*. London: Darton, Longman & Todd, 1985.

Delebecque, Édouard. *Évangile de Jean: Texte traduit et annoteé*. CahRB 23. Paris: Gabalda, 1987.

Evans, Craig A., and Stanley E. Porter, eds. *Dictionary of New Testament Background*. Downers Grove: InterVarsity Press, 2000.

Freedman, David N., ed. *Anchor Bible Dictionary*. 6 vols. New York: Doubleday, 1992.

García Martínez, Florentino, and Elbert J. Tigchelaar. *The Dead Sea Scrolls Study Edition*. 2 vols. New York: Brill, 1997.

Jasper, Ronald C. D., and G. C. Cuming, eds., *Prayers of the Eucharist: Early and Reformed*. New York: Oxford University Press, 1980.

Kittel, Gerhard, and Gerhard Friedrich, eds. *Theological Dictionary of the New Testament*. 10 vols. Grand Rapids: Eerdmans, 1964–1976.

Liddell, Henry George, and Robert Scott. *A Greek English Lexicon*. Oxford: Clarendon Press, 1971.

Lightfoot, John. *A Commentary on the New Testament from the Talmud and Hebraica*. 4 vols. Peabody, MA: Hendrickson, 1979.

Louw, Johannes P., and Eugene A. Nida, eds., *Greek-English Lexicon of the New Testament Based on Semantic Domains*. New York: United Bible Societies, 1988.

McNamara, Martin. *Targum Neofiti 1: Genesis*. The Aramaic Bible 1A. Edinburgh: T&T Clark, 1992.

Metzger, Bruce M. *A Textual Commentary on the Greek New Testament: A Companion Volume to the United Bible Societies' Greek New Testament* (3rd ed.). London: United Bible Societies, 1971.

Nestle, Eberhard, Erwin Nestle, Barbara Aland, and Kurt Aland, et al. *100 Jahre Novum Testamentum Graece, 1898–1998: Jubiläumsausgabe Nestle-Aland*. 27th ed. Stuttgart: Deutsche Bibelgesellschaft, 1998.

Neusner, Jacob, Alan J. Avery-Peck, and William Scott Green, eds. *The Encyclopedia of Judaism*. 5 vols. New York: Continuum, 1999–2003.

Spicq, Ceslas. *Theological Lexicon of the New Testament*. Translated and edited by James D. Ernest. 3 vols. Peabody, MA: Hendrickson, 1991–1994.

Strack, Hermann L., and Günter Stemberger. *Introduction to the Talmud and Midrash*. Translated by Markus Bockmuehl. 2nd ed. Edinburgh: T&T Clark, 1996.

Strack, Hermann L., and Paul Billerbeck. *Kommentar zum Neuen Testament aus Talmud und Midrasch*. 6 vols. Munich: C. H. Beck, 1922–1961.

VanGemeren, Willem A., ed. *New International Dictionary of Old Testament Theology and Exegesis*. 5 vols. Grand Rapids: Zondervan, 1997.

Winter, Jakob, and August Wünsche. *Mechiltha: Ein tannaitischer Midrasch zu Exodus*. Leipzig: J. C. Hinrichs, 1909.

Zerwick, Max, and Mary Grosvenor. *An Analysis of the Greek New Testament*. Vol. 1, *Gospels–Acts*. Rome: Biblical Institute Press, 1974.

Commentaries

Barrett, Charles Kingsley. *The Gospel According to St John*. 2nd ed. London: SPCK, 1978.

Brown, Raymond. *The Gospel According to John: Introduction, Translation, and Notes*. 2 vols. AB 29, 29a. New York: Doubleday, 1966, 1970.

Bultmann, Rudolf. *The Gospel of John: A Commentary*. Translated by G. R. Beasley Murray et al. Oxford: Blackwell, 1971.

Carson, D. A. *The Gospel According to John*. Grand Rapids: Eerdmans, 1991.

Dodd, Charles Harold. *The Interpretation of the Fourth Gospel*. Cambridge: Cambridge University Press, 1953.

Kysar, Robert. *John*. Augsburg Commentary on the New Testament. Minneapolis: Augsburg, 1986.

Léon-Dufour, Xavier. *Lecture de l'Évangile selon Jean*. 4 vols. Parole de Dieu. Paris: Éditions du Seuil, 1988, 1990, 1993, 1996.

Lindars, Barnabas. *The Gospel of John*. NCB. London: Oliphants, 1972.

Moloney, Francis. J. *Belief in the Word: Reading John 1–4*. Minneapolis: Fortress Press, 1993.

———. *Signs and Shadows: Reading John 5–12*. Minneapolis: Fortress Press, 1996.

———. *Glory not Dishonor: Reading John 13–21*. Minneapolis: Fortress Press, 1998.

————. *John.* SP 4. Collegeville: Liturgical Press, 1998.

Painter, John. *1, 2, and 3 John.* SP 18. Collegeville: Liturgical Press, 2002.

Schnackenburg, Rudolf. *The Gospel according to St John.* Translated by Kevin Smyth et al. 3 vols. HTCNT. London: Burns & Oates; New York: Herder & Herder, 1968–1982.

Witherington, Ben III. *John's Wisdom: A Commentary on the Fourth Gospel.* Louisville: Westminster John Knox, 1995.

Other Literature

Ashton, John. "The Transformation of Wisdom: A Study of the Prologue of John's Gospel." *New Testament Studies* 32 (1986) 161–86.

Asiedu-Peprah, Martin. *Johannine Sabbath Conflicts as Juridical Controversy.* WUNT 2nd ser. 132. Tübingen: Mohr Siebeck, 2001.

Aune, David E. *The Cultic Setting of Realized Eschatology in Early Christianity.* NovTSup 28. Leiden: Brill, 1972.

Balch, David L., and Carolyn Osiek, eds., *Early Christian Families in Context: An Interdisciplinary Dialogue.* Grand Rapids: Eerdmans, 2003.

Ball, David M. *"I AM" in John's Gospel: Literary Function, Background and Theological Implications.* JSNTS 124. Sheffield: Sheffield Academic Press, 1996.

Belleville, Linda L. "'Born of Water and Spirit:' John 3:5." *Trinity Journal* 1 (1980) 125–41.

Bieringer, Reimund, Didier Pollefeyt, and Frederique Vandecasteele-Vanneuville, eds., *Anti-Judaism and the Fourth Gospel.* Louisville: Westminster John Knox, 2001.

Blond, Georges. "Clement of Rome." In Willy Rordorf et al., eds., *The Eucharist of the Early Christians.* Translated by Matthew J. O'Connell. New York: Pueblo, 1978, 24–47.

Boismard, Marie-Émile. "L'ami de l'Époux (Jo., 111, 29)." In André Barucq, et al., eds., *A la rencontre de Dieu: Mémorial Albert Gelin.* Le Puy: Xavier Mappus, 1961, 289–95.

————. *Moses or Jesus: An essay in Johannine Christology.* Translated by Benedict T. Viviano. Minneapolis: Fortress Press, 1993.

————. *Our Victory over Death: Resurrection?* Translated by Madeleine Beaumont. Collegeville: Liturgical Press, 1999.

Borig, Rainer. *Der Wahre Weinstock. Untersuchungen zu Jo 15:1-10.* SANT 16. Munich: Kösel, 1967.

Bratcher, Robert G. "What does 'glory' mean in relation to Jesus? Translating *doxa* and *doxazo* in John." *Bible Translator* 42 (1991) 401–408.

Brightman, Frank E. *Liturgies Eastern and Western.* Oxford: Clarendon Press, 1896.

Brown, Raymond E. *The Death of the Messiah: From Gethsemane to the Grave.* 2 vols. New York: Doubleday, 1994.

————. *New Testament Essays.* Milwaukee: Bruce, 1965.

————. *Jesus God and Man: Modern Biblical Reflections.* New York: Macmillan, 1967.

————. "Roles of Women in the Fourth Gospel." *Theological Studies* 36 (1975) 688–99.

————. *The Community of the Beloved Disciple.* New York: Paulist, 1979.

————. "The Resurrection in John 20—A Series of Diverse Reactions." *Worship* 64 (1990) 194–206.

————. *An Introduction to the Gospel of John: Edited, updated, introduced and concluded by Francis J. Moloney.* ABRL. New York: Doubleday, 2003.

Bruce, Frederick F. "'Jesus is Lord.'" In J. McDowell Richards, ed., *Soli Deo Gloria: New Testament Studies in Honor of William Childs Robinson.* Richmond: John Knox, 1968, 23–36.

Büchsel, Friedrich. ἄνωθεν. TDNT 1 (1964–76) 378.

Byrne, Brendan. *Lazarus: A Contemporary Reading of John 11:1-46.* Homebush: St. Paul, 1991.

Chennattu, Rekha M. "On Becoming Disciples (John 1:35-51): Insights from the Fourth Gospel." *Salesianum* 63 (2001) 465–96.

————. *Johannine Discipleship as a Covenant Relationship.* Peabody: Hendrickson, 2005.

————, and Mary L. Coloe, eds., *Transcending Boundaries: Contemporary Readings of the New Testament.* Rome: Libreria Ateneo Salesiano, 2005.

Collins, John J. *Jewish Wisdom in the Hellenistic Age.* OTL. Edinburgh: T&T Clark, 1997.

————. "Marriage, Divorce and Family in Second Temple Judaism." In Leo G. Perdue, et al., *Families in Ancient Israel.* Louisville: Westminster John Knox, 1997, 104–62.

Collins, Raymond F. *These Things Have Been Written: Studies on the Fourth Gospel.* Louvain Theological and Pastoral Monographs 2. Louvain: Peeters, 1990.

————. "'Blessed are those who have not seen': John 20:29." In Rekha M. Chennattu, and Mary L. Coloe, eds., *Transcending Boundaries: Contemporary Readings of the New Testament.* Rome: Libreria Ateneo Salesiano, 2005, 173–90.

Coloe, Mary L. "Like Father, Like Son: The Role of Abraham in Tabernacles—John 8:31-59." *Pacifica* 12 (1999) 1–11.

————. "Households of Faith (Jn 4:46-54–11:1-44): A metaphor for the Johannine community." *Pacifica* 13 (2000) 326–33.

————. "Raising the Johannine Temple (Jn 19:19-37)." *Australian Biblical Review* 48 (2000) 47–58.

————. *God Dwells with Us: Temple Symbolism in the Fourth Gospel.* Collegeville: Liturgical Press, 2001.

————. "Welcome in the Household of God: The Footwashing in John 13." *Catholic Biblical Quarterly* 66 (2004) 400–15.

————. "Was there another vine? Questions on John 15:1a." *Australian E-Journal of Theology* 4, 2005. Accessed March 30th, 2006. Available from http://dlibrary.acu.edu.au/research/theology/ejournal/aejt_4/coloe.htm.

Cory, Catherine. "Wisdom's Rescue: A New Reading of the Tabernacles Discourse (John 7:1–8:59)." *Journal of Biblical Literature* 116 (1997) 95–116.

Couratin, Arthur H., and David H. Tripp, eds., *Liturgical Studies [of] E. C. Ratcliff*. London: SPCK, 1976.

Crosby, Michael H. *House of Disciples: Church, Economics and Justice in Matthew*. Maryknoll, NY: Orbis, 1988.

Cullmann, Oscar. *Early Christian Worship*. SBT 10. London: SCM, 1953.

Cullmann, Oscar, and Franz J. Leenhardt. *Essays on the Lord's Supper*. Ecumenical Studies in Worship. Richmond: John Knox, 1958.

Culpepper, R. Alan. *Anatomy of the Fourth Gospel: A Study in Literary Design*. Philadelphia: Fortress Press, 1983.

———. "The Johannine *hypodeigma*: A Reading of John 13." Semeia 53 (1991) 133–52.

———. *The Gospel and Letters of John*. Interpreting Biblical Texts. Nashville: Abingdon, 1998.

Dettwiler, Andreas. *Die Gegenwart des Erhöhten: Eine exegetische Studie zu den johanneischen Abschiedsreden (Joh 13,31–16,33) unter besonderer Berücksichtigung ihres Relecture-Charakters*. Göttingen: Vandenhoeck & Ruprecht, 1995.

Dodd, Charles Harold. "A Hidden Parable in the Fourth Gospel." In idem, *More New Testament Studies*. Manchester: Manchester University Press, 1968, 30–40.

Dupont, Liliane, Christopher Lash, and Georges Levesque. "Recherche sur la structure de Jean 20." *Biblica* 54 (1973) 482–98.

Ernst, Josef. *Johannes der Täufer: Interpretation—Geschichte—Wirkungsgeschichte*. BZNW 53. Berlin: de Gruyter, 1989.

Evans, Craig A., and Peter W. Flint. "Introduction." In Craig A. Evans and Peter W. Flint, eds., *Eschatology, Messianism, and the Dead Sea Scrolls*. Grand Rapids: Eerdmans, 1997, 1–9.

Feuillet, André. *Johannine Studies*. Staten Island: Alba House, 1965.

Fitzgerald, J. T. "Hospitality." In Craig A. Evans and Stanley E. Porter, eds., *Dictionary of New Testament Background*. Downers Grove: InterVarsity Press, 2000, 522–25.

Ford, J. Massyngberde. *Redeemer—Friend and Mother: Salvation in Antiquity and in the Gospel of John*. Minneapolis: Fortress Press, 1997.

Forestell, J. Terence. *The Word of the Cross: Salvation as Revelation in the Fourth Gospel*. AnBib 57. Rome: Biblical Institute Press, 1974.

Fortna, Robert T. *The Fourth Gospel and its Predecessor: From Narrative Source to Present Gospel*. Studies in the New Testament and its World. Edinburgh: T&T Clark, 1988.

Frey, Jörg. *Die johanneische Eschatologie: Die eschatologische Verkündigung in den johanneischen Texten*. 3 vols. WUNT 96. Tübingen: J.C.B. Mohr, 1997–2000.

Fuglseth, Kåre Sigvald. *Johannine Sectarianism in Perspective: A Sociological, Historical and Comparative Analysis of Temple and Social Relationships in the Gospel of John, Philo and Qumran*. NovTSup 119. Leiden: Brill, 2005.

Gadamer, Hans Georg. *Truth and Method.* Translated by John Cumming. 2nd ed. New York: Seabury Press, 1975.

Gamble, Harry Y. "The Formation of the New Testament Canon and its Significance for the History of Biblical Interpretation." In Alan J. Hauser and Duane F. Watson, eds., *A History of Biblical Interpretation: Volume One, The Ancient Period.* Grand Rapids: Eerdmans, 2003, 409–30.

Gaster, Theodor H. "Dead, Abode of the." *IDB* 1 (1962) 787–88.

Gehring, Roger W. *House Church and Mission: The Importance of Household Structures in Early Christianity.* Peabody, MA: Hendrickson, 2004.

George, Michele. "Domestic Architecture and Household Relations: Pompeii and Roman Ephesus." In Margaret MacDonald and Halvor Moxnes, eds., *Domestic Space and Families in Early Christianity.* JSNT 27 (New York: Continuum, 2004) 7–25.

Gese, Hartmut. *Essays on Biblical Theology.* Translated by Keith Crim. Minneapolis: Augsburg, 1981.

Goergen, Donald J. *The Death and Resurrection of Jesus.* A Theology of Jesus 2. Wilmington, DE: Michael Glazier, 1988.

Gowan, Donald E. *Eschatology in the Old Testament.* Philadelphia: Fortress Press, 1986.

Hahn, Ferdinand. *The Titles of Jesus in Christology: Their History in Early Christianity.* Translated by Harold Knight and George Ogg. London: Lutterworth Press, 1969.

Hakola, Raimo. *Identity Matters: John, the Jews and Jewishness.* NovTSup118. Leiden and Boston: Brill, 2005.

Hanson, Anthony T. *The New Testament Interpretation of Scripture.* London: SPCK, 1980.

Harrington, Daniel J. "Afterlife Expectation in Pseudo-Philo, 4 Ezra, and 2 Baruch, and Their Implications for the New Testament." In Reimund Bieringer, Veronica Koperski, and Bianca Lataire, eds., *Resurrection in the New Testament: Festschrift J. Lambrecht.* Leuven: Leuven University Press, 2002, 21–34.

Hatina, Thomas R. "John 20,22 in Its Eschatological Context: Promise or Fulfillment?" *Biblica* 74 (1993) 196–219.

Hays, Richard B. *Echoes of Scripture in the Letters of Paul.* New Haven: Yale University Press, 1989.

Heise, Jürgen. *Bleiben: Menein in den johanneischen Schriften.* HUT 8. Tübingen: J.C.B. Mohr (Paul Siebeck), 1967.

Hellerman, Joseph H. *The Ancient Church as Family.* Minneapolis: Fortress Press, 2001.

Hengel, Martin. "The Old Testament in the Fourth Gospel." In Craig A. Evans and W. Richard Stegner, eds., *The Gospels and the Scriptures of Israel.* Sheffield: Sheffield Academic Press, 1994, 380–95.

Hoegen-Rohls, Christina. *Der nachösterliche Johannes: Die Abschiedsreden als hermeneutischer Schlüssel zum vierten Evangelium.* WUNT 2nd ser. 84. Tübingen: J.C.B. Mohr, 1996.

Holst, Robert. "The one anointing of Jesus: Another application of the form-critical method." *Journal of Biblical Literature* 95 (1976) 435–46.

Hossfeld, Frank-Lothar. "Die alttestamentliche Familie vor Gott." In Josef Schreiner, ed., *Freude am Gottesdienst: Aspekte ursprünglicher Liturgie*. Stuttgart: Katholisches Bibelwerk, 1983, 217–28.

Hultgren, Arland. "The Johannine Footwashing (13.1-11) as Symbol of Eschatological Hospitality." *New Testament Studies* 28 (1982) 539–46.

———. "Eschatology in the New Testament: The Current Debate." In Carl E. Braaten and Robert W. Jenson, eds., *The Last Things: Biblical and Theological Perspectives on Eschatology*. Grand Rapids: Eerdmans, 2002, 67–89.

Hurtado, Larry W. *Lord Jesus Christ: Devotion to Jesus in Earliest Christianity*. Grand Rapids: Eerdmans, 2003.

Idelsohn, Abraham Z. *Jewish Liturgy and its Development*. New York: Schocken, 1932.

Jeremias, Joachim. νύμφη, νυμφίος. TDNT 4 (1967) 1099–1106.

Jones, Larry Paul. *The Symbol of Water in the Gospel of John*. JSNTSup 145. Sheffield: Sheffield Academic Press, 1997.

Jungmann, Josef A. *The Early Liturgy: To the Time of Gregory the Great*. Translated by Francis A. Brunner. London: Darton, Longman & Todd, 1959.

Käsemann, Ernst. *The Testament of Jesus according to John 17*. Translated by Gerhard Krodel. Philadelphia: Fortress Press, 1968.

Kilpatrick, George D. "'Kurios' in the Gospels." In Faculté autonome de théologie de Genève, *L'Évangile Hier et Aujourd'hui: Mélanges Offerts au Professeur Frans-J. Leenhardt*. Geneva: Labor et Fides, 1968, 65–70.

Kodell, Jerome. *The Eucharist in the New Testament*. Wilmington, DE: Michael Glazier, 1988.

Koester, Craig R. "Messianic Exegesis and the Call of Nathanael (John 1.45-51)." *Journal for the Study of the New Testament* 39 (1990) 23–34.

———. *Symbolism in the Fourth Gospel: Meaning, Mystery, Community*. Minneapolis: Fortress Press, 1995.

Labahn, Michael, Klaus Scholtissek, and Angelika Strotmann, eds., *Israel und seine Heilstraditionen im Johannesevangelium. Festgabe für Johannes Beutler SJ zum 70. Geburtstag*. Paderborn: Schöningh, 2004.

La Potterie, Ignace de. "Genèse de la Foi Pascale D'Après Jn. 20." *New Testament Studies* 30 (1984) 26–49.

———. "Le Verbe 'demeurer' dans la Mystique Johannique." *Nouvelle revue théologique* 117 (1995) 843–59.

LaVerdiere, Eugene. *The Eucharist in the New Testament and the Early Church*. Collegeville: Liturgical Press, 1996.

LaVerdiere, Eugene, and William G. Thompson. "New Testament Communities in Transition." *Theological Studies* 37 (1976) 567–97.

Leal, Juan. "El simbolismo histórico del IV Evangelio." *Estudios Bíblicos* 19 (1960) 329–48.

Lee, Dorothy A. *The Symbolic Narratives of the Fourth Gospel: The Interplay of Form and Meaning.* JSNTSup 95. Sheffield: JSOT Press, 1994.

———. "Beyond Suspicion? The Fatherhood of God in the Fourth Gospel." *Pacifica* 8 (1995) 140–54.

———. "Partnership in Easter Faith: The Role of Mary Magdalene and Thomas in John 20." *Journal for the Study of the New Testament* 58 (1995) 37–49.

———. "Abiding in the Fourth Gospel: A Case-study in Feminist Biblical Theology." *Pacifica* 10 (1997) 123–36.

———. "The Symbol of Divine Fatherhood." *Semeia* 85 (1999) 177–94.

———. *Flesh and Glory: Symbolism, Gender and Theology in the Gospel of John.* New York: Crossroad, 2002.

Léon-Dufour, Xavier. *Sharing the Eucharistic Bread: The Witness of the New Testament.* Mahwah, NJ: Paulist, 1987.

Leyerle, Blake. "Meal Customs in the Greco-Roman World." In Paul F. Bradshaw and Lawrence A. Hoffmann, eds., *Passover and Easter: Origin and History to Modern Times.* Notre Dame: University of Notre Dame, 1999, 29–61.

Lieu, Judith M. *Image and Reality: The Jews in the World of the Christians in the Second Century.* Edinburgh: T&T Clark, 1996.

———. *Neither Jew nor Greek? Constructing Early Christianity.* Studies of the New Testament and its World. Edinburgh: T&T Clark, 2002.

Loader, William R. G.. "John 1:50-51 and the 'Greater Things' of Johannine Christology." In Cilliers Breytenbach and Henning Paulsen, eds., *Anfänge der Christologie: Festschrift für Ferdinand Hahn zum 65. Geburtstag.* Göttingen: Vandenhoeck & Ruprecht, 1991, 255–74.

MacDonald, Margaret, and Halvor Moxnes, eds., *Domestic Space and Families in Early Christianity. JSNT* 27 (New York: Continuum, 2004). "Editors' Introduction," 3–6.

Madigan, Kevin, and Carolyn Osiek. *Ordained Women in the Early Church: A Documentary History.* Baltimore: John Hopkins University Press, 2005.

Malina, Bruce J. "The received view and what it cannot do: III John and Hospitality." *Semeia* 35 (1986) 171–89.

Manns, Frédéric. "Le Lavement des Pieds. Essai sur la structure et la signification de Jean 13." *Recherches de science religieuse* 55 (1981) 149–69.

———. *L'Evangile de Jean à la lumière du Judaïsme.* SBFA 33. Jerusalem: Franciscan Printing Press, 1991.

Marchadour, Alain. *Lazare: Histoire d'une Récit, Récit d'une Histoire.* LD 132. Paris: Éditions du Cerf, 1988.

Martyn, J. Louis. *History and Theology in the Fourth Gospel.* NTL. 3rd ed. Louisville: Westminster John Knox, 2003.

Mayer, Günter. ידה הֲדִי תֹּלשׁה תְדֶת *TDOT* V (1986) 427–43.

Maynard, Arthur H. *"Ti emoi kai soi." New Testament Studies* 31 (1985) 582–86.

McCaffrey, James. *The House With Many Rooms: The Temple Theme of Jn 14, 2-3.* AnBib 114. Rome: Biblical Institute Press, 1988.

Meier, John P. *A Marginal Jew: Rethinking the Historical Jesus.* 3 vols. Vol. 2: *Mentor, Message, and Miracles.* ABRL. New York: Doubleday, 1994– .

Menken, Maarten J. J. "The Translation of Ps 41:10 in John 13:18." *Journal for the Study of the New Testament* 40 (1990) 61–79.

———. *Old Testament Quotations in the Fourth Gospel: Studies in Textual Form.* CBET 15. Kampen: Kok Pharos, 1996.

———. "Interpretation of the Old Testament and the Resurrection of Jesus in John's Gospel." In Reimund Bieringer, Veronica Koperski, and Bianca Lataire, eds., *Resurrection in the New Testament: Festschrift J. Lambrecht.* Leuven: Peeters, 2002, 189–205.

Michaud, Jean-Paul. "Le signe de Cana dans son contexte johannique." *Laval Théologique et Philosophique* 18 (1962) 239–85.

Millgram, Abraham E. *Jewish Worship.* Philadelphia: Jewish Publication Society of America, 1971.

Moloney, Francis J. "The Johannine Son of God." *Salesianum* 38 (1976) 71–86.

———. *The Johannine Son of Man.* Biblioteca di Scienze Religiose 14. 2nd ed. Rome: LAS, 1978.

———. "When is John Talking about Sacraments?" *Australian Biblical Review* 30 (1982) 10–33.

———. "A Sacramental Reading of John 13:1–38." *Catholic Biblical Quarterly* 53 (1991) 237–56.

———. "The Fourth Gospel and the Jesus of History." *New Testament Studies* 46 (2000) 42–58.

———. "Can Everyone be Wrong? A Reading of John 11:1–12:8." *New Testament Studies* 49 (2003) 505–27.

———. "The Johannine Son of Man Revisited." In Gilbert van Belle, Jan Gabriël Van der Watt, and P. J. Maritz, eds., *Theology and Christology in the Fourth Gospel. Essays by the members of the SNTS Johannine Writings Seminar.* Leuven: Peeters, 2005, 177–202.

Moxnes, Halvor. "What is Family? Problems in constructing early Christian families." In idem, ed., *Constructing Early Christian Families: Family as Social Reality and Metaphor.* London and New York: Routledge, 1997, 13–41.

Murphy, Catherine M. *John the Baptist: Prophet of Purity for a New Age.* Interfaces. Collegeville: Liturgical Press, 2003.

Mussner, Franz. *Die johanneische Sehweise und die Frage nach dem historischen Jesus.* QD 28. Freiburg: Herder, 1965. English translation by W. J. O'Hara: *The Historical Jesus in the Gospel of John.* New York: Herder & Herder, 1967.

———. "Jesus und 'das Haus des Vaters'—Jesus als 'Tempel.'" In Josef Schreiner, ed., *Freude am Gottesdienst: Aspekte ursprünglicher Liturgie.* Stuttgart: Katholisches Bibelwerk, 1983, 267–75.

Neusner, Jacob. "Mekhilta Attributed to R. Ishmael (Exodus)." In Jacob Neusner, Alan J. Avery-Peck, and William Scott Green, eds., *The Encyclopedia of Judaism.* New York: Continuum, 1999–2003, 1161–163.

Neyrey, Jerome H. "The Jacob Allusions in John 1:51." *Catholic Biblical Quarterly* 44 (1982) 596–605.

Nielsen, Helge Kjaer. "Der erste Gottesdienst. Eine Analyse von Joh 20, 19–23." *Studien zum Neuen Testament und seiner Umwelt* 28 (2003) 65–81.

O'Brien, Mark. "Theodicy and Eschatology: Old Testament Considerations." In D. Neville, ed., *Theodicy and Eschatology*. Adelaide: Australian Theological Forum Press, 2005, 1–17.

Orlett, Raymond. "An Influence of the Early Liturgy Upon the Emmaus Account." *Catholic Biblical Quarterly* 21 (1959) 213–19.

Osiek, Carolyn. "The Family in Early Christianity: 'Family Values' Revisited." *Catholic Biblical Quarterly* 58 (1996) 1–24.

Osiek, Carolyn, and David Balch. *Families in the New Testament World: Households and House Churches*. Louisville: Westminster John Knox, 1997.

Painter, John. "The Farewell Discourses and the History of Johannine Christianity." *New Testament Studies* 27 (1981) 525–43.

———. *The Quest for the Messiah: The History, Literature and Theology of the Johannine Community*. 2nd ed. Nashville: Abingdon, 1993.

Perdue, Leo G. *Wisdom and Creation: The Theology of Wisdom Literature*. Nashville: Abingdon, 1994.

Porter, Stanley E. "Resurrection, the Greeks and the New Testament." In Stanley E. Porter, Michael A. Hayes, and David Tombs, eds., *Resurrection*. Sheffield: Sheffield Academic Press, 1999, 52–81.

Potin, Jean. *La Fête Juive de la Pentecôte: Étude des Textes Liturgiques*. LD 65. Paris: Éditions du Cerf, 1971.

Rad, Gerhard von. *Genesis: A Commentary*. Translated by John H. Marks. Revised ed. London: SCM Press, 1972.

Rad, Gerhard von, and Gerhard Kittel. Δόχα. *TDNT* 2 (1964) 233–55.

Radcliffe, Timothy. "'My Lord and my God': The Locus of Confession." *New Blackfriars* 65 (1984) 52–62.

Reese, James M. *The Book of Wisdom, Song of Songs*. Old Testament Message 20. Wilmington, DE: Michael Glazier, 1983.

Reinhartz, Adele, ed. *God the Father in the Gospel of John*. Semeia 85. Atlanta: Society of Biblical Literature, 1999.

Reumann, John. *The Supper of the Lord: The New Testament, Ecumenical Dialogues, and Faith and Order on Eucharist*. Philadelphia: Fortress Press, 1985.

Ricoeur, Paul. *Freud and Philosophy*. Translated by Denis Savage. New Haven: Yale University Press, 1970.

———. *Interpretation Theory: Discourse and the Surplus of Meaning*. Fort Worth: Texas Christian University Press, 1976.

———. *The Rule of Metaphor: Multidisciplinary Studies of the Creation of Meaning in Language*. London: Routledge & Kegan Paul, 1977.

———. *Hermeneutics and the Human Sciences: Essays on Language, Action and Interpretation*. Translated by John B. Thompson. Cambridge: Cambridge University Press, 1981.

Riesenfeld, Harald. "Sabbat et Jour du Seigneur." In Angus J. B. Higgins, ed., *New Testament Essays: Studies in Memory of Thomas Walter Manson*. Manchester: Manchester University Press, 1959, 210–17.

Ringe, Sharon H. *Wisdom's Friends: Community and Christology in the Fourth Gospel.* Louisville: Westminster John Knox, 1999.

Robinson, John A. T. "Elijah, John and Jesus: An Essay in Detection." *New Testament Studies* 4 (1957–58) 263–81.

Rüger, Hans Peter. "ΝΑΖΑΡΕΘ, ΝΑΖΑΡΑ, ΝΑΖΑΡΗΝΟΣ, ΝΑΖΩΡΑΙΟΣ." *Zeitschrift für die neutestamentliche Wissenschaft und die Kunde der älteren Kirche* 72 (1981) 257–63.

Rylaarsdam, John C. "Weeks, Feast of." *IDB* 4 (1962) 827–28.

Safrai, Shemuel. "Religion in Everyday Life." In Shemuel Safrai and M. Stern, in cooperation with David Flusser and W. C. van Unnik, eds., *The Jewish People in the First Century: Historical Geography, Political History, Social, Cultural and Religious Life and Institutions.* 2 vols. CRINT 1/1-2. Amsterdam: Van Gorcum; Philadelphia: Fortress Press, 1974–1976, 2:793–833.

Satlow, Michael L. *Jewish Marriage in Antiquity.* Princeton: Princeton University Press, 2001.

Saxby, Harold. "The Time-Scheme in the Gospel of John." *Expository Times* 104 (1992) 9–13.

Schlier, Heinrich. ὑπόδειγμα. *TDNT* 2 (1964) 32–33.

Schneiders, Sandra M. "The Johannine Resurrection Narrative: An Exegetical Study of John 20 as a Synthesis of Johannine Spirituality." D.S.T. (unpublished), Pontificia Universitas Gregoriana, 1975.

———. "History and Symbolism in the Fourth Gospel." In Marinus de Jonge, ed., *L'Évangile de Jean: Sources, rédaction, théologie.* BETL 44. Gembloux: J. Duculot, 1977, 371–76.

———. "Symbolism and the Sacramental Principle in the Fourth Gospel." In Pius-Ramon Tragan, ed., *Segni E Sacramenti Nel Vangelo Di Giovanni.* Rome: Editrice Anselmiana, 1977, 221–35.

———. "The Foot Washing (John 13:1-20): An Experiment in Hermeneutics." *Catholic Biblical Quarterly* 43 (1981) 76–92.

———. "Death in the Community of Eternal Life: History, Theology and Spirituality in John 11." *Interpretation* 41 (1987) 44–56.

———. *Written That You May Believe: Encountering Jesus in the Fourth Gospel.* New York: Crossroad, 1999.

———. "The Resurrection (of the Body) in the Fourth Gospel: A Key to Johannine Spirituality." In John R. Donahue, ed., *Life in Abundance: Studies of John's Gospel in Tribute to Raymond E. Brown.* Collegeville: Liturgical Press, 2005, 168–98.

Scholtissek, Klaus. "Mystagogische Christologie im Johannesevangelium?" *Geist und Leben* 68 (1995) 412–26.

———. *In Ihm sein und bleiben: Die Sprache der Immanenz in den johanneischen Schriften.* Herder Biblische Studien 21. Freiburg: Herder, 2000.

Scott, Martin. *Sophia and the Johannine Jesus.* JSNTSup 71. Sheffield: JSOT Press, 1992.

Seevers, B. צרר. In Willem A. VanGemeren, ed., *New International Dictionary of Old Testament Theology and Exegesis.* Grand Rapids: Zondervan, 1997, 3:527–31.

Segal, Samuel M. *The Sabbath Book.* 2nd ed. New York: Thomas Yoseloff, 1957.

Segovia, Fernando F. *Love Relationships in the Johannine Tradition: Agape/Agapan in 1 John and the Fourth Gospel.* SBLDS 58. Missoula: Scholars Press, 1982.

―――. *The Farewell of the Word: The Johannine Call to Abide.* Minneapolis: Fortress Press, 1991.

Seim, Turid Karlsen. "Roles of Women in the Gospel of John." In Lars Hartman and Birger Olsson, eds., *Aspects on the Johannine Literature.* Stockholm: Almqvist & Wiksell, 1987, 56–73.

Selms, Adrianus van. "The Best Man and the Bride: From Sumer to St John with a New Interpretation of Judges, Chapters 14 and 15." *Journal of Near Eastern Studies* 9 (1950) 65–75.

Setzer, Claudia. *Resurrection of the Body in Early Judaism and Early Christianity: Doctrine, Community and Self-Definition.* Boston and Leiden: Brill, 2004.

Simoens, Yves. *La gloire d'aimer: Structures stylistiques et interprétives dans le Discours de la Cène (Jn 13–17).* AnBib 90. Rome: Biblical Institute Press, 1981.

Sinnott, Alice M. "Wisdom as Saviour." *Australian Biblical Review* 52 (2004) 19–31.

Smith, Dennis E. *From Symposium to Eucharist: The Banquet in the Early Christian World.* Minneapolis: Fortress Press, 2003.

Spicq, Ceslas. Δόξα, Δοχάζω, Συνδοχάζω. In idem, *Theological Lexicon of the New Testament.* Translated and edited by James D. Ernest. 3 vols. Peabody, MA: Hendrickson, 1991–1994, 1:362–79.

Sproston North, Wendy E. *The Lazarus Story within the Johannine Tradition.* JSNTSup 212. Sheffield: Sheffield Academic Press, 2001.

Stapfer, Edmond. *Palestine in the Time of Christ.* Translated by Annie H. Holmden. New York: Armstrong and Son, 1885.

Strange, James F. "Nazareth." *ABD* 4 (1992) 1050–51.

Suggit, John. "The Eucharistic Significance of John 20:19-29." *Journal of Theology for Southern Africa* 16 (1976) 52–59.

Tatum, W. Barnes. *John the Baptist and Jesus: A Report of the Jesus Seminar.* Sonoma, CA: Polebridge Press, 1994.

Taylor, Joan E. *The Immerser: John the Baptist within Second Temple Judaism.* Grand Rapids: Eerdmans, 1997.

Thomas, John C. *Footwashing in John 13 and the Johannine Community.* JSOTSup 61. Sheffield: JSOT Press, 1991.

Tilborg, Sjef van. *Imaginative Love in John.* Biblical Interpretation Series 2. Leiden: Brill, 1993.

Trainor, Michael F. *The Quest for Home: The Household in Mark's Community.* Collegeville: Liturgical Press, 2001.

Trever, John C. "Fig Tree, Fig." *IDB* 2 (1962) 267.

Trocmé, Etienne. *The Passion as Liturgy: A Study in the Origin of the Passion Narratives in the Four Gospels.* London: SCM, 1983.

Trumbull, Henry Clay. *Studies in Oriental Social Life.* Philadelphia: The Sunday School Times Co., 1894.

Tsevat, Matitiahu. בְּכוֹר. *TDOT* 2 (1975) 121–27.

Van der Watt, Jan Gabriël. *Family of the King: Dynamics of Metaphor in the Gospel According to John*. Biblical Interpretation Series 47. Leiden: Brill, 2000.

Vanderkam, James C. "Weeks, Festival of." *ABD* 6 (1992) 895–97.

Von Wahlde, Urban C. "He Has Given to the Son To Have Life in Himself (John 5,26)." *Biblica* 85 (2004) 409–12.

Voorwinde, Stephen. *Jesus' Emotions in the Fourth Gospel*. Library of New Testament Studies 284. London: T&T Clark, 2005.

Wall, Robert W. "Divorce." *ABD* 2 (1992) 217–19.

Weiss, Herold. "Footwashing in the Johannine Community." *Novum Testamentum* 21 (1979) 298–325.

Wengst, Klaus. *Bedrängte Gemeinde und verherrlichter Christus. Ein Versuch über das Johannesevangelium*. Munich: Kaiser, 1990.

Westermann, Claus. *Genesis 12–36: A Commentary*. Translated by John J. Scullion. Minneapolis: Augsburg, 1985.

Wevers, John William. *Notes on the Greek Text of Genesis*. SBLSCS 35. Atlanta: Scholars Press, 1993.

Wight, Fred H. *Manners and Customs of Bible Lands*. Chicago: Moody Press, 1953.

Willett, Michael E. *Wisdom Christology in the Fourth Gospel*. San Francisco: Mellen Research University Press, 1992.

Willis, Geoffrey Grimshaw. *A History of Early Roman Liturgy: To the Death of Pope Gregory the Great*. Subsidia 1. London: Henry Bradshaw Society, 1994.

Wink, Walter. *John the Baptist in the Gospel Tradition*. SNTSMS 7. Cambridge: Cambridge University Press, 1968.

Winston, David. *The Wisdom of Solomon*. AB 43. New York: Doubleday, 1979.

Witherington, Ben III. "The Waters of Birth: John 3.5 and 1 John 5.6-8." *New Testament Studies* 35 (1989) 155–60.

Wright, N. T. *The Resurrection of the Son of God*. Christian Origins and the Question of God 3. London: SPCK, 2003.

Yamauchi, Edwin M. "Cultural Aspects of Marriage in the Ancient World." *Bibliotheca Sacra* 135 (1978) 241–52.

Yee, Gale A. *Jewish Feasts in John's Gospel*. Wilmington, DE: Michael Glazier, 1989.

Zimmermann, Ruben. *Christologie der Bilder im Johannesevangelium: Die Christopoetik des vierten Evangeliums unter besonderer Berücksichtigung von Joh 10*. WUNT 2nd ser. 171. Tübingen: Mohr Siebeck, 2004.

Zumstein, Jean. "Der Prozess der Relecture in der Johanneischen Literatur." *New Testament Studies* 42 (1996) 394–411.

———. "Foi et vie éternelle selon Jean." In Odette Mainville and Daniel Marguerat, eds., *Résurrection: L'après-mort dans le monde ancien et le Nouveau Testament*. Geneva: Labor et Fides; Montreal: Médiaspaul, 2001.

———. *Kreative Erinnerung: Relecture und Auslegung im Johannesevangelium*. 2nd revised and expanded ed. ATANT 84. Zürich: Theologischer Verlag Zürich, 2004.

Index of Authors

Index of Biblical References